The Best of SQLServerCentra

Alex Grinberg
Alex Kersha
Andre Quitta
Andy Warren
Anubhav Bansal
Aries Manlig
Brian Knight
Charles Hawkins
Chris Rock
Christoffer Hedgate
Darwin Hatheway
David Poole
Dinesh Asanka
Eli Leiba
Frederik Vandeputte
Grant Fritchey
Haidong Ji
Hugh Lynch
James Greaves
Jereme Guenther
Jonathan Stokes
Joseph Sack
Kathi Kellenberger
Ken Powers
Kristian Wedberg
Leo Peysakhovich
M. Choirul Amri
Michael Coles
Nanda Kishore
Peter He
Peter Ward
Raj Vasant
Rama Nageshwara
Ranga Narasimhan
Rob Scholl
Robert Davis
Roy Carlson
Satia Madimchetty
Sean McCown
Serhiy Snisarenko
Sloan Holliday
Steve Jones
Steve Moore
Subramanyam Krishnamurthy
Suresh Maganti
Sushila Iyer
Terry Troisi
Thomas LaRock
Tiago Andrade e Silva
Tim Chapman
Tim Mitchell
Tom Lodermeier
Vince Iacoboni
Zach Mattson

The Central Publishing Group
3186 Michaels Ct
Green Cove Springs, FL 32043
U.S.A

Disclaimer

The Central Publishing Group, SQLServerCentral.com, and the authors of the articles contained in this book are not liable for any problems resulting from the use of techniques, source code, or compiled executables referenced in this book. Users should review all procedures carefully, test first on a non-production server, and always have good backup before using on a production server.

Trademarks

Microsoft, SQL Server, Windows, and Visual Basic are registered trademarks of Microsoft Corporation, Inc. Oracle is a trademark of Oracle Corporation.

Editors

Steve Jones and Andy Warren

Cover Art

Sylvia Peretz of PeretzDesign.com

The Best of SQLServerCentral.com – Vol.

Table of Contents

Introduction

Welcome to The Best of SQLServerCentral.com – Vol. 4!

Our fourth year of producing a book that covers the best articles of the past year . This past year was a great one with the release of SQL Server 2005 in November and quite a few articles being written with the new paradigm of SQL Server development in mind.

We also wanted to give all our authors a chance to see their names in print as well as give you an off-line resource that you can take with you wherever you may need it-most likely at your bedside to help. This book is our way of saying thank you for the effort you put into producing great content for the community.

We would like to thank everyone for their support both on the website as well as by purchasing this book. Your visits to the site, clicking through to advertisers, purchasing products, registering for PASS, all help us continue this community and provide you with a valuable resource that hopefully helps you learn, perform better at your job, and grow your career. We'd like to encourage all of you to submit an article in the next year, whether you are working with SQL Server 2005 or SQL Server 2000! This is a community and we aren't looking for the gurus only to contribute. We love hearing about the real world you all live in and deal with on a daily basis. We plan to get at least one article from each author and send you a couple copies of the book. Great for your bookshelf and they make a great Mother's Day present.

Once again, thanks so much for your support and we look forward to 2006.

Andy Warren
Brian Knight
Steve Jones

Administration

This is what we do: administer servers and databases. Everyone has their own set of tricks, tips, scripts tailored to the quirks of their own systems. We can each get sidetracked into dealing with our own systems and miss out on understanding some other sections of SQL Server that we don't work with.

Here's a selection of articles to impart a little more information about the server, Autoclose, AWE, Traces and more. As we compile this 3rd edition, Microsoft SQL Server is a very mature product that is mostly being limited by its architecture as hardware continues to grow in power, loads increase, and many different stresses occur. Nothing earth-shattering here, just some good information that might help you save the day.

An Audit Trail Generator

By Leo Peysakhovich

Many companies which have transactional applications, working with government or for many other reasons they have very strong requirements for the audit of data changes. In many other cases data changes auditing is the internal business requirement. Many companies using audited data and shows it via front end or generate business reports from it.

In present days of increased corporate scrutiny and regulatory requirements, you want to be sure that your integration architecture does not introduce hidden decisions that may affect your compliance. For example, medical trial companies have a strong FDA regulation that required to keep record of basically any data changes in a database. In addition, clients very often would like to make sure that their data getting flagged and can't be modified silently without an ability to trace any modifications and in case of mistakenly modified the data have an ability to be corrected by setting the old value back.

In such cases I would suggest that you have to have full and detailed history of the record changes which can be shared with the business stakeholders of the system.

There are few ways the companies are trying to setup the audit solutions. One way is to use a third party products such Lumigent Entegra (http://www.lumigent.com/products/entegra_sql.html)

The other companies are trying to create their own home grown solutions.

There are many articles about different types and different ways for the audit architecture. The great series of articles (4 articles) posted in SQLServerCentral.com by Steve Jones http://www.sqlservercentral.com/columnists/sjones/auditingyoursqlserverpart4selectiveauditing.asp

And all the articles are great. But there is something in addition to the auditing theory and simple solution examples is missing in most of them.

Is your organization faced with pending audits resulting in long and tedious meetings to try to achieve compliance? Have you been trying to figure how you are going to develop a code to capture the data needed for the continuous audits in between the remainder of the company projects?

Did you try for example to implement those solutions in the environment with 100 and more tables, where each customer have their own similar but slightly different database (for example in medical trial or accounting firm) and number of new databases 100+ during the year? And you will figure out quickly that the manual creation of an audit objects is not really working.

In this article I am not going to explain various scenarios for auditing (it was done in many other articles) but would like to show the automated way to setup an audit system and describe the generator which is automatically creating the full audit solution regardless of the database structure. Eventually, it will be done for the one audit solution which was implemented for one of my clients. And I can say that solution is working without any issues for almost a year.

When I start working to architect the solution some of the requirements were already placed by business and application, and report developers. So, I was staying in boundaries and suppose to keep the minimal database changes

First, solution is based on the assumption that the audit trail tables should have the same structure as audited tables and will be created for each main table.

The code for this method is usually inserting the old row in the audit table when any data changes are in the main table.

This can be implemented by using a trigger that inserts the data in the audit table. This method also does not require a primary key as it is just saving the before versions of rows updated or inserted.

But to be able to distinguish the row that was modified or inserted each row from main table should have a row identifier or a key.

Further in the article I will use term modified for both updated and inserted rows. It was very sad that developers did the initial database design

without consideration of data auditing (what is surprise!) and only at the last moment DBA/Architect was invited when it was too late to make main

schema changes. Known history, isn't it? So, as an architect I placed some additional rules which were not really affecting any existing development.

1. Each table should have unique row identifier based on one column row_id

2. Column row_id will be an identity column in tables where there is no identity column and row_id will be a computed column with value equal the identity column value if table already has identity column. It may sound strange but applications required easily and uniquely identify the row if primary key consists of few columns or is not exists at all (should it be with proper design?). Is it surprise you that some tables are without primary keys?

Developers are telling me from time to time that this is a given design and I can't change it or that there are cases when primary key (even the fake one) is not necessary.

This is a known fact that many developers creating a unique index instead of a primary key arguing that it gets the same effect. But let's focus on our task instead of keeping good discussion about necessity of primary key.

3. Audit table is keeping the changed row, not an old row. This was done to increase performance of the reports and eliminate the necessity of audit and audited table joint to get the old and current values.

4. Each history table has modid field to show all the rows which are changed in one modification

5. Each audit table will have the same name as the main user table but with prefix 'a_'

Some other business requirements were posted to complicate an audit solution. But I am omitting them for sake of simplifying the article's implementation and give you a working idea of an audit generator. Let's check the solution for one table.

```
Create table customer ( cust_id int primary key, cust_name varchar(50), row_id int identity(1,1) )
Create table order ( order_id int  identity(1,1) primary key, order_desc varchar(50), row_id as
order_id)
```

Table customer created with row_id as identity column because cust_id is not an identity. Table order has row_id as computed column from order_id because order_id is identity column.General modification table can be created next way:

```
Create modif (modid int identity(1,1),
      tablenm varchar(50),
      dml_type char(1),
      insertdt datetime default getdate() ,
      insertuser varchar(128) default suser_sname(),
      insertmachine varchar(128) default host_name(),
      insertprocess varchar(128) default 'App=(' + rtrim(isnull(app_name(), '')) + ') Proc=(' +
            isnull(object_name(@@procid), '') +')' )
```

DML_type can be I for insert, U for update, D for delete.

```
Create table a_customer(cust_id int, cust_name varchar(50), row_id int,
            modid int, audit_id int identity(1,1) primary key)
Create table a_order ( order_id int  , order_desc varchar(50), row_id as order_id,
      modid int, audit_id int identity(1,1) primary key )
```

Next step shows the trigger for the table customer. This trigger is generic solution for any table in database. If multiple triggers exists for the same table for the same event (UPDATE, INSERT, and DELETE) then audit trigger should be the last one among them.

```
if exists (select * from dbo.sysobjects where
name = 't_customer_A' and type = 'TR' )
 drop trigger
dbo.t_customer_A
GO
CREATE TRIGGER t_customer_A
```

```
   ON customer AFTER INSERT,UPDATE,DELETE
AS
BEGIN
declare @tblname varchar(128)
SET NOCOUNT ON
set @tblname = 'customer'
select * into #td from deleted
select * into #ti from inserted
exec p_trigger @tblname = @tblname
END
GO
SET QUOTED_IDENTIFIER OFF
SET ANSI_NULLS  ON
GO
sp_settriggerorder @triggername= 't_customer_A', @order='LAST', @stmttype = 'INSERT'
sp_settriggerorder @triggername= 't_customer_A', @order='LAST', @stmttype = 'UPDATE'
sp_settriggerorder @triggername= 't_customer_A', @order='LAST', @stmttype = 'DELETE'
```

As you can see the only change for another table will be the value of the variable @tblname.

Now we need a stored procedure p_trigger to add record(s) to the audit table. This procedure dynamically creating the insert statement for the audit table and insert rows into the audit table based on the passed table name value. Procedure p_trigger is inserting the row with general information about the modification into the table modif. But before seeing the source code for the procedure p_trigger let's find out what is required to implement a generic solution for all tables in any database?

1. Generate script for each table to add column row_id and add it
2. Generate audit table script for each user table in database and create it
3. Generate trigger for each table
4. Create wrapper to get audit columns and objects for each table in database.

Set of stored procedures created in database is producing the necessary result.

Procedure p_add_row_id produces the statement to add the column row_id if column is not exists in table.

Procedure p_generate_audit_table generates drop and create statement for the audit table

Procedure p_generate_audit_trigger generates statement to drop and create the audit trigger for the table

And finally, procedure p_generate_audit is the wrapper which generating the script for all tables in database.

If you compile the stored procedures in database and run the wrapper p_generate_audit the script will be generated. Here is the output produced by the generator for the database Pubs Pubs_GeneratedOutput.txt

The last portion of the equation is generic stored procedure p_trigger. This procedure is actually inserting the rows to the audit and modification tables.

```
SET QUOTED_IDENTIFIER  ON
SET ANSI_NULLS  ON
GO
CREATE PROCEDURE p_trigger
   @tblname VARCHAR(128)
as
BEGIN
declare @cnti int, @cntd int, @maxid int, @minid int, @cmd varchar(4000), @audittblname varchar(128),
     @cmdINSERT varchar(1000), @cmdSELECT varchar(1000), @modif_id bigint,
     @cmdFROM varchar(255), @AUDITINSERT varchar(255), @DUI varchar(10)
set @audittblname = 'a_' + substring(@tblname,2,128)

declare @tmp table (cname varchar(128), cid int identity(1,1) )
select @cnti = count(*) from #ti
select @cntd = count(*) from #td
-- check how many rows changed. If 0 then do nothing
IF (@cnti = 0 and @cntd = 0)
   return 0
-- get all table columns
insert into @tmp(cname)
 select COLUMN_NAME from INFORMATION_SCHEMA.COLUMNS
  WHERE TABLE_NAME = @tblname

select @maxid = max(cid), @minid = min(cid) from  @tmp
set @cmdSELECT = ' SELECT '
```

```
set @cmdINSERT = ' INSERT INTO ' + @audittblname + ' ( '

while (@minid <= @maxid)
 begin
 -- begin while
   select @cmdINSERT = @cmdINSERT + cname + ',' ,  @cmdSELECT = @cmdSELECT + 'd.' + cname + ','
        FROM  @tmp
          where cid = @minid
       set @minid = @minid + 1
 end
 -- end while
-- always set new rows for the AUDIT
IF (@cnti = @cntd )
 begin
       set @DUI = ' ''U'' '
       SET @cmdFROM = ' FROM #ti d '
 END
IF (@cnti < @cntd)
 begin
       set @DUI = ' ''D'' '
       SET @cmdFROM = ' FROM #td d '
 END
IF (@cnti > @cntd)
 BEGIN
       set @DUI = ' ''I'' '
       SET @cmdFROM = ' FROM #ti d '
 END
-- insert record into table modif
insert into modif(tablenm, dml_type)
 select @tblname, @dui
-- get identity
select @modif_id  = SCOPE_IDENTITY( )
-- add modification column value
set @AUDITINSERT = ' modid )'
set @cmd = @cmdINSERT + @AUDITINSERT  + @cmdSELECT + cast(@modif_id as varchar) + @cmdFROM
exec (@cmd)
SET NOCOUNT OFF
END
```

CONCLUSION

It is possible to make all the procedures more sophisticated and add features such as index creation for the column modifid and row_id.

For my client I created generator the way that all procedures were created in one central location and one of the additional parameters was parameter for the audit database name. It allows centralize the stored procedures in one database per server. Some other parameters allowed exclude tables or include only specific tables in database by passing comma-delimited string. So, many additional features can be implemented in the audit generator to satisfy many other scenarios.

Are Your Database Backups Current and Available?

By Thomas LaRock

Background

Recently, the business side of our company requested that our team develop a process to ensure that the database backups were current and still available on disk. This decision was spurred by a recent disaster in which we could not bring one of our database servers back from the dead. As (bad) luck would have it, the backup jobs, along with our alert notifications, stopped working about three weeks previously, making for a rather uncomfortable Monday morning. The business wanted assurance that such an event would never happen again. Our team agreed and sat down to work out the details.

Like many shops, we use an in-house developed system for monitoring our database servers. It is called DBA_Perform and it has been built over the past eighteen months. The solution that our team was about to incorporate would involve the use of this system. Code for all of the tables and stored procedures for the solution can be found in the downloadable zip file here.

A Simple Plan

We came up with a simple idea. First, find the backup file information for each database from the msdb system database. Then, find out if the latest full or differential backup for that database is less than twenty-four hours old. Lastly, make certain that the backup files still exist on disk, to ensure a quick recovery without having to go to the tape backups. Simple, right? The only stumbling block at this point was how to verify if a file was still on disk.

I began to create a stored procedure that would do exactly that. It would take a filename as an input parameter and run a command shell in order to use the dir command in DOS. Details of this can be found in the DBA_Verify_File_Exists procedure in the downloadable zip file. And while I was quite proud that I was able to do this rather easily, a colleague then pointed out to me the undocumented extended stored procedure, xp_fileexist. As I was about to rewrite everything to use the extended stored procedure, I remembered that Microsoft always tells us that undocumented objects are subject to change without notice. So perhaps it is best to use the DIR command, but feel free to make modifications if you desire.

Wheels in Motion

With the procedure in place to check if a file exists on disk, we were ready to write the other procedures that would do the bulk of the work. First up was a stored procedure that would query the msdb database and retrieve the actual backup filename. It is named DBA_Recent_Backup_files, and is included the zip file. The procedure takes the name of a particular database as an input string, and based upon that database name it searches for any full and differential backup files by using the following code:

```
select @backup_set_full = max(bs.backup_set_id)
from msdb.dbo.backupset bs
where bs.database_name = @dbname
and bs.type = 'D'
and bs.server_name = @@servername

select @backup_set_diff = max(bs.backup_set_id)
from msdb.dbo.backupset bs
where bs.database_name = @dbname
and bs.type = 'I'
and bs.backup_set_id > @backup_set_full
and bs.server_name = @@servername
```

And from this, everything will fall into place. First, we find the backup_set_id for the most recent full backup. Then, using that backup_set_id, we find the most recent differential backup, if one is available. If there is no differential backup, then the @backup_set_diff variable is NULL, and we respond accordingly.

With no differential, then all we are concerned about is the time of latest full backup and if that file is still on disk. The following code will return the physical_device_name for the full backup, which is the filename that will be passed to the DBA_Verify_File_exists stored procedure. If the physical_device_name is NULL, then there is no full backup that is less than twenty-four hours old.

```
select @physical_device_name= '"'+convert(varchar(200),bmf.physical_device_name)+'"'
from msdb.dbo.backupset bs, msdb.dbo.backupmediafamily bmf
where bs.media_set_id = bmf.media_set_id
and ((bs.backup_set_id = @backup_set_full))    -- need full
and bs.server_name = @@servername
and bs.backup_finish_date > dateadd(hh, -24, getdate())     --we want to find a full backup within the
last 24 hours
order by bs.backup_set_id    --in case more than one is available, make certain we check only the most
recent
```

If a differential backup does exist, then we want to check to see if that differential backup is less than twenty-four hours old. Here things get a little trickier. It is not enough that we have a differential file available on disk that is less than twenty-four hours old. Why? Because the differential backup is useless unless you have the original database backup file to start with! So, we need to check that the differential is recent and available, and also check that the full backup is available on disk. So we insert into a temporary table two rows, one for the full backup filename, and one for the differential. From there, we verify that each file exists on disk. All the while, we are building our error message that will ultimately be inserted into the Backup_Verify table within our DBA_Perform database.

Create the Job

The last thing we needed to do was to put together a job that would run once a day and generate an email notification if necessary. We created a job that simply calls a procedure named DBA_Recent_Backups (also included in the zip file). This procedure creates a cursor that steps through all of the databases (filtering out pubs, tempdb, and Northwind, of course) and passes each database name to the DBA_Recent_Backup_files stored procedure. The DBA_Recent_Backups procedure will then retrieve a count of the rows in the Backup_Verify table that are less than 24 hours old.

Included in the email notification is a select statement to assist the DBA currently on call in troubleshooting the situation. It was discovered that inclusion of the filenames that are being retrieved from the msdb would greatly reduce the amount of time necessary to troubleshoot, as the DBA would not need to step through the code or look through the msdb database. We could have included the filenames in the email, and feel free to format the notification as you desire. The filenames are stored in the backup_verify table, and there is a filename for the latest full backup as well as the latest differential.

Conclusions

Face it, DBAs are working best when they are not seen. If you have six managers in your cube on Monday morning, something has gone horribly wrong. We all have our own tool boxes that we have built up over time, and in the end they all get some of the basics accomplished. Backup the databases, scan the error logs, check for failed jobs each morning, etc. But management will always want to know what will be done to minimize risk in the event of a disaster The attached code is yet another tool that can assist a DBA to assure their company that the database servers are as stable as possible.

Arriving at Database Growth Factor in SQL Server 2000

By Suresh Maganti

Introduction

This article explores the system table SYSALTFILES in the master database and the table, SYSFILES in each database, and figures out a method of arriving at the growth factor for each database file in an instance of Microsoft SQL Server 2000.

Detailed Discussion

The system table, SYSATLFILES resident in the master database stores information on the files of all the databases in the SQL Server instance. Similarly, the system table, SYSFILES resident in each database stores information on the files of that particular database only. The structure of the two system tables, SYSALTFILES and SYSFILES is similar and so is the information contained except that the former has information on all the databases and the latter has information on only the database in which it resides.

As we already know, every database would be comprised of at least one data file and at least one log file. If a database is set to grow automatically, user has the option to specify either the percentage by which it should auto-grow or a size in Megabytes by which the file should grow. Fetching the already specified auto-growth factor for a database file can be accomplished through Enterprise Manager. But such as exercise may be good at the beginning stages of one's career when speed of work is not a factor but at a later stage nothing beats the efficiency or speed of the prolific T-SQL.

The issue comes when a user has to get the growth factor for a database file using T-SQL. One would imagine that reading through SYSALTFILES instead of SYSFILES would be a better choice as information for all files of all databases can be gathered in a single operation. Such a perception is natural.

SQL Server Books Online specifies that if the status entry for a particular database file is 0x100000, the growth column entry in SYSALTFILES for that particular database file should be perceived as a percentage. If not, then the corresponding entry in the growth column should be read as number of pages. The same logic holds true for the system table, SYSFILES.

Issue

The column, STATUS of the system table, MASTER.DBO.SYSATLFILES does not always match the same column, STATUS of the system table, SYSFILES for the same database file. This leads to erroneous interpretation of growth factor at times. Let me clarify this point with the situation that I encountered recently. The column, Status was 3 and the column, Growth was 10 in MASTER.DBO.SYSATLFILES for a particular database file. When I perform the T-SQL AND operator on the status column as follows, the result is 0:

```
select 3 & 0x100000
```

A value of 0 means that the growth is not in percentage but it is in number of 8K pages. SO I should assume that the Growth factor is 10 pages. When I looked up the growth factor in the Enterprise Manager for the same database file, the value was 10 percent. So my interpretation of the STATUS column in MASTER.DBO.SYSALTFILES for this file was wrong.

Now, in Query Analyzer, I choose the database in question and read from the table SYSFILES for the same database file. The column, Status was 1048579 and the column, Growth was 10 for the same database file (the Status column-value in SYSALTFILES was 3). And the AND operation of Status with 0x100000 was non-zero. That means, The Growth value of 10 in this case means the data file is set to auto-grow by 10% each time it runs out of space. This is validated by the reading in the Enterprise Manager.

Solution

Based on the above analysis, it could be concluded that SYSFILES is absolutely reliable for interpreting data-file growth factors. I have validated the same with several databases in our environment and each time the value of Growth in SYSFILES has been consistent with that in the Enterprise Manager, but the value of Growth in MASTER.DBO.SYSALTFILES has not.

I have created a script based on this conclusion. The script traverses the system table, SYSFILES in each of the databases in an instance of SQL Server and provides consistent results on database-files' growth factor removing all ambiguity on whether the growth factor is in pages or in percentage.

Again, in case of growth by number of pages, SQL Server Enterprise Manager considers whole numbers only. For example, for the system database MSDB, the growth factor is 32 pages for the data file MSDBData, which is equivalent to

$$(32 * 8192)/(1024 * 1024) \text{ MB} = 0.25 \text{ MB}.$$

0.25 MB is interpreted as a whole number in Enterprise Manager as 1 MB. Such a consideration has also been handled in the script.

The T-SQL script is available for download at www.sqlservercentral.com.

Conclusion

In all cases where database file sizes and their growth factors need to be studied, it would be better to use the system table SYSFILES present in each database rather than the system table, SYSALTFILES present only in the master database. Although a lengthier approach, the results are perfect. In these days where a DBA has less and less time and more and more databases to manage, T-SQL instead of Enterprise Manager comes in handy in terms of fast results and portable code as shown in this article.

Differential Backup Prediction

By Darwin Hatheway

A while back, I was thinking about my backup strategy and it occurred to me that I might be able to optimize it if I could predict, in advance, how much disk space a differential backup would consume. If a database hasn't changed much - or at all - since yesterday's full backup, why not save space and time by doing incremental backups until it's worthwhile to do another full? Since differential backups run very quickly on even very large databases when little has changed, there must be some structure in the database that accelerates finding the changed pages.

"Surely," I thought, "this information must be available to the DBA."

So, I started hunting through "Books On Line" and trolling through the SQL-DMO Object Model looking for the function that would tell me what percentage of a database had changed through the last full backup or a function that would list the affected pages or ... something useful... but I couldn't find anything obviously helpful.

The best I could find was a brief description of the Differential Change Map (DCM) page, in Kalen Delaney's book, "Inside SQL Server 2000," and a briefer description of how to locate the page in the database. Armed with this meager store of knowledge, I started working with the DBCC PAGE utility to see if I could locate and decode the information on that page.

I ran into trouble right away. "Inside SQL Server" said that page 6 would be a DCM page and, sure enough, it was. However, it also said that a DCM page occurred every 511230 pages and that wasn't quite the case. Fortunately, the actual value was very close (511232) and I was able to locate the second DCM page in one of my larger databases after a brief search just ahead of and just beyond the expected page. I'm still not sure why the published value is off by two.

To see an example DCM page, execute the following:

```
DBCC TRACEON (3604)
GO
DBCC PAGE('<database>',1,6,3)
GO
```

The parameters to this DBCC command are:
DatabaseName
FileNumber
PageNumber
Formatting

I ran this command against a couple of small test databases, trying various formats. As it turns out, a format value of 3 formats a DCM page very nicely. The output (minus a lot of page header information) looked like this:

```
DIFF_MAP: Extent Alloc Status @0x1A14C0C2
-----------------------------------------
(1:0)        - (1:8)       =      CHANGED
(1:16)       -             = NOT  CHANGED
(1:24)       -             =      CHANGED
(1:32)       - (1:56)      = NOT  CHANGED
...
```

What we see here are extents or extent ranges described by their first page number for a single extent or first page number of first extent and first page number of last extent for a range.

Dividing the page numbers by 8 gives the extent numbers that are marked changed or unchanged. So, for the dbcc ouptut fragment above, we determine that:

Extents 0 to 1 - changed (pages 0 to 7 and 8 to 15)
Extent 2 - not changed (pages 16 to 23)
Extent 3 - changed (pages 24 to 31)
Extent 4 to 7 - not changed (pages 32 to 63)

Awkwardly, DMO and DBCC do not agree on terminology. To tally up all the changed extents for a database, you also have to look through all files in the database. I was planning to discover all the databases and files on a server by looping through DMO objects. In DMO, a database can have one or more File Groups, referenced by FileGroupNumber. I had to do a little experimentation to be sure that a FileNumber parameter for DBCC would be the same as FileGroupNumber in DMO and it is.

The next step was to try and tally up the list of changed extents, run a differential backup and see how my tally compared to reality. Even tallying a small-but-still-large-enough database for test purposes would require me to get started with programming at this point, rather than spend a lot of time with a calculator.

My plan was to use VB to execute the DBCC calls and get the output from the 3604 trace flag into a message buffer. Unfortunately, the there's considerable gark included with the output, along with some seemingly unpredictable extra cr/lf pairs, and parsing this looked like it was going to be a true pain in the...

Then I got unlucky and lucky at the same moment. While I was thinking about how I'd do the decoding and tallying, I noticed that the largest message buffer returned was just about 64K in length and quite a few of the message buffers returned were that size. That seemed highly suspicious. A little more investigation persuaded me that, between SQL-DMO and VB, something was limiting the maximum size of the return message buffer to 64K (I use VB 6). If the call wouldn't return the entire message buffer of page information, there was no point writing a ton of code to plow through it. This seemed very unlucky. Thinking there was no feasible way to do this, I set the project aside for the rest of the day.

The next day, I realized that hitting the 64K limit was actually a lucky thing. It caused me to stop and think. I realized that I had foolishly overlooked the "with tableresults" option to the DBCC command. I tried that and found using a result table was more promising. Still using 3 as the format parameter, we get a nicely formatted group of records to scroll through that looks (minus the header records) like this:

```
DIFF_MAP: Header @0x1A14C064 Slot 0, Offset 96 DIFF_MAP: Extent Alloc Status @0x1A14C0C2 (1:0)  -
(1:8) CHANGED
DIFF_MAP: Header @0x1A14C064 Slot 0, Offset 96 DIFF_MAP: Extent Alloc Status @0x1A14C0C2 (1:16) -
NOT CHANGED
DIFF_MAP: Header @0x1A14C064 Slot 0, Offset 96 DIFF_MAP: Extent Alloc Status @0x1A14C0C2 (1:24) -
CHANGED
DIFF_MAP: Header @0x1A14C064 Slot 0, Offset 96 DIFF_MAP: Extent Alloc Status @0x1A14C0C2 (1:32) -
(1:56)NOT CHANGED
```

Using the table result, it was fairly easy to set up a program to scroll through the result set and select only the records marked "CHANGED" and tally up the changed extents. My code examines the field that contains "CHANGED" or "NOT CHANGED" and, when it finds a match on "CHANGED" the page range is parsed and the modified extent(s) are added to the tally.

Then, the final step was to compare the results to reality. A small VB program modeled on the above, scanned 25GB of databases on our server in well under a minute and I arranged to write out the change tallies to a listbox. Running this just before our periodic differential backups, I found my differential size prediction was within 256K of every differential backup. Apparently, each differential includes 128K to 256K of header information, which accounts for the small difference. It also appears that the differential backups are done by extent; if the extent is marked changed, the entire extent is written to the backup.

OK, what good is this? Well, I'm working on that. With reliable differential size prediction, I can set up optimized backup processes that will minimize the number of backup pages written to disk while still maximizing the protection given to the databases. Most of us run some sort of automatic database backup process on a scheduled basis. Knowing the size of an expected differential (and it takes just a very few seconds to get this information), your periodic automatic backups could include code to "decide" whether or not to run a differential or a full backup. If a differential will be truly small, a full backup plus a number of differential backup will both minimize disk space taken for backups and allow for quick restores. Databases which change little over the course of an entire week could be differentialed every day for a week, saving considerable time spent running disk backups. If one of these databases suddenly undergoes massive changes, the next and all subsequent differentials would all be very large. Doing a full at this point and then switching back to differentials might save considerable disk space on the next few days' worth of backups.

However, at this point, I haven't quite figured out how I'm going to set up the automatic process. I'll probably end up with a system that contains history information, so the backup routine can make good guesses as to best strategy and I might include override options the DBA can set to force certain behaviors.

While you're waiting for me to figure out how to use differential prediction in practice, you could look into it on your own. I'm including three files that provide just about all the code you need for a complete differential predictor:

- DifferentialPredictorMain.frm, which is principally the code to loop through the databases on a server and write the predictions to a listbox. The complete form will need about four objects on it, which are described in the comments.
- DBAUtil.bas, which is a module that does most of the heavy lifting in this project. It includes the routines to locate the DCM pages and decode the results.
- UTIL.bas, which contains a few of my library routines I found useful for this project.

You will need to include references to the SQL-DMO objects in your project. As a security note, my code is set up for trusted connections.

Dynamic Management Objects

By Christoffer Hedgate

Introducing Dynamic Management Objects

Performance tuning and troubleshooting in SQL Server has always been something of a black art. To be effective at it you need to know how to use a large set of tools, including Profiler, Perfmon, DBCC commands and stored procedures. Sometimes it can seem almost random which tool you should use for a specific issue. They will often affect performance themselves, so you might not always be able to use them. Another problem is undocumented DBCC commands or system tables. More or less everyone who knows something about tuning, know and use a couple of these. But the advice has always been that you should not use these unless you really know what you are doing or you are told to use them by a Microsoft support professional. For all of these reasons SQL Server 2000 can be seen as a black box that can be quite difficult to penetrate. SQL Server 2005 changes all this by introducing the new Dynamic Management Objects (DMO)*.

Note: Dynamic Management Objects have absolutely nothing to do with SQL-DMO, the old technique for programmatically accessing the server, which has now been replaced by SMO.

The dynamic management objects introduce a very transparent view into what is going on inside SQL Server at any time. There are two types of DMO; Dynamic Management Views (DMV) and Dynamic Management Functions (DMF). These are similar in the same way as any view and function, with the difference being that the DMFs take arguments that refine the output. They both generate tabular resultsets with dynamically generated information regarding the state and health of the server. There are 75 dynamic management views and dynamic management functions fully documented in SQL Server Books Online.

The information returned by the DMOs is collected by the engine itself from lots of different sources and the DMOs make it easy for you to use it by simply querying them using SELECT statements. Since the information shows the current state of the server this means that when the server is restarted the information collected is lost and the engine starts collecting a fresh set.

* I do not know if DMO is actually an officially used abbreviation. The term dynamic management objects is used however in Books Online for referring to dynamic management views and dynamic management functions as a whole.

Categories of DMOs

The DMOs are divided into different categories and named accordingly to be easy to find and distinguish. All DMO names start with the prefix dm_ (no difference between DMVs and DMFs). Next follows a prefix identifying the category a DMO belongs to. For instance, the prefix dm_io_ is used for dynamic management objects that return information regarding disk and network I/O. Another category is dm_clr_ which is used for DMOs that return information regarding the hosting of the CLR (.NET Common Language Runtime) in SQL Server. Below is a listing of the complete set of categories of dynamic management objects.

- dm_broker_* - Service Broker
- dm_clr_* - Common Language Runtime
- dm_db_* - Database related
- dm_db_index_* - Indexes
- dm_db_mirroring_* - Database mirroring
- dm_exec_* - Execution
- dm_fts_* - Full-Text Search
- dm_io_* - I/O
- dm_os_* - SQL Operating System (SQLOS)
- dm_qn_* - Query Notification
- dm_repl_* - Replication
- dm_tran_* - Transactions

The following query lists all the dynamic management objects that are available:

```
SELECT [name], [type], type_desc
FROM sys.system_objects
WHERE NAME LIKE 'dm%'
ORDER BY [name]
```

Viewing a currently executing query

Now, lets have a look at a typical usage of the dynamic management objects. One problem that a DBA sometimes faces is when some connection is executing something that seems to be blocking resources and making the system run slowly. Prior to SQL Server 2005, you needed to have a trace running already in Profiler (or a server-side trace of course) when the blocking statement was executed. A trace started after the connection had already started the execution of the blocking statement would not be able to show you what that connection was actually doing. You could always try DBCC INPUTBUFFER, but depending on the situation you might not get all the information you wanted from it. For instance, it only shows the first 255 characters of the statement that was executed, or if it was a procedure that was executed only the procedure name is shown. Lets see what options SQL Server 2005 and the dynamic management objects gives us in this case.

There are three scripts at the end of this article that you can use to follow the action. Script 1 creates a simple stored procedure that starts a transaction, updates all the rows in a table and then sits back and waits for an hour. Script 2 executes this procedure. Note the session ID for the query window where script 2 is executed. Enter this session ID in Script 3 for the variable @sessionid. The rest of the code in Script 3 is the interesting part. First we query sys.dm_exec_requests using the session id. Some of the output in this dynamic management view should look familiar since it is similar to what sp_who returns in SQL Server 2000. However, there is a lot more information in this dynamic management view. We are particularly interested in two columns here, sql_handle and plan_handle. These are hash values of the SQL text and execution plan respectively used for the request we are looking at. With these handles we can move on and look closer at what this request is doing.

The dynamic management view sys.dm_exec_query_stats can tell us a lot about the amount of resources used by a query plan given a sql_handle or plan_handle. However, we are simply interested in reviewing what the request is doing right now, so we instead use the dynamic management function sys.dm_exec_sql_text. This table-valued function takes a sql_handle as input and returns a table where the column text contains the actual SQL statement(s) that corresponds to that hash. If we pass it the sql_handle we got from sys.dm_exec_requests we get the text of the stored procedure executed in Script 2. But we are not finished yet. There is one further step we can take to really understand what is going on. By passing the plan_handle from sys.dm_exec_requests into the dynamic management function sys.dm_exec_query_plan we can get the actual query plan that was used to execute the request. The output column query_plan contains the query plan in the new showplan XML format. Like all columns that return XML data in SQL Server Management Studio we can click the contents of the column and a new window is opened with the XML data indented and fully readable. Even better, if we save the xml with a . sqlplan extension we can then double-click the saved file and SQL Server Management Studio will show the graphical query plan that the showplan XML describes. At this stage we should be able to tell exactly what is causing the problem.

Summary

The dynamic management objects gives us a very transparent view of what is going on inside various areas of SQL Server 2005. By using them we will be able to query the system for information about it's current state in a much more effective and easy way than ever before. For performance tuning and troubleshooting they will be an essential tool to use. This article has shown a small glimpse of what they are and how you can use them, now it is time to start taking a look at all the other available dynamic views and functions.

Scripts for demo

Script 1

```
USE AdventureWorks
GO
CREATE PROCEDURE dbo.updater
AS
BEGIN TRAN
UPDATE Person.Contact WITH (HOLDLOCK)
SET FirstName = 'Chris'
WAITFOR DELAY '01:00:00'
```

```
ROLLBACK TRAN
GO
```

Script 2

```
-- Execute the line below and note the session ID for the query window executing this part
-- SELECT @@SPID

EXEC dbo.updater
```

Script 3

```
DECLARE @sessionid INT
SET @sessionid = 52 -- Change to the session ID script 2 was executed in
DECLARE @sqlhandle VARBINARY(64)
DECLARE @planhandle VARBINARY(64)

SELECT @sqlhandle = sql_handle, @planhandle = plan_handle
FROM sys.dm_exec_requests
WHERE session_id = @sessionid
SELECT *
FROM sys.dm_exec_sql_text(@sqlhandle)
SELECT *
FROM sys.dm_exec_query_plan(@planhandle)
```

Detecting Performance Issues With Sysprocesses

By Terry Troisi

Using Master..Sysprocess to Isolate Performance Issues - Part 1

It's 4:30 on Friday and your boss comes to you in a panic. The e-commerce system is down, and the database is to blame. You go through your usual what's-going-on checklist and all you can tell is the CPU on the SQL Server is pegged at 100%. You check Profiler, but no high CPU commands seem to hitting the database. Looks like it's going to be a late Friday.

Checking the Sysprocesses table

Finding the solution to this weekend killing scenario is often quite simple. The sysprocesses table in the master database holds information about each unique process, or SPID, running on the SQL Server. To view information about these processes, run the following command in Query Analyzer:

```
select * from master..sysprocesses
```

The output will be a row for each unique SPID on the server. SPIDs 1 thru 50 are reserved for internal SQL Server processes, while SPIDs 51 and above are external connections.

Finding high CPU activity

Since the issue appears to be a CPU intensive process, you will be particularly interested in the CPU column in the result set. The value in this column is cumulative over the period the process has been connected to the server, so a high value doesn't necessarily indicate a problem. However, combined with the status column, you may be able to narrow down on the particular process that is causing you to stay late on Friday. If the sysprocesses table holds many rows, narrowing down to processes that are currently active as follows might be helpful:

```
select * from master..sysprocesses
where status = 'runnable'
order by CPU desc
```

The status = 'runnable' clause will return only processes that are currently running. You can now look at the top couple of rows that were returned. Do any have values in the CPU column that seem excessively high? Generally, a value in the thousands might indicate a problem.

Assigning blame

Now that we have isolated the process that is causing the pegged CPU scenario we can look further into exactly what this process is. The following columns in the master..sysprocesses table will help shed light on the culprit:

loginname - The login used to connect to SQL for this process. This can be a SQL Server login, or a Windows domain account.
hostname - The NetBios name of the computer where the process originated.
program_name - The name of the application that opened the connection

Furthermore, the exact command currently being run can usually be determined. On SQL 7.0 or SQL 2000 sp2 or below servers, the following command will output the first 255 characters of the command currently being run for a particular SPID:

```
DBCC INPUTBUFFER (spid)    -- replace spid with the actual numeric value
```

The above command will also work on SQL 2000 sp3 and SQL 2005 servers (with SQL 2005 up to 4000 characters may be returned). These SQL editions have three additional columns in the master..sysprocesses table: `sql_handle, stmt_start,` and `stmt_end`. These columns can be used to obtain additional information on the command being run as follows:

```
DECLARE@handle binary(20)
SELECT @handle = sql_handle FROM master..sysprocesses
WHERE spid = SPID  -- replace with actual numeric value
SELECT [text] FROM ::fn_get_sql(@handle)
```

Now that you know who is running what from where and why it is pegging your CPU, you may choose to contact them and ask them to stop their process, or if you are really ready to start your weekend, terminate the process using the KILL command:

```
KILL SPID  -- replace with actual numeric value
```

Conclusion

The sysprocesses table holds valuable information on the processes running on your server. There are several SQL management tools on the market today that make great use in leveraging this information to generate all kinds of useful reports on your databases - Periscope for SQL Server by Highwire Development and i/3 by Veritas are two examples.

In Part 2 we will examine how to use the sysprocess table to create an automated job to monitor another common performance bottleneck - blocking. Until then, enjoy your Friday.

Enterprise Manager Tricks for Newbies

By Sushila Iyer

Introductory warnings!

If you're one of those that heap scorn on Enterprise Manager (EM) and the people that use it, please note that this article has been written exclusively with the newbie in mind. One of the members of this site - Erik Little - once said something so remarkably enthusiastic that I was immediately struck by how much all of us can benefit by adopting such a novel and refreshing outlook towards being a rookie! Erik said - "Man, it's great being a newbie, feels like Christmas every day!" - I'm sure all of you agree that this can't be topped for a positive attitude. EM and "newbieness" are tied together in that this tool can teach a lot to someone just starting out with SQL Server and who has some basic knowledge of T-Sql syntax. So while there are still people on SQL Server 2000 and before the Yukon gold rush knocks this great tool off the map, let's proceed to make good use of some EM basics with some Query Analyzer (QA) magic. Before we start, I must redeem myself with the disclaimer that all the database objects in this article have been created for demonstration purposes only and even the slightest similarity to any real world database is completely unintentional!

Let's learn how to create tables, views and stored procedures using both EM and QA to our advantage:

1. Expand **Databases**, right click on **Tables** and select **New Table...**

2. In the grid provided for **Column Name**, **Data Type**, **Length** and **Allow Nulls**, type in 3 column names and select their datatypes as you see below (leave the SQL Server defaults for varchar lengths and Allow Nulls as is):

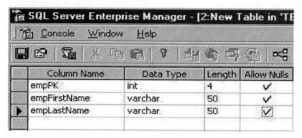

3. Select the **empPK** column and in the Column details box provided at the bottom of the screen

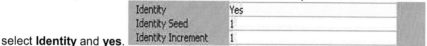

select **Identity** and **yes**.

4. Save this table as **EmpDetails**.

5. Right click on the **EmpDetails** table and select **Design Table**. With **empPK** selected, click on the

Set primary key icon on the menu bar and **Save**.

6. The exercise behind setting the primary key **after** the table creation is to enable us to view the **alter table** script.

   Right click on **EmpDetails** again and select **All Tasks - Generate SQL Script...** In the **Options** tab, under **Table Scripting Options**, check the two boxes that say **Script indexes** and **Script PRIMARY keys, FOREIGN keys, defaults, and check constraints**. Go back to the **General** tab and click on the **Preview** button on the top right of screen. Click on the **Copy** button of your preview window.

   Open Query Analzyer and paste the SQL script and there you have it....the script for both the **Create table** as well as the **Alter Table** where we set the primary key constraint on the **empPK** column.

```
if exists (select * from dbo.sysobjects where id = object_id(N'[dbo].[EmpDetails]') and
OBJECTPROPERTY(id, N'IsUserTable') = 1)

drop table [dbo].[EmpDetails]
GO
CREATE TABLE [dbo].[EmpDetails] (
        [empPK] [int] IDENTITY (1, 1) NOT NULL ,
        [empFirstName] [varchar] (50) COLLATE SQL_Latin1_General_CP1_CI_AS NULL ,
        [empLastName] [varchar] (50) COLLATE SQL_Latin1_General_CP1_CI_AS NULL
) ON [PRIMARY]
GO
ALTER TABLE [dbo].[EmpDetails] WITH NOCHECK ADD
        CONSTRAINT [PK_EmpDetails] PRIMARY KEY  CLUSTERED
        ( [empPK]
        ) ON [PRIMARY]
GO
```

7. Delete the **ALTER TABLE** section and modify the remaining script to create a new table called **EmpAccounts**:

```
if exists (select * from dbo.sysobjects where id = object_id(N'[dbo].[EmpAccounts]') and
OBJECTPROPERTY(id, N'IsUserTable') = 1)
drop table [dbo].[EmpAccounts]
```

```
GO
CREATE TABLE [dbo].[EmpAccounts] (
        [empFK] [int] NOT NULL ,
        [empAccountNumber] [int] NULL ,
        [empBankName] [varchar] (50) NULL
) ON [PRIMARY]
GO
```

8. Run the script by clicking on the **Execute Query** Play button or **F5** on your keyboard and you have just created a new table and learnt a little of T-SQL syntax along the way. Go back to EM and you will see the new table that you have just created.
Now let's insert data into the two tables using EM for one and the QA for the other:

9. Right click on **EmpDetails** table, **Open Table**, **Return all rows** and insert 6 sample rows - you do not have to insert any values in the **empPK** column as it is an identity column and SQL Server will generate this automatically for you. These are the rows that I created for demonstration purposes:

Before we insert rows into the **EmpAccounts** table using QA we will create a view - the reasons for creating one will become apparent as we go along - but essentially we need this view to tell us what **empAccountNumber** and **empBankName** to enter against a given **empFK**.

Now for views:

10. Right click on **Views** in EM and select **New View....** Right click on the upper pane and select **Add Table** - from the list of tables, double click and open **EmpDetails** first and then the **EmpAccounts** table - click **Close**. So far the two tables are not linked by any relationships and you will see that the T-Sql generated in the bottom pane reads:

```
SELECT
FROM        dbo.EmpDetails CROSS JOIN
                 dbo.EmpAccounts
```

Select the **empPK** column and keeping your mouse pressed, select the **empFK** column from the second table. Notice how the T-Sql immediately changes to:

```
SELECT
FROM        dbo.EmpDetails INNER JOIN
                 dbo.EmpAccounts ON dbo.EmpDetails.empPK = dbo.EmpAccounts.empFK
```

Note also that a **link** has been created between the two tables represented iconically by the diamond shaped inner join.
For now let's select all the columns in the order they appear in the two tables, so the first column selected is **empPK** and the last one is **empBankName** and the T-Sql generated is:

```
SELECT     dbo.EmpDetails.empPK, dbo.EmpDetails.empFirstName, dbo.EmpDetails.empLastName,
 dbo.EmpAccounts.empFK, dbo.EmpAccounts.empAccountNumber, dbo.EmpAccounts.empBankName
FROM        dbo.EmpDetails INNER JOIN
                 dbo.EmpAccounts ON dbo.EmpDetails.empPK = dbo.EmpAccounts.empFK
```

The first change we're going to make is to concatenate the first name and last name into one column for readability. Your T-Sql will look like this after concatenation:

```
SELECT     dbo.EmpDetails.empPK, dbo.EmpDetails.empFirstName + ' ' +
dbo.EmpDetails.empLastName AS empName, dbo.EmpAccounts.empFK,
                 dbo.EmpAccounts.empAccountNumber, dbo.EmpAccounts.empBankName
FROM        dbo.EmpDetails INNER JOIN
                 dbo.EmpAccounts ON dbo.EmpDetails.empPK = dbo.EmpAccounts.empFK
```

If you click on **run** represented by the **exclamation mark** on the menu bar, you will not get any rows back. The two tables are joined by an inner join - simply put - the inner join will return only those rows where for each **empPK** in **EmpDetails** you have corresponding **empFK** rows in **EmpAccounts**. Since EmpAccounts does not have any data, you will not see any rows. To ensure that you get the resultset from both tables, let's change the inner join. Right click on the **link icon** between the two tables and select **Select All Rows from EmpDetails**. Notice how the T-Sql immediately changes to:

```
SELECT      dbo.EmpDetails.empPK, dbo.EmpDetails.empFirstName + ' ' +
dbo.EmpDetails.empLastName AS empName, dbo.EmpAccounts.empFK,
            dbo.EmpAccounts.empAccountNumber, dbo.EmpAccounts.empBankName
FROM        dbo.EmpDetails LEFT OUTER JOIN
            dbo.EmpAccounts ON dbo.EmpDetails.empPK = dbo.EmpAccounts.empFK
```

Now if you click on **Run**, you will see **all** the rows from **EmpDetails** with null values in the **EmpAccounts** table. Note also that the diamond shaped **inner join** icon now changes to represent a **left outer join** one.

11. Save this view as **vwEmpInfo** and let's move back to QA to enter values into the **EmpAccounts** table using the newly created view to help us.

12. In QA, type **SELECT * FROM vwEmpInfo** and run the query. Using the resultset in the bottom pane, you can now start inserting the values for the **EmpAccounts** table since you can now see the employee details against which you can enter corresponding account data. These are the values I inserted into my **EmpAccounts** table using **Insert into**:

```
INSERT INTO EmpAccounts (empFK, empAccountNumber, empBankName) VALUES(1, 1000, 'Wachovia')
INSERT INTO EmpAccounts (empFK, empAccountNumber, empBankName) VALUES(2, 1001, 'Sun Trust')
INSERT INTO EmpAccounts (empFK, empAccountNumber, empBankName) VALUES(3, 1002, 'Amro Bank')
INSERT INTO EmpAccounts (empFK, empAccountNumber, empBankName) VALUES(4, 1003, 'Credite
Suisse')
INSERT INTO EmpAccounts (empFK, empAccountNumber, empBankName) VALUES(5, 1004, 'Central
Fidelity')
INSERT INTO EmpAccounts (empFK, empAccountNumber, empBankName) VALUES(6, 1005, 'Wachovia')
```

13. Now back to our view in EM where we will **uncheck** the **empPK** and **empFK** columns since these were checked only so we could use the **empPK** as reference to enter values into the **EmpAccounts** table. Change the link back to an **INNER JOIN** either by using the **icon - properties** or by directly typing it in the T-Sql pane. Save the view again with the new changes.

Now for the very last object - stored procedure:

14. A stored procedure is (simply explained) one or more T-Sql statements stored in Sql Server. Right click **Stored Procedure** and **New Stored Procedure....** I usually use a **comments template** at the beginning of each of my procedures which is infinitely more detailed than what is shown here. Please substitute with your own customised version. Here's the procedure I created:

```
/*****************************************************************************
Name:       procEmpInfo
Details:    View employee name, account number and bank info from
            EmpDetails & EmpAccounts tables.
            Date            Who             Comments
History:    08/10/2005      Sushila         Created initial.
*****************************************************************************/
CREATE PROCEDURE procEmpInfo
AS
SELECT * FROM vwEmpInfo
GO
```

15. When creating and saving a new stored procedure, EM offers us the opportunity to also **Save as Template**. Once it is saved as a template, it is presented to you everytime you want to write a new procedure - you only have to modify the existing template and thus save on typing, editing etc. As indicated by the **Create** syntax, save this procedure as **procEmpInfo**.

16. Now for the very last step - using QA, run your new procedure - **EXEC procEmpInfo** to view the results and you should see all the employee names with the corresponding account numbers and bank names.

Summary

Now let's review everything that we've accomplished with the exercises listed above:

1. Created table **EmpDetails** using EM.
2. Set primary key on **EmpDetails** after saving it so that we could get the **Alter Table** syntax.
3. Generated script for **EmpDetails** using EM - modifying this script in QA to create new table **EmpAccounts**.
4. Inserted values into **EmpDetails** table via EM.
5. Created view in EM - initial T-Sql was **Cross Join** when there was no relationship between the two tables. Created relationship using the **Design** interface and stepped through the process of **Inner Join** and **Left Outer Join** learning a lot of useful join syntax along the way. Concatenated **empFirstName** and **empLastName** to get **empName**.
6. Used view in QA to insert values into **EmpAccounts**.
7. Modified view in EM and changed the join back to **INNER** and selected only the three columns that were required.
8. Created stored procedure in EM (along with template for future use) - using the view.
9. Executed stored procedure in QA.

Conclusions

All the exercises listed were primarily to demonstrate that both EM and QA are closely interwoven; We can always use EM for its' ease of use and the fact that it is a great learning tool to get acquainted with T-Sql syntax - to a point where with enough practice, we can comfortably start leaving the EM wizards behind to command some T-Sql wizardry of our own. In the next article in the **newbie series**, we'll look at yet another way to create tables using EM and also have some fun with learning how to create a computed column and a trigger.

More Intelligent Backup and Restore

by Vince Iacoboni

Backup and Restore - More Intelligent Than Before

Backups and restores are some of the primary responsibilities of a DBA, but they're not very fun. Especially when you've got to concoct the correct MOVE statement when restoring from one server to another, or find the latest YYYYMMDDHHMM filename to use for a restore, or get the quoting just right if calling a third-party backup/restore utility such as Imceda's SQL Litespeed or Redgate's SQL Backup. And how many times have you started a restore but forgot to kill existing connections? Or, after the restore from another server, forgot to run sp_change_user_login to match logins with newly restored user ids?

To alleviate some of the pain, I wrote the procedures sp_ABBackupDb and sp_ABRestoreDb. My goal was to make backup/restore as easy as it could be for me. Download the zip file here.

Naming convention note: sp_ is the magical prefix that looks in the master database for a stored procedure, and uses the current database's system tables when doing so. The AB portion follows a Microsoft convention of using sp_MS* names for additional stored procedures they added but didn't document as well. AB is the pre-merger initials of the company I work for.

Features

- Determines whether SQL Litespeed or SQL Backup is present, and by default uses them if they are
- Can backup/restore a list of databases, including {UserDbs}, {SystemDbs}, or {AllDbs}
- Intelligent file specifications than can include:
  - Database name
  - Current datetime (backup only)
  - Wildcards that match the most recent file

- Prepend backup path if relative filespec provided
- Sensible defaults when no filespec provided
- Multiple filespecs can be specified for parallel backup/restore
- Dynamic construction of the MOVE clause on restores:
  - If database to restore exists, use existing database physical filenames
  - If database to restore doesn't exist, put data on the Default Data and Default Log paths specified in Enterprise Manager and saved in the registry
  - If logical filenames on existing database and file to restore differ, match them intelligently
  - Give up if the number of logical files by type (data,log) in the backup differs from the database
- Kill existing database users before restore
- Fixup user logins after restore with sp_change_user_login
- Remove old backups after any number of hours, days, or weeks
- Can specify additional WITH clause options to pass through to backup or restore
- Optionally verify backups

To use the procedures, call them from any database (except, of course, a database that you wish to restore) using EXEC. The return code of the procedure is zero if no errors occur, otherwise the highest-numbered error encountered is returned (but see the Limitations section for a caveat).

sp_ABBackupDb Parameters

Parameter	Default	Information
@Databases	DB_NAME ()	Comma-separated list of databases to backup. Can include {UserDbs}, {SystemDbs}, or {AllDbs}. {SystemDbs} and {AllDbs} include master on backup.
@FileSpec	&\&_db_@ or &_db_@	File specification that determines the name of the backup output file(s). & is replaced by the name of the database, and @ is replaced by the current datetime in YYYYMMDDHHMM format. The specification may include the wildcards * and ?, in which case the LATEST file matching the pattern is used. If no drive letter or UNC path is given, prepends the path specified in the BackupDirectory registry key. If no extension is provided, will use .BAK for native SQL and Litespeed backups and .SQB for SQL Backup. If the parameter is not provided, will use the specification &\&_db_@ or &_db_@ if @CreateDir = 0.
@Options		Additional backup options to be appended to the WITH clause. For SQL Litespeed backups, options starting with @ are additional stored procedure parameters rather than added to the @With parameter.
@Type	(dynamic)	The backup vendor. Valid values are "SQL" for native SQL Server backup, "Litespeed" for Imceda's SQL Litespeed and "SQB" for Redgate's SQL Backup. If not supplied, checks for the existence of extended stored procedures to determine if the third-party backup products should be used.
@Verify	0	Verifies backup file after completion of each backup if set to 1.
@DeleteAfter		Deletes backup files matching the file specification if the YYYYMMDDHHMM component is older than the specified time interval and the backup (and verify if specified) succeeded. Format is a number followed by a space and one of the words "hour", "day", or "week" with an optional plural. The file specification must contain @.
@CreateDir	1	Creates file directories if not already existing. Also, if the @FileSpec parameter is not supplied, places the backup in directories named for the database. If 0, aborts the backup if directory does not exist.
@DryRun	0	If 1, does not perform any backup or file deletions, but displays commands that would be run.

sp_ABRestoreDb Parameters

Parameter	Default	Information
@Databases	(required)	Comma-separated list of databases to restore. Can include {UserDbs}, {SystemDbs}, or {AllDbs}. {SystemDbs} and {AllDbs} DO NOT include master for restores, since this would stop the current instance of SQL Server. This parameter is required.
@FileSpec	&\&* or &*	File specification that determines the name of the backup file(s) to restore. & is replaced by the name of the database. The specification may include the wildcards * and ?, in which case the LATEST file matching the pattern is used. If no drive letter or UNC path is given, prepends the path specified in the BackupDirectory registry key. If the parameter is not provided, will use the specification &\&* if ALL databases to be restored have such directories existing, otherwise the specification &* will be used.
@Options		Additional restore options to be appended to the WITH clause. For SQL Litespeed backups, options starting with @ are additional stored procedure parameters rather than added to the @With parameter. Do not include the MOVE clause, as this is handled automatically.
@Type	(dynamic)	The backup vendor. Valid values are "SQL" for native SQL Server backup, "Litespeed" for Imceda's SQL Litespeed and "SQB" for Redgate's SQL Backup. If not supplied, checks for the existence of extended stored procedures to determine if the third-party backup/restore products should be used.
@DryRun	0	If 1, does not perform any restores, but displays commands that would be run.

Backup Examples

```
-- Backup Northwind to E:\MSSQL\MSSQL$Inst\BACKUP\Northwind_db_HHHHMMDDHHMM.xxx
-- If SQL Backup present use it, xxx extension will be .SQB
-- If Litespeed present use it otherwise native, xxx extension will be .BAK
EXEC sp_ABBackupDb 'Northwind', 'E:\MSSQL\MSSQL$Inst\BACKUP\&_db_@'

-- Backup Northwind to [BackupDir]\Northwind\Northwind_db_HHHHMMDDHHMM.xxx
USE Northwind
EXEC sp_ABBackupDb

-- Differential Backup of Northwind and pubs.  Replace the most recent file
-- in the pattern [BackupDir]\Northwind\Northwind_diff_* and [BackupDir]\pubs\pubs_diff_*
-- Use native SQL backup.  Verify backup file after each backup completes.
EXEC sp_ABBackupDb 'Northwind,pubs', '&_&_diff_*', @Options = 'DIFFERENTIAL', @Type = 'SQL',
@Verify=1
-- Backup all databases except master, model, msdb, and tempdb to backup directory. Do not put
--  files in subdirectories. Filename defaults to [Database]_db_YYYYMMDDHHMM.xxx, where xxx is
--  either SQB or BAK.  Delete backups that are 3 days or more old.
EXEC sp_ABBackupDb '{UserDbs}', @DeleteAfter = '3 days', @CreateDir = 0
-- Backup master, model, msdb, and also pubs, with filenames as above.
EXEC sp_ABBackupDb '{SystemDbs},pubs'
-- Backup Northwind and pubs using three backup files.
EXEC sp_ABBackupDb @Databases = 'Northwind,pubs', @FileSpec = '&_part1,&_part2,&_part3'
```

Restore Examples

```
-- Restore Northwind from most recent backup found in E:\MSSQL\MSSQL$Inst\BACKUP
--  with a filename starting with Northwind_db_.
-- If SQL Backup or Litespeed is present, assume it was used to make the backup.
EXEC sp_ABRestoreDb 'Northwind', 'E:\MSSQL\MSSQL$Inst\BACKUP\&_db_*'
-- Restore Northwind from most recent file matching [BackupDir]\Northwind\Northwind*
--  or [BackupDir]\Northwind* if Northwind dir not present.
EXEC sp_ABRestoreDb 'Northwind'
-- Restore Northwind and pubs.  Use the most recent file.
-- in the pattern [BackupDir]\Northwind\Northwind_diff_* and [BackupDir]\pubs\pubs_diff_*
-- Use native SQL restore.  Use the NORECOVERY option to permit additional log restores.
EXEC sp_ABRestoreDb 'Northwind,pubs', '&_&_diff_*', 'NORECOVERY', 'SQL'
-- Restore all databases (master is intentionally excluded from {AllDbs} and {SystemDbs}).
-- Look for most recent file like [BackupDir]\[Database]\[Database]* if [BackupDir]\[Database]
-- exists for ALL databases, otherwise look for files like [BackupDir]\[Database]*.
USE master
EXEC sp_ABRestoreDb '{AllDbs}'
```

```
-- Restore Northwind and pubs using three backup files each.
EXEC sp_ABBackupDb 'Northwind,pubs', '&_part1,&_part2,&_part3'
-- Create a new database NewPubs from the most recent backup of pubs on the
--    share \\Prod\share\.
-- Create the new database devices in the default data and log device locations.
EXEC sp_ABRestoreDb 'NewPubs', '\\Prod\share\pubs_db_*'
```

Benefits

Using sp_ABBackupDb provides the benefits of simplicity and consistency to your scheduled backups. You can get away with a single backup command for all of your databases. You can use the same backup command across multiple servers, even when paths to the backups differ, by allowing the default backup directory to be prepended. You can replace backups that are part of a database maintenance plan by using the @DeleteAfter option. When you have a mix of third-party and native backup software in your environment, you can handle them consistently. Adhoc backups become simple.

The major benefits, though, are seen on the restore side. Coding your cross-server restore directly requires fiddling with the MOVE clause, unless the paths on the two servers are identical. Then you need to lookup just what those logical file names are, and get the pathing correct to the current database physical filenames. Of course, for adhoc restores you can use the restore wizards within SQL Enterprise Manager, SQL Litespeed MMC console, or the SQL Backup GUI. Maybe it's just me, but these seem to require lots of clicks, and tend to confuse my little brain. And of course, if you forgot to kill the existing connections first, you get to start over at square one with the GUIs. Once it starts, you get to watch the status bar grow. Then, what are the chances you remember to run sp_change_users_login? How fun is it to do so for every stinking user account? Oh, and hope you only needed a single restore, or you get to play again.

sp_ABRestoreDb solves all these niggling issues. It's great for restoring the latest production database backups to a disaster recovery, QA, or development machine. You can literally get the restores down to a single stored procedure call, supplying the list of databases and an optional file specification.

SQL Backup Gotchas Avoided

Redgate's SQL Backup is great product for the price, and we use it on most of our servers. To be sure, though, it has its quirks. Most insidious is its instance handling. Assume you have two instances of SQL Server on a single machine, one on the default instance and one on a named instance, and the SQL Backup extended stored procedure is installed on both. If you connect to the named instance and call the extended procedure master.dbo.sqlbackup, you backup or restore a database on that instance, right? Wrong! By default, the interface assumes the default instance, no matter which instance it is called from. Yikes! sp_ABBackupDb and sp_ABRestoreDb always pass the name of the current instance to master.dbo.sqlbackup to avoid this gotcha.

Another fun exercise is SQL Backup error detection. If there's one place I don't want a silent failure, it's on my backups and restores. But I've found SQL Backup to be inconsistent at returning an error code, even at the latest version (v3.2.05) that was supposed to help with this. To detect SQL Backup errors, the extended procedure output is sent to a table and then parsed. The highest numbered error code will be saved and used as the return code. A return code of 0 from sp_ABBackupDb or sp_ABRestoreDb means no errors detected.

Speaking of parsing, one little issue spun me in circles for hours. The output from SQL Backup is a C-style string terminated with a zero-byte. But SQL Server doesn't see the zero-byte as a termination. There could be, and is, lots of junk after that byte that SQL happily considers part of the string. However most output tools, including Query Analyzer, don't display past a zero byte! Unless you issue a len() or datalength() command (as I did in my third debugging hour) you can't tell that SQL has more string than it shows. The solution is to use LEFT(col1, charindex(char(0), col1) - 1) when reading from the output table.

Helper Function and Procedures

The procedures sp_ABBackup and sp_ABRestore make use of a custom system function named ::fn_Split. By creating this as a system function, it will be found in the master database regardless of the current database (much like an sp_* procedure). This function splits a string on a delimiter, and returns the result as a two column table. Column Item contains an instance of the data, and column ItemId holds an identity column identifying the sequence of this instance. Parsing comma-separated input is easy with this function. It gets used to piece apart the database string, the file specification string (when multiple filespecs are specified), and to separate Litespeed's stored procedure-based options from the typical WITH-based options.

Before restoring, procedure sp_ABKillDbUsers is called to clear existing database connections. This could be done inline to the procedure, but separating it out makes it available for other uses. After the restore, we need to run sp_change_users_login procedure across all SQL (non-Windows) logins. sp_ABFixUsersLogin does the job nicely.

Coding Techniques

Using ::fn_Split works well to parse apart comma-separated values, but how do we get them back together again? A WHILE loop can be used, but that's a lot of error prone coding. At several points in the code, you'll find statements like this:

```
SELECT  @String = NULL
SELECT  @String = ISNULL(@String + ', ', '') + Item
  FROM  ::fn_Split(@ParmString, ',')
  ORDER BY ItemId
```

The second SELECT statement does the work by appending a comma and adding the current row for every row after the first. On the first row, @String IS NULL and is changed to an empty string, so that just the first row's data is added.

Another technique is to be wary of SQL injection. Since we're executing using the EXEC() statement, we need to be cautious of hackers inputting unwanted SQL Syntax within the parameters. A quick check at the start of the procedure helps prevent this, though I'm not at all certain its foolproof. Execute rights for these procedures should be limited to administrators.

Limitations

Presently sp_ABBackupDb can't determine which additional options should be used for the verify command. I didn't want to add another parameter for what seemed of limited use.

Native SQL Backups will often handle errors by blowing up the batch, so you can't rely on an error code return in that case.

Feedback

If you find the procedures here to be of use, let me know in the "Your Opinion" section. If you find bugs or want to suggest some enhancements, I'll do like my kindergartner and put my listening ears on.

No Outlook for Alerts!

By Roy Carlson

No email client for alerts! Then apply here.

There is an old philosophical controversy "If a tree falls in the forest, and no one is around, does it still make a sound." If the tree fell on my car, then there would definitely be a sound - my scream. If the SQL server errors, nobody reads the logs, it does not crash and nothing is on fire should we care? I think so. But how do you remember to read the logs, handle all the day's challenges, and get from server to server scattered throughout the forests and sites? Even if we had the time, event logs are located on the best seller reading list somewhere near the phone book. We are not implying the content is not important, but like the phonebook 99.9% of the content is not important to the reader and there is a lot of content.

Let me relate to you the tragic tale of the "Great Write Protect Incident at the Not Okay Corral." One dark and stormy night, the SQL tape backup failed. SQL server dutifully entered the event into the Event Logs. This process repeated every night. When the tape was changed and checked there was no data on the tape. The full and incremental backups for that week didn't exist. Someone had enabled the write protect. We checked with everyone they all swore that it was "not me." An immediate search for Mr. NotMe was undertaken, but he has managed to remain undetected, undiscovered, unnoticed, unobserved, unobtrusive, and unperceived.

We knew that if we had Exchange or Outlook we could be notified by e-mail if a SQL job failed. We had neither. We decided that we needed a means to read the event logs and the ability to notify key personnel of certain errors and warnings. The following script reads the application log looking for any error. We set up ours to e-mail our tape monkey when a category of 6, EventCode of 17055 error happens (for the Not Okay Corral this is a SQL server 3041 backup job failure). It also uses a CDO method for the e-mail function.

You are not limited to a single event error. You can scan the system logs and advise the LAN Team of events of interest. It is also possible to scan the Security logs, but this is a trickier subject reserved for later discussion. The neat thing about this script is that you can send an alert relating to errors, like a transaction log fill in the msdb, that do not stop things but can affect performance or are precursors to gloom and doom. You can even select warnings of a specific type to alert you of less-serious but important issues.

The Changes:

The script is relative simple to use but you will need to change the following:

- strComputer = "yourSQLserver" add your server name or if you run it on the server just add a period. strComputer = "." You can also run it on your workstation using the strComputer = "." designation.
- The e-mail stuff, From user, Recipient(s), The subject, Text body, and Mailserver.

```
objEmail.From = "SQLLords@company.com"
objEmail.To = "tapemonkey@company.com,boss@company.com"
objEmail.Subject = "SQL ERROR"
objEmail.Textbody = "The sky is falling!  The Sky is falling!"
objEmail.Configuration.Fields.Item _
    ("http://schemas.microsoft.com/cdo/configuration/sendusing") = 2
                        'name of notesserverhost ?
objEmail.Configuration.Fields.Item _
    ("http://schemas.microsoft.com/cdo/configuration/smtpserver") = _
                        "mailserver"
Note: quotations marks are required.

The Code (alert.vbs):
'- - - - - - - - - - - - - - - - - - - - - - - - - - - - -
' remove the comment marker (') from On Error Resume Next
' when code runs without error
' On Error Resume Next
' declaring variables
DIM strComputer,dtmDate,dtmDay,dtmMonth,dtmYear,strDate
DIM intCounter,intCount,dtmWritDate,dtmWritDateY
DIM dtmWritDateM,dtmWritDateD,strWritDate
' initializing some variables
intCounter = 0
strComputer = "yourSQLserver"
dtmDate = Now-1
dtmDay = Right(("0" & Day(dtmDate)),2)
dtmMonth = Right(("0" & Month(dtmDate)),2)
dtmYear = Year(dtmDate)
strDate = dtmYear & dtmMonth & dtmDay
' attaching to WMI provider on server
Set objWMIService = GetObject("winmgmts:" _
    & "{impersonationLevel=impersonate}!\\" & strComputer & "\root\cimv2")
' the query
Set colLoggedEvents = objWMIService.ExecQuery _
    ("Select * from Win32_NTLogEvent Where Logfile = 'Application' " & _
    "AND Type = 'Error' AND Category = 6 AND EventCode = 17055")
For Each objEvent in colLoggedEvents
        dtmWritDate = objEvent.TimeWritten
        dtmWritDateY = Left(dtmWritDate, 4)
        dtmWritDateM = Mid(dtmWritDate,5,2)
        dtmWritDateD = Mid(dtmWritDate,7,2)
        strWritDate = dtmWritDateY & dtmWritDateM & dtmWritDateD
        intCounter = intCounter + 1
        If strWritDate >= strDate Then
        intCount = intCounter
        End If
Next
If intCount > 1 Then
' e-mail section
        Set objEmail = CreateObject("CDO.Message")
        objEmail.From = "SQLLords@company.com"
        objEmail.To = "tapemonkey@company.com,boss@company.com "
        objEmail.Subject = "SQL ERROR"
        objEmail.Textbody = "The sky is falling!  The Sky is falling!"
```

```
    objEmail.Configuration.Fields.Item _
        ("http://schemas.microsoft.com/cdo/configuration/sendusing") = 2
                                'name of notesserverhost ?
    objEmail.Configuration.Fields.Item _
        ("http://schemas.microsoft.com/cdo/configuration/smtpserver") = _
                    "mailserver"
    objEmail.Configuration.Fields.Item _
                ("http://schemas.microsoft.com/cdo/configuration/smtpserverport") = 25
    objEmail.Configuration.Fields.Update
    objEmail.Send
' end of e-mail section
End If
' - - - - - - - - - - - - - - - - - - - - - - - - - - -
```

The Query: The SQL query can be changed to meet your needs:

```
("Select * from Win32_NTLogEvent Where Logfile = 'Application' " & _
"AND Type = 'Error'")
```

Which will send an e-mail when any error is written to the application log. This can be changed to:

```
("Select * from Win32_NTLogEvent Where Logfile = 'Application' " & _
"AND Type = 'Error' AND Category = 6 AND EventCode = 17055")
```

Which only returns an e-mail when this very specific error occurs. We recommend that you start with the simpler version. As your needs become more focused, the responsibilities more defined, that is when you make the query more specific. Some errors might be automatically handled by your maintenance plan and you can set the query to ignore them.

Queries in VB scripting are written in WQL, similar to SQL, but there are differences. The & _ is a way to break up and concatenate a script to make it more readable.

Date handling:

"Now-1" gets yesterday's date. It is broken up into component parts and reassembled as YYYYMMDD. The Right(("0" & Month(dtmDate)),2) is a trick to assure single month and days are preceded by a "0" and that the reassembled date will always have eight characters.

```
dtmDate = Now-1
dtmDay = Right(("0" & Day(dtmDate)),2)
dtmMonth = Right(("0" & Month(dtmDate)),2)
dtmYear = Year(dtmDate)
strDate = dtmYear & dtmMonth & dtmDay
```

The dtmWritdate object returned is either in Cuniform or Mesopotanian code, I am not sure which. We convert it to its component parts and reassemble to the YYYYMMDD to compare it to yesterdays result. This could be simplified, but we use the Month and Day components in another part of the actual script we use which is a little more complex.

```
    dtmWritDate = objEvent.TimeWritten
        dtmWritDateY = Left(dtmWritDate, 4)
        dtmWritDateM = Mid(dtmWritDate,5,2)
        dtmWritDateD = Mid(dtmWritDate,7,2)
        strWritDate = dtmWritDateY & dtmWritDateM & dtmWritDateD
```

CDO e-mail

If there is more than one error in the last two days the e-mail is sent. We chose to use a two day window in case the e-mail server is down for a day. It's a comfort thing. It is wise to have some date determinant in the script otherwise you will get all errors based on your query for the entire length of the log.

More on e-mailing scripting with Exchange or CDO is found here:
http://www.microsoft.com/technet/scriptcenter/scripts/message/default.mspx

Depending on your security set-up, this e-mail process may not be allowed. You option here is to replace the e-mail section with a line like: Wscript.Echo "THERE IS AN ERROR IN THE APPLICATION LOG." You would run the script from the command line as cscript alert.vbs and the message will appear. You can then run the bonus script - "cscript event.vbs > eventError.txt." Note: Change the server array to the specific server with the error and change the query to report only error ids, dates and messages. Either delete the unwanted lines or use a single quote to comment them out.

Rest of Script:

We connect to the provider and query Win32_NTLogEvent Logfile =application , Type = error. If one or more errors occurred within the last two days we index the counter variable intCount. If the intCount is greater than or equal to one then an e-mail will be sent using the CDO method. Telling you to go an read the application event log for errors within the last two days.

The batch file: alert.bat Note that the batch file is run using cscript and not wscript. Running any of these scripts from wscript could have you closing message boxes for the next century. You can use the Windows Scheduler or a third party scheduler to run the batch file at whatever interval you want.

Contain your excitement but we are adding a Bonus script. The following "event.vbs" will extract the events in your application and system event logs. Copy and paste it. Call it event.vbs and run it from a command line c:> cscript event.vbs > c:\event.txt . Note: do not run it under wscript or event.vbs > c:\event.txt unless you have changed the default to cscript. Also the command Ctrl-C stop the script.

Select a comfy chair and have a long, long, long evenings read . . . yawn! The value of this is to help you determine what objects to add to your query to make it more specific to your needs making the script actually useful

Notice also that the date codes are thoughtfully converted from Mesopotanian into English for you at no additional charge.

The bonus script: Event.vbs: (This script was generated using the ScriptoMatic 2 - available from the Microsoft Web Site - http://www.microsoft.com/technet/scriptcenter/tools/scripto2.mspx)

```
' - - - - - - - - - - - - - - - - - - - - - - - - - - - - -
cscript Alert.vbs
' - - - - - - - - - - - - - - - - - - - - - - - - - - - -
On Error Resume Next
Const wbemFlagReturnImmediately = &h10
Const wbemFlagForwardOnly = &h20

' The following can be an array ("Server1","Server2",..,..,"ServerN")
' But be careful this can return a lot of data, the (".") returns info from your computer.
arrComputers = Array(".")
For Each strComputer In arrComputers
    WScript.Echo
    WScript.Echo "=========================================="
    WScript.Echo "Computer: " & strComputer
    WScript.Echo "=========================================="

    Set objWMIService = GetObject("winmgmts:\\" & strComputer & "\root\CIMV2")
    Set colItems = objWMIService.ExecQuery("SELECT * FROM Win32_NTLogEvent", "WQL", _
                                        wbemFlagReturnImmediately + wbemFlagForwardOnly)

    For Each objItem In colItems
        WScript.Echo "Category: " & objItem.Category
        WScript.Echo "CategoryString: " & objItem.CategoryString
        WScript.Echo "ComputerName: " & objItem.ComputerName
        strData = Join(objItem.Data, ",")
            WScript.Echo "Data: " & strData
        WScript.Echo "EventCode: " & objItem.EventCode
        WScript.Echo "EventIdentifier: " & objItem.EventIdentifier
        WScript.Echo "EventType: " & objItem.EventType
        strInsertionStrings = Join(objItem.InsertionStrings, ",")
            WScript.Echo "InsertionStrings: " & strInsertionStrings
        WScript.Echo "Logfile: " & objItem.Logfile
        WScript.Echo "Message: " & objItem.Message
        WScript.Echo "RecordNumber: " & objItem.RecordNumber
        WScript.Echo "SourceName: " & objItem.SourceName
        WScript.Echo "TimeGenerated: " & WMIDateStringToDate(objItem.TimeGenerated)
        WScript.Echo "TimeWritten: " & WMIDateStringToDate(objItem.TimeWritten)
        WScript.Echo "Type: " & objItem.Type
        WScript.Echo "User: " & objItem.User
        WScript.Echo
    Next
Next

Function WMIDateStringToDate(dtmDate)
WScript.Echo dtm:
        WMIDateStringToDate = CDate(Mid(dtmDate, 5, 2) & "/" & _
        Mid(dtmDate, 7, 2) & "/" & Left(dtmDate, 4) _
        & " " & Mid (dtmDate, 9, 2) & ":" & Mid(dtmDate, 11, 2) & ":" & Mid(dtmDate,13, 2))
```

```
End Function
` - - - - - - - - - - - - - - - - - - - - - - - - - - - -
```

The use of vbs to get SQL server information is a valuable tool to allow hands free administration, filtering vast amounts of information and making sure the server is healthy. This is just another tool in your arsenal that you can make very general or super specific as your needs dictate. We also use this script to monitor other non-Microsoft OEM database application functions proactively preventing troubles. Since we now monitor the tape function, Mr. NotMe seems to have left the building. Hope you find it a helpful tool.

Caveat: Like any script you download or discover in a magazine or book, try this script in a development environment, not on a production server. You do not want to slow up a production server if you have issues. You can even run this on your work station to examine your logs before taking it to the SQL world.

Small Scale SQL Server Deployment

By Tim Mitchell

Much has been written about large scale database deployments, and the later versions of SQL Server – including the upcoming version of SQL Server 2005 – fit well into VLDB (very large database) configurations. However, for every VLDB setup there are dozens if not hundreds of small (under 500 megabytes) to medium (500 megabytes to 10 gigabytes) database deployments. This is an often overlooked element of the SQL Server community; there are many fine books and other publications that focus on VLDBs but few if any that are geared toward those who support much smaller databases. To that end, I have assembled a broad view of using Microsoft SQL Server to deploy less-than-enterprise level databases.

Availability and Disaster Recovery

Key elements to any SQL Server deployment include performance, availability, and disaster recovery. The architect of the database solution must ask the following questions:

- How much performance do I need?
- How much downtime is considered acceptable?
- How much data can we afford to lose?

The answer to these three questions will be the driving force behind the architecture decisions. It has been my experience that many smaller database implementations do not require the level of availability or performance as larger systems. For example, I work daily with an internal trouble ticket tracking system that is available throughout the day, but is rarely if ever accessed outside of normal weekday business hours. Another ticket tracking system I developed is accessible from the Internet via a web application and is continuously available, but has a minimal number of concurrent users. Neither of these systems requires high availability, and neither has performance demands to necessitate high-end hardware or software; since they are not core to our operations, it would be an unnecessary drain on our very small budget to pour money into enterprise software or expensive metal for these applications. By the way, both systems have been running well with excellent performance and very little downtime.

Choosing the Right Software

Critical to a successful small implementation of SQL Server is determining which version of the software your deployment will require. SQL Server 2005 comes available in three different flavors for production use: Enterprise, Standard, and Workgroup. The Enterprise version is the all-inclusive release, and includes the full suite of features including high availability, business intelligence, and a rich set of client tools. The Standard version includes many of the same features, but lacks several of the enterprise-level elements such as database partitioning, online indexing and restore, and other advanced BI and high availability features, and has a limit of 4 CPUs. The Workgroup edition is limited to 2 CPUs and 3GB of RAM, and does not include Notification Services, Analysis Services, or Integration Services, all of which are extremely useful but may be of little benefit on smaller implementations. Fortunately, the core database engine is identical on all versions, allowing for maximum throughput regardless of the version you choose. If your organization's policy or budget requires the use of SQL Server 2000, it is available in Enterprise and

Standard edition, which has similar limitations between the two versions as its successor. Microsoft's website can provide more detailed information about product features by version for SQL Server 2005 and 2000 .

In choosing the correct version of SQL Server for your small implementation, don't forget to consider SQL Server Express, the free version of SQL Server 2005. Although it lacks the high-availability features and the rich GUI client of its more glamorous cousins, the database engine in the Express version is identical to that of the costlier flavors. The predecessor to this product was MSDE (Microsoft SQL Desktop Engine), which had a throughput throttle of five simultaneous queries; fortunately, no such limitation exists on SQL Server Express. The Express edition also has a scaled-down administrative tool called Express Manager, a welcome addition since MSDE did not include any GUI tools. In addition, like its predecessor, SQL Server Express may be freely redistributed to end users and clients after proper registration with Microsoft. For many small to medium sized database deployments that do not require high availability, the new SQL Server Express may be the perfect low-cost solution.

Choosing the Right Hardware

Extreme databases require extreme hardware, and I've had my share of both. But many database implementations have far less stringent requirements. The last two new databases I deployed were on less-than-enterprise hardware; in fact, one was set up on a converted desktop machine. The hardware requirements for installing SQL Server 2005 are well within reach of any one or two year old desktop machine. For the record, all commercial versions of SQL Server 2005 require at least a P3/600 processor and 512MB of RAM, while the Express edition requires only 192MB of RAM. Even when operating at or just above the minimum hardware requirements , I have found that query responses are more than adequate in low- to moderate-volume systems. SCSI drives are great, but a set of good 7200RPM IDE drives will yield good results in less demanding systems. Further, it is possible to configure a software RAID setup on IDE drives within Windows 2000 or XP (see Darrell Brown's how-to on this) for increased disk performance and fault tolerance. In fact, you could configure a fully capable small- to medium-sized database server with just the spare parts you find lying around your shop.

Backup

Many organizations choose to use third-party tools to back up VLDBs, and with good reason: an online backup operation on a large database can take several hours using the integrated Microsoft SQL backup utility. However, for small to moderately sized databases, the backup tools within SQL Server generally work fine. I am able to back up the aforementioned ticket tracking system, currently somewhere around 500MB in size, in under 30 seconds. Further, one can configure a remote network location - for example, a share folder on a desktop machine or small backup server - as a backup storage target to avoid using costly and troublesome tape systems.

Conclusion

There are many cases in which a high-end server and a full-blown Enterprise copy of SQL Server are essential. But for many small companies, or even large companies needing a small database deployment, Microsoft has provided some scaled-down options - including one that is free - for implementing SQL Server, which may be deployed on relatively minimal hardware. There is a correct tool for every job, and for many smaller tasks, these tips could provide just the right solution.

SQL Server Agent 2005

By Dinesh Asanka

What is new in SQL Server 2005 Agent?

It has been well over five months since SQL Server 2005 was released. Market research has shown that it is still gathering momentum among the software community. If you meet a person who is new to SQL Server 2005, the obvious question that they will ask is "What is new in SQL Server 2005?". Well, obviously there are lots of differences.

To start with it does have a nice UI. You can rename the databases, which you could not do in earlier versions. With these simple (but important) enhancements, there are a few major changes as well. DDL triggers and peer-to-peer replication can be considered as major changes.

So, it is obvious that the above question needs a lengthy answer, which cannot be completed in one article. So I thought to identify a major component of SQL Server 2005 that has had drastic changes. SQL Agent is one of them, so this series of articles will discus the changes in SQL Server 2005 Agent.

This article will describe about security and performance improvements are done to the SQL Server Agent.

Security Improvements

In SQL Server 2000, the SQL Server Agent service account had to be a member of the local administrators group when executing Jobs owned by users who were not members of the sysadmin fixed server roles. In order to give more control to the administrators, new three roles have been added in SQL Server 2005. These roles are SQLAgentUserRole, SQLAgentReaderRole, and SQLAgentOperatorRole.

After the initial installation, only sysadmin users can edit, view and execute SQL Server jobs. These roles exists only in msdb database. The following screen will show you how to create a user with above mentioned roles.

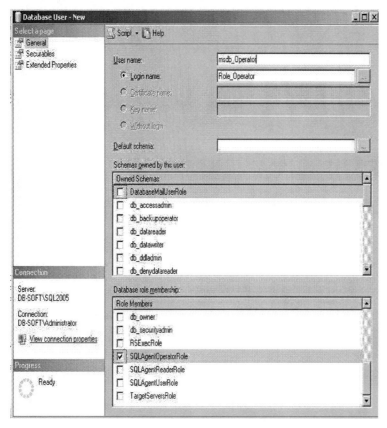

With SQL Server 2005, a user must be a member of one of the new fixed database roles or a member of the **sysadmin** fixed server role to use SQL Server Agent. When users who are not members of one of these roles are connected to SQL Server in SQL Server Management Studio, the SQL Server Agent node in Object Explorer is not visible. After this basic introduction let us identify what are the specific uses of each role.

SQLAgentUserRole

This is the least privileged role among new three new fixed server roles. This role has permissions only on operators, local jobs, and job schedules. These types of users can only view the operator but they can't create, modify or delete operators. They cannot change job ownership to gain access to jobs that they do not already own. SQLAgentUserRole members can view a list of available proxies only in the Job Step Properties dialog box of SQL Server Management Studio. These users cannot delete job history.

SQLAgentReaderRole

SQLAgentReaderRole has all the options that SQLAgentUserRole has. In addition, it does have permissions to view the list of available multiserver jobs, their properties, and their history. Members of this role can also view the list of all available jobs and job schedules and their properties, not just those jobs and job schedules that they own.

SQLAgentOperatorRole

SQLAgentOperatorRole is the most privileged of the SQL Server Agent fixed database roles. It includes all the permissions of SQLAgentUserRole and SQLAgentReaderRole. Members of this role can also view properties for operators and proxies, and enumerate available proxies and alerts on the server. SQLAgentOperatorRole members have additional permissions on local jobs and schedules. They can execute, stop, or start all local jobs, and they can delete the job history for any local job on the server.

Performance Improvements

When a job is running in SQL Server 2005, at the end of the each job step, the thread goes back to SQL Server Agent and check whether there is another job step of the same type waiting to be executed. If there is, the thread will execute that job step. If there is no similar job steps the thread terminates. This modification has allowed SQL Server Agent to execute jobs more efficiently than the SQL Server 2000 jobs.

In SQL Server 2000, registry entry determines how many threads of a subsystem could be activated at once. the **max_worker_thread** settings is stored in registry. For the default instance, this setting is in **HKEY_LOCAL_MACHINE\SOFTWARE\Microsoft\MSSQLServer\SQLServerAgent\Subsystems** registry key. Last part of each key is a number which specifies the **max_worker_thread** setting for the subsystem. For **QueueReader** subsystem , in my SQL Server instance it has the value **C:\Program Files\Microsoft SQL Server\MSSQL\BINN\SQLREPSS.DLL,C:\Program Files\Microsoft SQL Server\80\COM\QRDRSVC.EXE,ReplStart,ReplEvent,ReplStop,100.** This means that **max_worker_thread** value is 100.

In addition to the above improvement, new four performance counter objects have introduced in SQL Server 2005 Agent. These objects can be used to improve the performance of your SQL Server.

SQLAgent:Alerts

SQLAgent:alrets counter object gives information about the SQL Server Agent alerts. This object has two counters.

Counter Name	Description
Activated alerts	The total number of alerts that SQL Server Agent has activated since the last time that SQL Server Agent restarted.
Alerts activated/minute	This counter reports the number of alerts that SQL Server Agent activated within the last minute.

Events are generated by Microsoft SQL Server and entered into the Microsoft Windows application log. SQL Server Agent reads the application log and compares events written there to alerts that you have defined. When SQL Server Agent finds a match, it fires an alert. So from the above counters, a system admin can examine the alert pattern and their quantity. If the Alert count is high it needs to prompt immediate actions. **Alerts activated/minute** is more important as it gives the density of alerts.

Only users who are member of the sysadmin fixed server role can use this counter object.

SQLAgent:Jobs

SQLAgent:Job counter object will give information about SQL Server Jobs. Following table shows available conunters.

Counter Name	Description

Active Jobs	the number of jobs currently running.
Failed jobs	the number of jobs that exited with failure.
Job success rate	the percentage of executed jobs that completed successfully.
Jobs activated/minute	the number of jobs launched within the last minute.
Queued jobs	the number of jobs that are ready for SQL Server Agent to run, but which have not yet started running.
Successful jobs	the number of jobs that exited with success.

Each counter contains the following instances:

Instance	Description
_Total	Information for all jobs.
Alerts	Information for jobs started by alerts.
Others	Information for jobs that were not started by alerts or schedules.
Schedules	Information for jobs started by schedules.

SQLAgent:JobSteps

SQL Server Agent:JobSteps object has the counter to report information about SQL Server Agent job steps. Following table shows available counters.

Counter Name	Description
Active steps	reports the number of job steps currently running.
Queued steps	reports the number of job steps that are ready for SQL Server Agent to run, but which have not yet started running.
Total step retries	reports the total number of times that Microsoft SQL Server has retried a job step since the last server restart.

Following are the instances for each counter listed above.

Instance	Description
_Total	Information for all job steps.
ActiveScripting	Information for job steps that use the **ActiveScripting** subsystem.
ANALYSISCOMMAND	Information for job steps that use the ANALYSISCOMMAND subsystem.
ANALYSISQUERY	Information for job steps that use the ANALYSISQUERY subsystem.
CmdExec	Information for job steps that use the **CmdExec** subsystem.
Distribution	Information for job steps that use the **Distribution** subsystem.
Dts	Information for job steps that use the Integration Services subsystem.
LogReader	Information for job steps that use the **LogReader** subsystem.
Merge	Information for job steps that use the **Merge** subsystem.
QueueReader	Information for job steps that use the **QueueReader** subsystem.
Snapshot	Information for job steps that use the **Snapshot** subsystem.
TSQL	Information for job steps that execute Transact-SQL.

SQLAgent:JobStaticstics

This object has only one object named **SQL Server Restarted.** This counter gives number of times the Microsoft SQL Server has been successfully restarted by SQL Server Agent since the last time that SQL Server Agent started.

Conclusion

The availability of these roles have given administrators more flexibility when defining users for Jobs. Consider your requirements and associate the necessary fixed role that fit them.

SQL Server 2005 Agent also has four new performance counters. Using these counters, administrators can fine tune their jobs to a great extent.

In the next article we will take about few more additions that are introduced to SQL Server Agent 2005. Until then , do not hesitate to send your comments to dineshasanka@gmail.com

SQL Server 2005 Best Practices

By Nanda Kishore

Introduction

SQL Server 2005 provides more new language constructs and primitives for the T-SQL language than can be enumerated here. The enhancements to the T-SQL language reflect greater conformity to the ANSI-99 SQL specification and ease of use for developers. Many of the improvements in T-SQL are focused on greater expressiveness in queries. There are several new query types that allow for common scenarios to be covered in T-SQL code.

T-SQL in SQL Server 2005 provides new PIVOT and UNPIVOT operators which are very useful while generating the user defined reports. Previously developers have to write a huge code for converting rows into columns and vice versa. These operators perform a manipulation on an input table-valued expression and produce an output table as a result set. The PIVOT operator rotates rows into columns, optionally performing aggregations or other mathematical calculations along the way. It widens the input table expression based on a given pivot column and generates an output table with a column for each unique value in the pivot column. The UNPIVOT operator performs an operation opposite to the one PIVOT performs; it rotates columns into rows. The UNPIVOT operator narrows the input table expression based on a pivot column.

SQL Server 2005 introduces an excellent, simple but very powerful exception handling mechanism in the form of a TRY/CATCH T-SQL construct. This facility gives the developers to write more secured/managed code. Transaction abort errors that used to cause a batch to terminate can now be caught and handled.

In this article I am covering the key points to be remembered while performing migration from earlier versions of SQL Server to SQL Server 2005.

Migration Best practices - Upgrade options

We can upgrade an existing SQL Server 2000 database to SQL Server 2005 using the below methods:

1. Upgrade through Backup/Restore
2. Upgrade through Attach/Detach
3. Upgrade using Copy Database Wizard
4. Upgrade through an in-place install/upgrade

Compatibility

Once database is restored we need to set the compatibility to SQL server 2005. To achieve the compatibility we need to execute the below command

- **sp_dbcmptlevel < restored database name >, 90**

Points to remember - SQL Server 2005

- If the user database contains a user named "sys", it will not upgrade. "sys" is a reserved schema name in SQL Server 2005
- If you are using any object type code as "S" this will not work. System tables (S) are not exposed
- Updating system tables is not supported. Direct catalog updates are not supported in SQL Server 2005.

- Code will not work if it tries to GRANT, DENY, REVOKE, and DROP on system objects. Catalog and system objects are not modifiable.
- Code will not work if it accesses undocumented tables or columns

  Usage of DBCC commands is not supported in SQL Server 2005.

List of Documented columns

Here is the list of documented columns from the SQL 2000 System tables that currently return NULL or 0 in Microsoft® SQL Server™ 2005:

- sysobjects.schema_ver
- sysindexes.first
- sysindexes.FirstIAM
- sysindexes.root
- sysindexes.minlen
- sysindexes.xmaxlen
- sysindexes.maxirow
- sysindexes.keys
- syscomments.compressed
- syscomments.ctext
- syslogins.password
- sysremotelogins.status
- sysoledbusers.rmtpassword
- sysdevices.size
- Avoid using columns that SQL Server Books Online describes as: "Reserved", "For future use", or "For internal use only"
- Use two-part names to refer to system objects. For example EXEC sys.sp_help Select * from sys.tables
- Avoid code that assumes all metadata is publicly visible
- By default, stored procedures run in caller's execution context
- Use "EXECUTE AS OWNER" for owner's execution context

  GRANT VIEW DEFINITION if necessary

New Features in SQL Server 2005

Database Mirroring

Database mirroring is a solution to provide high availability at the database level as opposed to clustering which satisfies the need for high availability at the instance level. Maintaining synchronized copies of a database on two separate servers allows switching between them on an as needed basis allows automatic failover incase of failure of primary server.

Mirrored server can be used as report server for generating various reports by creating the snapshots on the mirrored database. Creating snapshots will not consume resources and are very fast while creating.

Note: Snapshots should be dropped once the purpose is completed, other wise snapshots will not allow you to restore database.

CLR Integration

Microsoft SQL Server 2005 significantly enhances the database programming model by hosting the Microsoft .NET Framework 2.0 Common Language Runtime (CLR). .Net CLR hosted inside SQL Server to improve performance, security and reliability. This enables developers to write procedures, triggers, and functions in any of the CLR languages.

If the procedure involves both significant data access and computation, consider separating the procedural code into a CLR portion that calls into a T-SQL procedure to perform data access, or a T-SQL procedure that calls into the CLR to perform computation. Another alternative is to use a single T-SQL batch that includes a set of queries that are executed once from managed code to reduce the number of round trips of submitting T-SQL statements from managed.

In previous releases of SQL Server, extended stored procedures (XPs) were the only alternative to T-SQL with which to write server-side code. CLR integration provides a more robust alternative to extended stored procedures (XPs).

T-SQL Enhancements

Most of SQL Server 2005's T-SQL enhancements focus on offering greater expressiveness to queries. The list of enhancements includes:

- Relational operators
- Changes to TOP
- New types of Exception handling
- XML formatted showplan
- Snapshot isolation level
- Recursive queries
- New Data types
- DDL triggers (You can use these triggers for Field auditing purpose)
- DML with output (access to Inserted and Deleted tables)

Partitioned Tables and Indexes

The ability to partition tables and indexes has always been a design tactic chosen to improve performance and manageability in larger databases. Microsoft SQL Server 2005 has new features that simplify the design of using this feature. Please refer to this white paperfor a better understanding of partitions in SQL server 2005.

Reporting services

There are many features of Reporting Services that can be beneficial to customers. These features include centralized report storage and management, control over how reports are processed or administered, and the ability to quickly change report formats (HTML, Excel, PDF, etc.). With these capabilities, Reporting Services is valuable client application implementations

The main strength of Web-based reporting is the ability to make up-to-date information available to a distributed group of users. SQL Server Reporting Services is Microsoft's server-based reporting solution. While Reporting Services provides a way for people to find and view reports, the Reporting Services interface may not be the most appropriate one for all report users

Native Xml Web services

SQL Server 2005 provides a standard mechanism for accessing the database engine using SOAP via HTTP. Using this mechanism, you can send SOAP/HTTP requests to SQL Server to execute T-SQL batch statements, stored procedures, extended stored procedures, and scalar-valued user-defined functions with or without parameters.

Setting up SQL Server as a Web Service that can listen natively for HTTP SOAP requests requires creating an HTTP endpoint and defining the methods that the endpoint exposes. When an HTTP endpoint is created, it must be created with a unique URL that it uses to listen for incoming HTTP requests.

Providing SOAP/HTTP access enables a broader range of clients to access SQL Server, including "zero foot print" clients, because there is no longer a need to have a Microsoft Data Access Components (MDAC) stack installed on the client device trying to connect to SQL Server. It facilitates interoperability with .NET, SOAP Toolkit, Perl, and more on a variety of platforms. Since the SOAP/HTTP access mechanism is based on well-known technologies such as XML and HTTP, it inherently promotes interoperability and access to SQL Server in a heterogeneous environment. Any device that can parse XML and submit HTTP requests can now access SQL Server

SQL Server 2005 Logon Triggers

By Frederik Vandeputte

Introduction

Oracle introduced logon triggers in Oracle 8i, which make it very easy to do some basic logging on logons. Every time a user connects to the database a trigger is fired. In the logon trigger you simple insert a row into an auditing table. A very easy to read example can be found on http://www.dba-oracle.com/art_builder_sec_audit.htm.

Microsoft introduced the Service Broker in SQL Server 2005. Service broker is an advanced architecture for building asynchronous distributed database applications. Along with SQL Server 2005 and the Service Broker came event notifications.

Event Notifications allow you to capture events on your SQL Server instance or database and respond to them. Event Notifications are similar to DDL triggers (another nice new feature in SQL Server 2005). However, event notifications are more advanced than DDL triggers. First of all they are handled asynchronous which make them ideal for logging. Secondly, event notifications allow you to respond to more events than DDL triggers. DDL triggers can only respond to DDL events, that's why they are called DDL triggers after all. Event notifications can respond to DDL events, but also to SQL Server Profiler events. And that's where we find the login related events.

Implementing Logon Triggers in SQL Server 2005 Using Event Notification

Before we start off we create a new "Logging_demo" database and add an audit table called Logging. We must enable the Service Broker on the database as well since it is disabled by default.

```
--Create Logging DB and table
CREATE DATABASE Logging_demo
GO
--Enable service broker
ALTER DATABASE Logging_demo SET ENABLE_BROKER
GO
USE Logging_demo

CREATE TABLE Logging (

LoggingID int IDENTITY(1,1),
EventTime DATETIME,
EventType VARCHAR(100),
LoginName VARCHAR(100),
HostName VARCHAR(100),
NTUserName VARCHAR(100),
NTDomainName VARCHAR(100),
Success INT,
FullLog XML
)
GO
```

Event notifications (and also Service Broker) work with 3 important objects: Queues, Services and Routes. Queues are very simple; they hold the messages (events) we want to process. The service will be listening on the queue, and the route makes it possible to read the queue. OK, I admit it is a little bit more complex than this, but we are focusing on our logon trigger. Detailed information about queues, services and routes can be found in books online.

Below we will create all three of these: the queue, the service, and the route.

```
--The queue
CREATE QUEUE LoggingQueue
GO
--The service
CREATE SERVICE LoggingService
ON QUEUE LoggingQueue
([http://schemas.microsoft.com/SQL/Notifications/PostEventNotification])
GO
--The route
CREATE ROUTE LoggingRoute
```

```
WITH SERVICE_NAME = 'LoggingService',
ADDRESS = 'LOCAL'
GO
```

Next we create our event notification object. We are interested in auditing successful and failed logons on the server. We use the appropriate events and link it to the service we created before.

```
CREATE EVENT NOTIFICATION Logging_Event_Notification
ON SERVER
FOR AUDIT_LOGIN, AUDIT_LOGOUT, AUDIT_LOGIN_FAILED
TO SERVICE 'LoggingService', 'current database'
GO
```

Now everything is in place to start our logging. If you open new connections to your server those logon attempts will be captured and send to our LoggingQueue. The SELECT below will show you what is on the queue.

```
SELECT * FROM LoggingQueue
```

Great, we have messages in the queue, but how do we get them from the queue into our logging table? We use the new RECEIVE statement to receive messages from the queue and put them into variables.

```
 WAITFOR (
         RECEIVE TOP(1)
@message_type_name=message_type_name,
@message_body=message_body,
@dialog = conversation_handle
FROM LoggingQueue
    ), TIMEOUT 2000
```

All the information about the event can be found in the @message_body variable. This is a XML type variable and we can use XQuery to retrieve the information we want and store it in our logging table.

```
INSERT INTO Logging (
EventTime,
EventType,
LoginName,
HostName,
NTUserName,
NTDomainName,
Success,
FullLog )
VALUES
(
CAST(CAST(@message_body.query('/EVENT_INSTANCE/PostTime/text()') AS VARCHAR(64)) AS DATETIME),
CAST(@message_body.query('/EVENT_INSTANCE/EventType/text()') AS VARCHAR(100)),
CAST(@message_body.query('/EVENT_INSTANCE/LoginName/text()') AS VARCHAR(100)),
CAST(@message_body.query('/EVENT_INSTANCE/HostName/text()') AS VARCHAR(100)),
CAST(@message_body.query('/EVENT_INSTANCE/NTUserName/text()') AS VARCHAR(100)),
CAST(@message_body.query('/EVENT_INSTANCE/NTDomainName/text()') AS VARCHAR(100)),
CAST(CAST(@message_body.query('/EVENT_INSTANCE/Success/text()') AS VARCHAR(64)) AS INTEGER),
@message_body)
```

Based on those RECEIVE and INSERT statements we create a stored procedure to handle our logon event:

```
--The proc to handle the events
-- Set options required for the XML data type.
SET ANSI_NULLS ON
GO
SET QUOTED_IDENTIFIER ON
GO
CREATE PROCEDURE LoggingProc
AS
SET NOCOUNT ON;

DECLARE      @message_body XML,
```

```
                @message_type_name NVARCHAR(256),
                @dialog UNIQUEIDENTIFIER ;

--Endless loop
WHILE (1 = 1)
BEGIN
    BEGIN TRANSACTION ;
    -- Receive the next available message
    WAITFOR (
        RECEIVE TOP(1)
            @message_type_name=message_type_name,
            @message_body=message_body,
            @dialog = conversation_handle
        FROM LoggingQueue
    ), TIMEOUT 2000
        --Rollback and exit if no messages were found
        IF (@@ROWCOUNT = 0)
        BEGIN
            ROLLBACK TRANSACTION ;
            BREAK ;
        END ;

    --End conversation of end dialog message
    IF (@message_type_name = 'http://schemas.microsoft.com/SQL/ServiceBroker/EndDialog')
    BEGIN
        PRINT 'End Dialog received for dialog # ' + cast(@dialog as nvarchar(40)) ;
        END CONVERSATION @dialog ;
    END ;
    ELSE
    BEGIN
        INSERT INTO Logging ( EventTime, EventType, LoginName,
                              HostName, NTUserName, NTDomainName,
                              Success, FullLog )
        VALUES
        (
        CAST(CAST(@message_body.query('/EVENT_INSTANCE/PostTime/text()') AS VARCHAR(64)) AS DATETIME),
        CAST(@message_body.query('/EVENT_INSTANCE/EventType/text()') AS VARCHAR(100)),
        CAST(@message_body.query('/EVENT_INSTANCE/LoginName/text()') AS VARCHAR(100)),
        CAST(@message_body.query('/EVENT_INSTANCE/HostName/text()') AS VARCHAR(100)),
        CAST(@message_body.query('/EVENT_INSTANCE/NTUserName/text()') AS VARCHAR(100)),
        CAST(@message_body.query('/EVENT_INSTANCE/NTDomainName/text()') AS VARCHAR(100)),
        CAST(CAST(@message_body.query('/EVENT_INSTANCE/Success/text()') AS VARCHAR(64)) AS INTEGER),
        @message_body)
    END
END
COMMIT TRANSACTION
END
GO
```

In the last step we just link the stored procedure to our queue.

```
ALTER QUEUE LoggingQueue
WITH ACTIVATION (
STATUS = ON,
PROCEDURE_NAME = LoggingProc ,
MAX_QUEUE_READERS = 2, EXECUTE AS SELF )
```

From now on all logon attempts will be monitored and logged in our audit table.

```
SELECT * FROM Logging
```

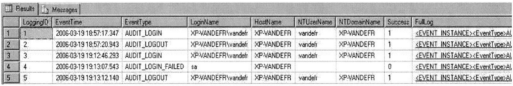

	LoggingID	EventTime	EventType	LoginName	HostName	NTUserName	NTDomainName	Success	FullLog
1	1	2006-03-19 18:57:17.347	AUDIT_LOGIN	XP-VANDEFR\vandefr	XP-VANDEFR	vandefr	XP-VANDEFR	1	<EVENT_INSTANCE><EventType>Al
2	2	2006-03-19 18:57:20.943	AUDIT_LOGOUT	XP-VANDEFR\vandefr	XP-VANDEFR	vandefr	XP-VANDEFR	1	<EVENT_INSTANCE><EventType>Al
3	3	2006-03-19 19:12:46.293	AUDIT_LOGIN	XP-VANDEFR\vandefr	XP-VANDEFR	vandefr	XP-VANDEFR	1	<EVENT_INSTANCE><EventType>Al
4	4	2006-03-19 19:13:07.543	AUDIT_LOGIN_FAILED	sa	XP-VANDEFR			0	<EVENT_INSTANCE><EventType>Al
5	5	2006-03-19 19:13:12.140	AUDIT_LOGOUT	XP-VANDEFR\vandefr	XP-VANDEFR	vandefr	XP-VANDEFR	1	<EVENT_INSTANCE><EventType>Al

Conclusion

I admit it is a little bit more complex to setup than it is in Oracle. However event notifications can do a lot more and it is really a nice tool to do all kinds of monitoring on your SQL Server 2005 databases and installations. When you are ready with event notifications go out and play with service broker and create some cool asynchronous applications.

You can download the code from www.sqlservercentral.com.

SQL 2005 Symmetric Encryption

By Michael Coles

Introduction

One of the most exciting new features of SQL Server 2005 is the built-in encryption functionality. With this new version of SQL Server, the SQL Server Team has added encryption tools, certificate creation and key management functionality directly to T-SQL. For anyone who males their living securing data in SQL Server tables because of business requirements or regulatory compliance, these new features are a godsend. For those trying to decide whether to use encryption to secure their data, the choice just got a lot easier. This article describes how the new encryption tools work, and how you can use them to your advantage.

T-SQL now includes support for symmetric encryption and asymmetric encryption using keys, certificates and passwords. This article describes how to create, manage and use symmetric keys and certificates.

Because of the amount of information involved, I've divided this article into three sections:

- Part 1: Service and Master Keys
-
- Part 2: Certificates
- Part 3: Symmetric Keys

 Part 1: Service and Database Master Keys

The SQL 2005 Encryption Hierarchy

SQL Server 2005 encryption functionality uses a hierarchical model that looks like this:

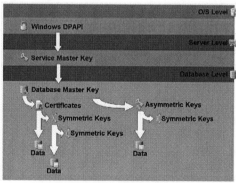

SQL Server 2005 Encryption Hierarchy

Service Master Key

Each SQL Server 2005 installation has exactly one Service Master Key (SMK), which is generated at install time. The SMK directly or indirectly secures all other keys on the server, making it the "mother of all SQL Server encryption keys." The Windows Data Protection API (DPAPI), at the higher O/S level, uses the SQL Server service account credentials to automatically encrypt and secure the SMK.

Because it is automatically created and managed by the server, Service Master Keys require only a few administrative tools. The SMK can be backed up via the `BACKUP SERVICE MASTER KEY` T-SQL statement. This statement has the following format:

```
BACKUP SERVICE MASTER KEY TO FILE = 'path_to_file'
    ENCRYPTION BY PASSWORD = 'password'
```

Path_to_file is the local path or UNC network path to the file in which the SMK will be backed up. *Password* is a password which is used to encrypt the SMK backup file.

 You should backup your Service Master Key and store the backup in a secure off-site location immediately after installing SQL Server 2005.

Should you ever need to restore the Service Master Key from the backup copy, you can use the RESTORE SERVICE MASTER KEY statement:

```
RESTORE SERVICE MASTER KEY FROM FILE = 'path_to_file'
    DECRYPTION BY PASSWORD = 'password' [FORCE]
```

The `path_to_file` is the UNC or local path to the backup file. `Password` is the same password previously used to encrypt the backup. When restoring the SMK, SQL Server first decrypts all keys and other encrypted information using the current key. It then re-encrypts them with the new SMK. If the decryption process fails at any point, the entire restore process will fail. The FORCE option forces SQL Server to ignore decryption errors and force a restore.

 If you have to use the FORCE option of the RESTORE SERVICE MASTER KEY statement, you can count on losing some or all of the encrypted data on your server.

If your Service Master Key is compromised, or you want to change the SQL Server service account, you can regenerate or recover the SMK with the ALTER SERVICE MASTER KEY statement. The format and specific uses of the ALTER SERVICE MASTER KEY statement are available in Books Online.

Because it is automatically generated by SQL Server, there are no CREATE or DROP statements for the Service Master Key.

Database Master Keys

While each SQL Server has a single Service Master Key, each SQL database can have its own Database Master Key (DMK). The DMK is created using the CREATE MASTER KEY statement:

```
CREATE MASTER KEY ENCRYPTION BY PASSWORD = 'password'
```

This statement creates the DMK, encrypts it using the supplied password, and stores it in the database. In addition, the DMK is encrypted using the Service Master Key and stored in the master database; a feature known as "automatic key management." We'll talk more about this feature later.

Like the Service Master Key, you can backup and restore Database Master Keys. To backup a DMK, use the BACKUP MASTER KEY statement. The syntax is analogous to backing up a Service Master Key.

```
BACKUP MASTER KEY TO FILE = 'path_to_file'
    ENCRYPTION BY PASSWORD = 'password'
```

Restoring the Database Master Key requires that you use the DECRYPTION BY PASSWORD clause, which specifies the password previously used to encrypt the backup file. In addition you must use the ENCRYPTION BY PASSWORD clause, which gives SQL Server a password to encrypt the DMK after it is loaded in the database.

```
RESTORE MASTER KEY FROM FILE = 'path_to_file'
    DECRYPTION BY PASSWORD = 'password'
    ENCRYPTION BY PASSWORD = 'password'
    [ FORCE ]
```

Like restoring the Service Master Key, the DMK restore statement has a FORCE option which will ignore decryption errors.

 It is recommended that you immediately create backups of Database Master Keys and store them in a secure off-site location immediately after creating them. Also, the FORCE option of the RESTORE MASTER KEY statement can result in encrypted data loss.

To drop a DMK, use the DROP MASTER KEY statement:

```
DROP MASTER KEY
```

This statement drops the Database Master Key from the current database. Make sure you are in the correct database before using the `DROP MASTER KEY` statement.

Automatic Key Management

When you create a Database Master Key, a copy is encrypted with the supplied password and stored in the current database. A copy is also encrypted with the Service Master Key and stored in the master database. The copy of the DMK allows the server to automatically decrypt the DMK, a feature known as "automatic key management." Without automatic key management, you must use the `OPEN MASTER KEY` statement and supply a password every time you wish to encrypt and/or decrypt data using certificates and keys that rely on the DMK for security. With automatic key management, the `OPEN MASTER KEY` statement and password are not required.

The potential downfall of automatic key management is that it allows every sysadmin to decrypt the DMK. You can override automatic key management for a DMK with the `DROP ENCRYPTION BY SERVICE MASTER KEY` clause of the `ALTER MASTER KEY` statement. `ALTER MASTER KEY` and all its options are described in full detail in Books Online.

 Part 2: Certificates

Creating Certificates

Once you have your Service Master Key and Database Master Key configured, you're ready to begin making certificates. SQL Server 2005 has the ability to generate self-signed X.509 certificates. The flexible `CREATE CERTIFICATE` statement performs this function:

```
CREATE CERTIFICATE certificate_name [ AUTHORIZATION user_name ]
    { FROM <existing_keys> | <generate_new_keys> }
    [ ACTIVE FOR BEGIN_DIALOG =  { ON | OFF } ]
<existing_keys> ::=
    ASSEMBLY assembly_name
    | {
        [ EXECUTABLE ] FILE = 'path_to_file'
        [ WITH PRIVATE KEY ( <private_key_options> ) ]
      }
<generate_new_keys> ::=
    [ ENCRYPTION BY PASSWORD = 'password']
    WITH SUBJECT = 'certificate_subject_name'
    [ , <date_options> [ ,...n ] ]
<private_key_options> ::=
    FILE = 'path_to_private_key'
    [ , DECRYPTION BY PASSWORD = 'password' ]
    [ , ENCRYPTION BY PASSWORD = 'password' ]
<date_options> ::=
    START_DATE = 'mm/dd/yyyy' | EXPIRY_DATE = 'mm/dd/yyyy'
```

There are a lot of options associated with the `CREATE CERTIFICATE` statement. Fortunately few are needed most of the time. The following statement will create a certificate encrypted by password:

```
CREATE CERTIFICATE TestCertificate
    ENCRYPTION BY PASSWORD = 'thisIsAP@$$w0rd'
    WITH SUBJECT = 'This is a test certificate',
    START_DATE = '1/1/2006',
    EXPIRY_DATE = '12/31/2008';
```

If you leave off the `ENCRYPTION BY PASSWORD` clause, the Database Master Key is used to encrypt the certificate. Leaving the `START_DATE` out will result in the current date being used as the default start date for your certificate.

You can also use the CREATE CERTIFICATE statement to import an existing certificate into your SQL Server.

In addition to CREATE CERTIFICATE, SQL Server provides additional statements to manage certificates. These include DROP CERTIFICATE, ALTER CERTIFICATE, and BACKUP CERTIFICATE.

 There is no RESTORE statement for certificates. Use the CREATE CERTIFICATE statement to restore a backed-up certificate.

Encryption and Decryption by Certificate

Certificates can be used to encrypt and decrypt data directly by using the built-in EncryptByCert, DecryptByCert and Cert_ID functions. The Cert_ID function returns the ID of the certificate with the specified name. The format of the Cert_ID function is:

```
Cert_ID ( 'cert_name' )
```
The 'cert_name' is the name of the certificate. The EncryptByCert function requires the Certificate ID and has the following format:

```
EncryptByCert ( certificate_ID , { 'cleartext' | @cleartext } )
```

The certificate_ID is acquired by using the Cert_ID function. 'Cleartext' is the clear text string to encrypt. The clear text can be a char, varchar, nchar, nvarchar or wchar value. The EncryptByCert function returns a varbinary result of up to 8,000 bytes.

The DecryptByCert function is used to decrypt data that was previously encrypted by certificate. The format for DecryptByCert looks like this:

```
DecryptByCert (certificate_ID,
              { 'ciphertext' | @ciphertext }
              [ , { 'cert_password' | @cert_password } ]
              )
```

Like EncryptByCert, certificate_ID can be obtained using the Cert_ID function. 'Ciphertext' is the previously encrypted text. If you created your certificate with the ENCRYPT BY PASSWORD clause, 'cert_password' must be the same password you used when you created the certificate. If you did not use ENCRYPT BY PASSWORD to create the certificate, leave out 'cert_password'.

The following sample script creates a Database Master Key, a test certificate and demonstrates how to encrypt/decrypt data using the certificate.

```
-- Sample T-SQL Script to demonstrate Certificate Encryption
-- Use the AdventureWorks database
USE AdventureWorks;
-- Create a Database Master Key
CREATE MASTER KEY ENCRYPTION BY PASSWORD = 'p@ssw0rd';
-- Create a Temp Table
CREATE TABLE Person.#Temp
 (ContactID    INT PRIMARY KEY,
  FirstName    NVARCHAR(200),
  MiddleName   NVARCHAR(200),
  LastName     NVARCHAR(200),
  eFirstName   VARBINARY(200),
  eMiddleName  VARBINARY(200),
  eLastName    VARBINARY(200));
-- Create a Test Certificate, encrypted by the DMK
CREATE CERTIFICATE TestCertificate
    WITH SUBJECT = 'Adventureworks Test Certificate',
    EXPIRY_DATE = '10/31/2009';
-- EncryptByCert demonstration encrypts 100 names from the Person.Contact table
INSERT INTO Person.#Temp (ContactID, eFirstName, eMiddleName, eLastName)
SELECT ContactID, EncryptByCert(Cert_ID('TestCertificate'), FirstName),
        EncryptByCert(Cert_ID('TestCertificate'), MiddleName),
        EncryptByCert(Cert_ID('TestCertificate'), LastName)
FROM Person.Contact
WHERE ContactID <= 100;
-- DecryptByCert demonstration decrypts the previously encrypted data
UPDATE Person.#Temp
SET FirstName = DecryptByCert(Cert_ID('TestCertificate'), eFirstName),
        MiddleName = DecryptByCert(Cert_ID('TestCertificate'), eMiddleName),
        LastName = DecryptByCert(Cert_ID('TestCertificate'), eLastName);
-- View the results
SELECT * FROM Person.#Temp;
-- Clean up work:  drop temp table, test certificate and master key
DROP TABLE Person.#Temp;
DROP CERTIFICATE TestCertificate;
DROP MASTER KEY;
```

 Part 3: Symmetric Keys

Creating Symmetric Keys

You can use certificates to create symmetric keys for encryption and decryption within the database. The CREATE SYMMETRIC KEY statement has the following syntax:

```
CREATE SYMMETRIC KEY key_name [ AUTHORIZATION owner_name ]
    WITH <key_options> [ , ... n ]
    ENCRYPTION BY <encrypting_mechanism> [ , ... n ]

<encrypting_mechanism> ::=
    CERTIFICATE certificate_name |
    PASSWORD = 'password' |
    SYMMETRIC KEY symmetric_key_name |
    ASYMMETRIC KEY asym_key_name

<key_options> ::=
    KEY_SOURCE = 'pass_phrase' |
    ALGORITHM = <algorithm> |
    IDENTITY_VALUE = 'identity_phrase'

<algorithm> ::=
    DES | TRIPLE_DES | RC2 | RC4 | DESX | AES_128 | AES_192 | AES_256
```

Like the CREATE CERTIFICATE statement, CREATE SYMMETRIC KEY is very flexible. In most situations you will probably use a small subset of the available options. As an example, this statement creates a symmetric key and encrypts it with the Test Certificate created in the previous section:

```
CREATE SYMMETRIC KEY TestSymmetricKey
    WITH ALGORITHM = TRIPLE_DES
    ENCRYPTION BY CERTIFICATE TestCertificate;
```

Symmetric keys can be secured via other symmetric keys, asymmetric keys and passwords, as well as by certificates. SQL Server also provides ALTER SYMMETRIC KEY and DROP SYMMETRIC KEY statements to manage your symmetric keys. Specific syntax for these statements can be found in Books Online.

 When dropping keys and certificates, the order is important. SQL 2005 will not allow you to DROP certificates or keys if they are being used to encrypt other keys within the database.

Symmetric Key Encryption

SQL Server provides a set of functions to encrypt and decrypt data by symmetric key. These functions are EncryptByKey, DecryptByKey and Key_GUID. The Key_GUID function returns the unique identifier assigned to a specific symmetric key. The format of the function is:

```
Key_GUID( 'Key_Name' )
```

The EncryptByKey function requires a reference to the symmetric key GUID in order to encrypt data. The format of the EncryptByKey function is:

```
EncryptByKey( key_GUID, { 'cleartext' | @cleartext }
          [ , { add_authenticator | @add_authenticator }
           , { authenticator | @authenticator } ]
          )
```

The key_GUID is the symmetric key GUID, 'cleartext' is the plain text to be encrypted. Add_authenticator and authenticator are optional parameters that can help eliminate post-encryption patterns from your data.

The DecryptByKey function performs the reverse of EncryptByKey. This function decrypts your previously encrypted data. The format for DecryptByKey is:

```
DecryptByKey( { 'ciphertext' | @ciphertext }
          [ , add_authenticator
           , { authenticator | @authenticator } ]
          )
```

'Ciphertext' is the encrypted text. Add_authenticator and authenticator, if present, must match the values used in the EncryptByKey function. The DecryptByKey function doesn't require you to explicitly specify the symmetric key GUID. The symmetric key used previously to encrypt the data must be open, however. The OPEN SYMMETRIC KEY statement is used to open a symmetric key.

Here is a sample T-SQL script demonstrating encryption and decryption by symmetric key:

```
-- Use the AdventureWorks database
USE AdventureWorks;
-- Create a Database Master Key
CREATE MASTER KEY ENCRYPTION BY PASSWORD = 'p@ssw0rd';
-- Create a Temp Table
CREATE TABLE Person.#Temp
(ContactID    INT PRIMARY KEY,
 FirstName    NVARCHAR(200),
 MiddleName   NVARCHAR(200),
 LastName     NVARCHAR(200),
 eFirstName   VARBINARY(200),
 eMiddleName  VARBINARY(200),
 eLastName    VARBINARY(200));
-- Create a Test Certificate
CREATE CERTIFICATE TestCertificate
    WITH SUBJECT = 'Adventureworks Test Certificate',
    EXPIRY_DATE = '10/31/2009';
-- Create a Symmetric Key
CREATE SYMMETRIC KEY TestSymmetricKey
        WITH ALGORITHM = TRIPLE_DES
    ENCRYPTION BY CERTIFICATE TestCertificate;
OPEN SYMMETRIC KEY TestSymmetricKey
    DECRYPTION BY CERTIFICATE TestCertificate;
-- EncryptByKey demonstration encrypts 100 names from the Person.Contact table
INSERT INTO Person.#Temp (ContactID, eFirstName, eMiddleName, eLastName)
SELECT ContactID,
        EncryptByKey(Key_GUID('TestSymmetricKey'), FirstName),
        EncryptByKey(Key_GUID('TestSymmetricKey'), MiddleName),
        EncryptByKey(Key_GUID('TestSymmetricKey'), LastName)
FROM Person.Contact
WHERE ContactID <= 100;
-- DecryptByKey demonstration decrypts the previously encrypted data
UPDATE Person.#Temp
SET FirstName = DecryptByKey(eFirstName),
        MiddleName = DecryptByKey(eMiddleName),
        LastName = DecryptByKey(eLastName);
-- View the results
SELECT * FROM Person.#Temp;
-- Clean up work:  drop temp table, symmetric key, test certificate and master key
DROP TABLE Person.#Temp;
CLOSE SYMMETRIC KEY TestSymmetricKey;
DROP SYMMETRIC KEY TestSymmetricKey;
DROP CERTIFICATE TestCertificate;
DROP MASTER KEY;
```

Conclusions

SQL Server 2005 includes several new functions to securely create, manage and use encryption keys and certificates to secure sensitive data. Taking advantage of this new functionality can greatly enhance your database and application security.

Reference

SQL Books Online References:

- ALTER CERTIFICATE
- ALTER MASTER KEY
- ALTER SERVICE MASTER KEY
- ALTER SYMMETRIC KEY
- BACKUP CERTIFICATE
- BACKUP MASTER KEY
- BACKUP SERVICE MASTER KEY
- Cert_ID
- CLOSE MASTER KEY
- CLOSE SYMMETRIC KEY
- CREATE CERTIFICATE
- CREATE MASTER KEY
- CREATE SYMMETRIC KEY
- DecryptByCert
- DecryptByKey

- DROP CERTIFICATE
- DROP MASTER KEY
- DROP SYMMETRIC KEY
- EncryptByCert
- EncryptByKey
- Key_GUID
- OPEN MASTER KEY
- OPEN SYMMETRIC KEY
- RESTORE MASTER KEY
- RESTORE SERVICE MASTER KEY

SQL Server Job Scheduling

By Peter He

If a job needs to run hourly from 3AM to 7AM, once at 12:00AM, and hourly from 6PM to 9PM everyday, how would you schedule the job in SQL server? If your answer to the question is to define three individual jobs, you will get a better way after reading this article.

SQL server has a very flexible scheduling system. This article will focus on the following topics:

- Attach multiple schedules to a job
- Schedules for frequent execution (schedule interval <1 minute) jobs
- Start a job whenever CPU is idle
- Start a job when SQL Agent server starts

Attach multiple schedules to a job

This answers the question in the beginning of the article. SQL server allows to define multiple schedules to a job. In SQL agent job schedule tab, click "New Schedule..." button will add schedules to a job.

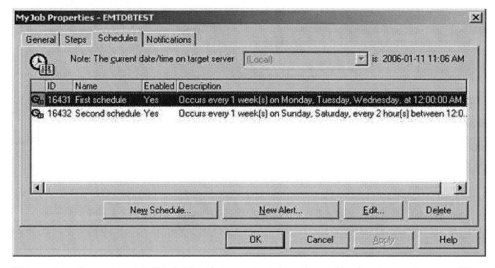

This script will create a job "MyJob" with two schedules showed in the above diagram. The schedules are saved in msdb..sysjobschedules table. We can run msdb..sp_help_jobschedule to check the schedules, e.g.:

```
msdb..sp_help_jobschedule @job_name='MyJob'
```

The results:

schedule_id	schedule_name	enabled	freq_type	freq_interval	freq_subday_type	freq_su
16431	First schedule	1	8	14	1	0
16432	Second schedule	1	8	65	8	2

The time frame (active start and end date) and daily running time (active start and end time) of schedules attached to a job can be overlapped. SQL server calculates the next run time in the following way:

- Calculate the next run time for each enabled schedule based on its definition
- Among them, find the soonest time as the next run time of the job
- The time and the schedule will be the next run schedule and next run time for the job
- If more schedules produce the same next run time, the schedule with the smallest schedule_id will be the next run schedule.

E.g., for the job with the following schedules, the execution history will be as follows:

Schedule_id	Schedule_name	Schedule description
16431	First schedule	Every day every 4 minute(s) between 00:00:00AM and 08:00:00PM
16432	Second schedule	Every day every 2 minute(s) between 11:22:00AM and 10:00:00AM

No.	Time	Next run schedule	Next run time
1	2006-01-11 11:13:00	First schedule	2006-01-11 11:16:00
2	2006-01-11 11:17:00	First schedule	2006-01-11 11:20:00
3	2006-01-11 11:21:00	Second schedule	2006-01-11 11:22:00
4	2006-01-11 11:23:00	First schedule	2006-01-11 11:24:00
3	2006-01-11 11:25:00	Second schedule	2006-01-11 11:26:00
4	2006-01-11 11:27:00	First schedule	2006-01-11 11:28:00

Schedules for frequent executing jobs

SQL server jobs can have high running frequency with interval less than 1 minute. But this capability is not exposed to SQL agent GUI, only "Hours" and "Minutes" are supported.

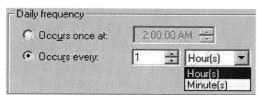

This can be achieved by calling the stored procedure msdb.dbo.sp_add_jobschedule or msdb.dbo.sp_update_jobschedule.

The stored procedures have a parameter **@freq_subday_type**, it has three values according to BOL:

Value	Description (unit)
0x1	At the specified time.
0x4	Minutes.
0x8	Hours.

For the same column in msdb..sysjobschedules table, it has four values, which includes 0x2 for seconds. Though 0x2 is not documented for the two stored procedures, it can accept the value and create the schedule correctly, e.g. this script will create a job runs every 30 seconds everyday. When a job is scheduled to run in the interval less than 1 minute, the schedule showed up in SQL agent GUI will not be correct, e.g. for the job created by the previous script, the schedule will be showed as following:

Jobs with less than 1 minute daily frequency may use lots of resources and may have negative impact on overall server performance.

Start a job whenever CPU is idle

SQL server can run jobs based on CPU utilization if the CPU idle condition is enabled and met. First of all we need to define the threshold for CPU idle in SQL agent property -> Advanced tab:

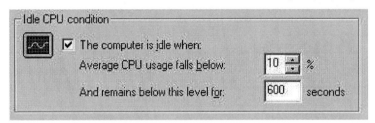

According to BOL: Average CPU usage falls below: Specify the idle CPU condition by percentage. Idle is when the average CPU usage remains below the selected percent for the specified number of seconds.

·   And remains below this level for Specify the idle CPU condition by seconds. Idle is when the average CPU usage remains below the selected percentage for the specified number of seconds.

If the Idle CPU condition is not defined, SQL server does not give any error messages when you define jobs to run on CPU idle. However, SQL Agent server gives a message in the error log when it starts up if the idle condition is not defined:

2006-02-07 08:24:00 - + [396] An idle CPU condition has not been defined - OnIdle job schedules will have no effect

To use this schedule, in SQL agent job property -> schedule tab, select "New Schedule…" or "Edit…", and select the second option in "Schedule Type" as following:

To define the schedule by calling stored procedure *msdb.dbo.sp_add_jobschedule*, we need to pass 128 for **@freq_type.**

Please keep in mind that CPU idle does not mean the server is idle, e.g. the I/O subsystem may be very busy at the time. So this type of schedule is suitable for jobs with light I/O and heavy CPU utilization, and the job is recurring with short running duration.

Start a job when SQL Agent server starts

The job with this type of schedule runs once SQL Agent server starts. It's suitable to clean up or set up running environment for other jobs, e.g. create or clean up certain folder etc. To use this schedule, in SQL agent job property -> schedule tab, select "New Schedule…" or "Edit…", and select the first option in "Schedule Type" as following:

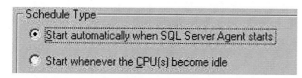

To define the schedule by calling stored procedure *msdb.dbo.sp_add_jobschedule*, we need to pass 64 for **@freq_type.**

Conclusion

SQL server has a very flexible scheduling system. Special irregular schedules can be defined for a job by combining different type of schedules, such as recurring, one time or CPU idle etc. SQL server 2005 separated job and schedule. So schedules can be shared by multiple jobs.

Triggers for Auditing

by Tiago Andrade e Silva

Have you ever had the need to know when a given row in a table was last changed? Maintaining a *last_modified* date field at the application level would give you more work and would not be the most correct way because somebody might just open Enterprise Manager and change the data directly.

In order to implement this functionality at the database level and never more worry about the update of that field we will need to use Triggers. A trigger is a set of statements that automatically executes after a data modification takes place on a table. We can register triggers for the 3 events that can occur on a table: Insert, update and delete.

In our case we would only need to create an UPDATE trigger in order to keep the *last_modified* field updated. Two approaches can be taken regarding the creation date, either we put a default value that uses the getdate() function, or we leave it null indicating it was never changed.

Available to the triggers is a virtual table that has the data that is about to be deleted or inserted or both in case of the update. If it is an update trigger, the *deleted* table has the record as it was before the update, and the *inserted* has the values that we are about to change.

One might be tempted to think that we would just need to change the *last_modified* field at the end of the trigger with the actual time and date and the magic would be done. But it's not so simple! The normal triggers which are called AFTER Triggers do not allow you to change the data on the virtual tables. So SQL Server 2000 has extended the power of triggers by letting you create a second kind of trigger, called an **INSTEAD OF**.

What the **INSTEAD OF trigger** does is override the normal insert,delete or update statement and leave that responsibility to your Trigger. You will be responsible for inserting, deleting or updating the data to the database.

Imagine we have a table with a *last_modified* column:

```
CREATE TABLE [Table_Name] (
        ...
        [last_modified] [datetime] NULL DEFAULT (getdate()),
        ...
) ON [PRIMARY]
```

The trigger to automatically update the *last_modified* date column would be:

```
CREATE TRIGGER TriggerName ON [Table_Name]
INSTEAD OF UPDATE
AS
   UPDATE [Table_Name]
      SET  field1=(select field1 from inserted),
              'Put Here all the fields of the table
         last_modified=getdate() 'this will do the magic
   WHERE id =(select id from inserted)
```

Conclusions

If you change the row you will notice that the field is automatically updated. If you manually change the *last_modified* your changes will be overridden by the actual time and date.

T-SQL and Programming

The basis of any relational database system is the SQL manipulation language. In this section we've compiled the best articles that work with the T-SQL language in SQL Server. Complicated queries, unusual methods of getting data, a look at some of the more interesting ways that people have written their queries.

Updated SQL Injection

By Michael Coles

Introduction

For many years now, SQL Injection attacks on large corporate websites have been highly publicized. Several articles around the Web have described what an injection attack is, how it works, and the basics of how to defend against it. A couple of very good articles here at SQL Server Central also delve into this topic (SQL Injection by Christoffer Hedgate and SQL Injection - Part 1 by Randy Dyess).

So why did I feel the need to write another article on SQL Injection? For three reasons:

1. The good work by Mr. Dyess and Mr. Hedgate offer code samples and examples for ASP. I felt that a sample pertaining to ASP.NET, for those without the ASP background, was in order.
2. These two authors focus on using parameterized queries; and in the case of Mr. Hedgate, validating user input. Excellent advice all around, but I feel there are other lines of defense which should be addressed as well.
3. Finally, no matter how many SQL Injection articles are posted around the Web, DBA's and developers continue to post highly exploitable code samples to newsgroups and discussion boards.

In this article, I hope to build upon the good work of Mr. Hedgate and Mr. Dyess, and provide updated samples as well as a more complete defensive strategy for dealing with SQL Injection.

What Is SQL Injection

SQL Injection is a method of exploiting databases via the user interface. The method takes advantage of the fact that SQL allows multiple commands on a single line, separated by semicolons. SQL Injection also takes advantage of the way SQL handles single quotes.

We'll create a sample using a fictitious Database Admin. We'll call him Ima D. Ba. Ima has to create a login table for Northwind that contains the usernames and passwords of all employees. He creates the following table, called Test_Logins, in the Northwind Database:

	EmployeeID	Username	Password
▶	1	NancyD	test
	2	AndrewF	pass
	3	JanetL	1234
	4	MargaretP	hello
	5	StevenB	mypassword
	6	MichaelS	wowsa
	7	RobertK	wait
	8	LauraC	linda
	9	AnneD	candy
✳			

Ima then made a SQL Login for the local ASPNET user. He made ASPNET the database owner (dbo) for the Northwind Database and also made ASPNET a SQL system administrator.

One of the company developers then wrote a simple ASP.NET login webform that asks for username and password, which it then validates against Ima's Test_Logins table.

```
Private Sub LoginButton_Click(ByVal sender As System.Object, ByVal e As System.EventArgs) &_
        Handles LoginButton.Click
    Dim success As Boolean = False
    Dim sqlcon As New System.Data.SqlClient.SqlConnection("SERVER=(local);" & _
                                                "INITIAL CATALOG=Northwind;" & _
                                                "INTEGRATED SECURITY=SSPI;")
    sqlcon.Open()
    Dim sqlstr As String = "SELECT * " & _
                    "FROM Test_Logins " & _
                    "WHERE UserName = '" & Username.Text & "' " & _
                    "AND Password = '" & Password.Text & "'"
    Dim sqlcmd As New System.Data.SqlClient.SqlCommand(sqlstr, sqlcon)
    Dim sqldr As System.Data.SqlClient.SqlDataReader = sqlcmd.ExecuteReader()
    If sqldr.HasRows Then
        success = True
    End If
    sqldr.Close()
    sqlcmd.Dispose()
    sqlcon.Dispose()
    If success Then
        Server.Transfer("Success.aspx")
    End If
End Sub
```

The login code basically performs five steps:

1. User enters username and password
2. Web form opens a connection to the Northwind Database
3. Web form dynamically builds a SQL query: `SELECT * FROM Test_Logins WHERE UserName = 'username' AND Password = 'password'`
4. Web form performs the SQL query over the open connection
5. If there are any rows in our resultset, we know that the user has entered a good username and password.

Enter The Hacker

Our hacker Yuri picks up one of Andrew Fuller's business cards at a tech convention. The business card has Andrew's title ("Vice President of Sales") in big 12 point type. So Yuri decides that Andrew probably has access to a lot of confidential company information. Andrew is now targeted.

This is a very simplified example, but it demonstrates several avenues of attack. The first is to trick the server into believing we are actually logging in as someone else. We can enter the following as a username:

Enter your username and password below, then press Login.

Username: AndrewF'; --

Password:

Login

The resulting SQL query is:

`SELECT * FROM Test_Logins WHERE UserName = 'AndrewF'; -- AND Password = ''`

Everything after the -- is a comment, so the password check is completely bypassed, allowing us to successfully log in as AndrewF without a password!

Alternatively Yuri could append DROP statements, DELETE statements or any other valid T-SQL commands to our username to produce intrusive or destructive results, as in these examples. We could even potentially access stored procedures and extended stored procedures (like xp_cmdshell) to wreak havoc all over the corporate network!

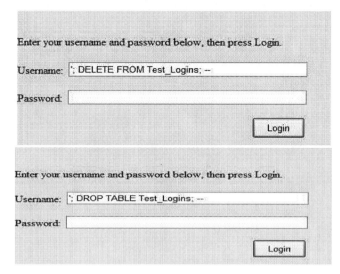

How To Avoid SQL Injection

So now that we know what SQL Injection is, how can we avoid it? Let's look at the mistakes Ima and his developer made:

 ### The Developer Did Not Validate User Input

Your first line of defense against SQL Injection is always input validation. Any time an application accepts input from a user and uses it in a query against a database, it absolutely has to be validated. This validation can be done server-side, client-side, or even both. In our example, we know that certain special characters in input strings can open us up to SQL injection: double-dash (--), single-quote(') and semi-colon (;) are the primary trouble-makers. We can check for these and other special characters on the client or server side and eliminate them before we dynamically build queries based on user input.

A good rule of thumb is if you don't allow certain characters in the input string, eliminate them completely (or throw an exception) during the validation phase. For instance, all our usernames consist of only alphabetic characters, so we could limit input in that form field to letters 'A' - 'Z' and 'a' - 'z'. Anything the user inputs, including drop-down box form inputs, should be validated before you try to query with it.

 ### The Developer Built A Query Dynamically

Our next line of defense is to avoid building queries dynamically when possible. Always look to parameterized queries (sp_executesql in T-SQL) first.

But if you do need to build a query dynamically, validate your input well and be certain to replace single quotes (') with escaped single quotes ('') in string constants. This can be done with the T-SQL Replace() function, or the .NET String.Replace() method can be used for this purpose.

For this particular application, however, it makes much more sense for Ima and the Developer to use a Parameterized Query to validate our user. Parameterized queries pass the input values to the server separately from the actual SQL Query. The server then provides a level of safety by using sp_executesql with parameters instead of dynamically building the query string.

Build queries dynamically only when you have to. And when you do have to, be sure to validate all input to the generated query string before running it against the server. Also when building dynamic SQL Queries, you generally should not need to dynamically insert table names, column names, etc. (unless you're building some sort of SQL DDL/Admin tools). If you find that you are generating a lot of dynamic queries with dynamic table and column names, it might be a good idea to take a closer look at your database implementation.

Ideally, Ima will build a stored procedure that accepts the username and password as parameters. This procedure will validate the user and return a success or failure code and any other pertinent information. The stored procedure model will add a layer of abstraction that will keep the hacker a little further away from our base tables.

 ### The DBA Gave Away The Farm

You might notice in the example attacks that the hacker was able to run such commands as DELETE FROM Test_Logins and DROP TABLE Test_Logins. This is because Ima made the ASPNET user the Northwind dbo. Also, Ima gave the ASPNET user SysAdmin rights. Our DBA needs to scale back the rights for the ASPNET user to something more reasonable. Most likely this user will have read-only rights to most information; and Ima's ASPNET user should never, ever have rights to run DDL commands such as CREATE TABLE, DROP TABLE, etc. Ima also needs to lock down the master database to ensure the ASPNET user doesn't grab all available information about the server configuration.

 ### The Developer Is Sending Too Much Information Across The Wire

In our sample, our Developer is sending much more information across the wire (between the IIS and SQL Server) than is necessary. All we need to know is if our username and password matched. So all we really need to return from SQL Server is a single number, not a complete table row! We could change the SELECT statement to return the EmployeeID of the logged in user with `SELECT EmployeeID FROM ....` The less information we have to pass along, the better our security.

 ### The DBA Is Storing Plain Text In Critical Columns

Closely related to the previous problem, Ima is storing passwords in plain text format in the Test_Logins table. This is a big no-no. Sensitive information such as passwords should be stored in encrypted or hashed format. That way, even if our hacker happens to get past all the other lines of defense and is able to view the data in our tables, it will be unusable to him. One method of protecting passwords is to hash the passwords using a hash algorithm (like MD5) before storing them in your table. Then when you go to compare passwords at login time, hash the password in your ASP.NET code or your Windows Forms code before sending it to the SQL Server. Any time we can prevent sending sensitive information across the wire in plain text format, we should take advantage of it.

 ## Conclusions

SQL Injection is a tactic used by hackers to gain unauthorized access to confidential data stored in SQL Server. Proper planning and development practices can help secure your system against SQL Injection and other types of attacks.

Resources

- MSDN Entry: sp_executesql Microsoft
- MSDN Entry: EXECUTE
- SQL Injection by Christoffer Hedgate
- SQL Injection Part 1 by Randy Dyess

Introduction to SQLCMD

By Haidong Ji

In SQL Server 2005, Microsoft introduced a new command line tool, SQLCMD, as a replacement for osql and isql. In a series of articles, I will give you a brief introduction to this versatile and powerful tool. In this installment, I will talk about differences among SQLCMD, osql, and isql. I will also give you some pointers on SQLCMD customization.

SQLCMD, osql, and isql

Microsoft has announced before that isql was on its way out. Sure enough, isql is not included in SQL Server 2005 RTM. osql eventually will be phased out also, although it is still included in SQL Server 2005 binary install. With the historical SQL Server release cycle in mind, maybe osql will bid us adieu in 2010;)

Migration to SQLCMD should be easy, since most of the command line switches are identical. The only difference would be that more switches are added in SQLCMD. To see the differences, open a DOS command line, and type sqlcmd /? and osql /?, this will give you a general idea of switches of them.

Most, if not all, your existing SQL script files should run as is under SQLCMD, without any modifications. So migration should not be a problem.

Like osql, SQLCMD has batch and interactive modes. You use batch mode mainly for scripting and automation tasks, whereas interactive mode is for ad-hoc query analysis.

In addition, you can run SQLCMD within SQL Server Management Studio (SSMS). There are some limitations on that. For example, certain commands will not within SSMS. More information on that can be obtained through BOL.

Setup an initialization script for SQLCMD

SQLCMD provides a few variables you can customize to suit your needs. To see a full list of available SQLCMD variables, when you are in SQLCMD command line, type:

```
:listvar
```
will give you a list of all available variables. I will show you how to customize 2 settings here: sqlcmdini and sqlcmdeditor.

You can set sqlcmdini so that sqlcmd would run a query whenever you launch it from the command line interactively. For example, you can let it run a query and return some useful information like version number, edition level, and patch level. All these are great to know for a DBA. Here are steps to set it up:

- Create the script file. Let's call it c:\work\scripts\SQL\Initialization.SQL. For example, you can put statements below, customize it to suit your needs:

```
--Begin script
set nocount on
go
print 'You are connected to ' + rtrim(CONVERT(char(20), SERVERPROPERTY('servername')))
+ ' (' + rtrim(CONVERT(char(20), SERVERPROPERTY('productversion'))) + ')' + ' '
+ rtrim(CONVERT(char(30), SERVERPROPERTY('Edition'))) + ' '
+ rtrim(CONVERT(char(20), SERVERPROPERTY('ProductLevel'))) + char(10)

:setvar SQLCMDMAXFIXEDTYPEWIDTH 20
set nocount off
go
:setvar SQLCMDMAXFIXEDTYPEWIDTH
--End script
```

- In DOS prompt, type:

```
set sqlcmdini=c:\work\scripts\SQL\Initialization.SQL
```

Here are some sample results:

```
C:\Documents and Settings\Haidong\sqlcmd
You are connected to MARIALAPTOP (8.00.194) Enterprise Evaluation Edition RTM
1. exit
C:\Documents and Settings\Haidong\sqlcmd -S.\ssistest
You are connected to MARIALAPTOP\SSISTEST (9.00.1399.06) Standard Edition RTM
1. exit
```

Customize SQLCMD editor

In SQLCMD, if you type ed, it will invoke a text editor and put the last command you run in the editor buffer. The default editor is Edit, a command line editor of DOS. This behavior is very similar to Oracle SQL Plus, by the way. The difference is that in SQL Plus, you can use / to run the command after you finished editing, whereas in SQLCMD you still need to type go for it, well, to go;)

Anyway, the really neat thing is you can change the default editor to whatever you like. I know many DBAs /

developers have their own preferred editors, like Edit Plus, TextPad, or even plain old Notepad. This is exciting because if you work in your favorite editor, you feel you are in control and your productivity increases. For me, I have changed the default editor to VIM, a clone of VI.

This is how you do it:

- Open a DOS prompt;
- Type set sqlcmdeditor=vim, or notepad or whatever;
- Go to sqlcmd, enter and execute a sql statement, then type ed;
- Your editor of choice opens. Edit away, after you are done, save and close;

I am very happy to find this feature. It is a real productivity enhancer.

I hope you have some general understanding of SQLCMD after reading this article. I will write about SQLCMD variables in the next installment.

Customer Database Update – A Practical Solution

By Serhiy Snisarenko

Introduction

If you are a DBA in a company that develops and maintains various database products for its customers, you know that the release and implementation of a new product version can be a challenge, since you are probably responsible for preparing of the database update packages and their installation on the customer sites. Since any product changes over time, and different clients often run different product versions, you need an efficient strategy to perform and keep track of regular database updates (by "update" in this article I mean implementation of a new version of the client-server application with the database on the back end). Ideally this strategy should work with all types of database and product changes, and be applicable to all your customers regardless of the product version they run, and the differences in the customer business rules.

One approach is to change only the objects that have to be changed the way they have to be changed for each client. Another solution is to only change the database schema, and then recreate everything else anew based on the specific client requirements. This method is clean and much less error-prone, but is complicated and requires a lot of work performed in a very strict order, so it is hard - unless we can automate it.

The key points of the article are:

- updating databases of any size and complexity with a single command
- implementation of a simple, clear and convenient structure for the database update package
- generating correct creation order for database objects that can have hierarchical dependencies
- creating a program that generates the full set of the database update scripts that comprise the package

Simply put, this article describes my approach to the problem, in form of the notes on preparing the database update package for the new product release. It suggests the folder structure, files, scripts and settings that I believe could be useful and convenient. I will discuss some common problems that you might face, and offer a solution for them, including code examples that could be helpful if you decide to apply this approach in your own database. The final result of these efforts is a program that automatically generates a database update package containing a number of always-up-to-date scripts that can be run on the customer site with one mouse click. This way, the update can be performed even by low-qualified personnel, and even if you are not given the access to the customer database.

Parsing Update Script

Whenever developers release a new product version, you have to make the necessary database and client updates. If the customer company has DBAs on staff, then they can implement the required changes. However, you problem becomes slightly more complex if the customer does not have its own DBAs. In this case you have to find a way to help a non-qualified employee do it.

The common way of doing it is to write the scripts, which are making the changes and updates, to be run in the target database; these scripts can be tested in the dedicated environment, and leave the trail of changes for future audits. Then they are shipped to every customer – since most of them do not usually give you access to their databases. Even in your own database, scripting the changes is more convenient and secure.

In my opinion, main database/client releases and patches/hot fixes should be implemented in different ways. In this article we will discuss the first one; implementing patches is the subject of the next article.

Let's now review our own sample set of scripts. Imagine the ideal folder and file structure of the script written for the standard pubs database. As a customer you receive a compressed file called "pubs20.zip". I usually include database name and version into the file name. When the zip file is unpacked, a customer has the following directory and file tree structure (see Figure 1):

Figure 1. Folder and file structure.

With this structure it is easier to explain which way the update will be done and what exactly will be updated.

Three major things to be updated are database schema, database objects, and the data itself. Changing the schema is the significant update but curiously enough it is the only thing we will change; the database objects and the data, which need changes, will be completely replaced.

Let's review the schema updates. There are at least two ways of doing it. One way is to unload data from the database into flat or XML files, change the database structure, and load the data back into the database. This will require reformatting data on either load or unload, or both, and is complicated and time-consuming method. It is worth only when the schema is being significantly changed. We are not reviewing such a case in this article.

In the majority of cases the other approach is taken. It involves keeping the detailed history of the previous database changes, and requires developers to thoroughly review them when writing the scripts for the next schema update. The "schema" folder, from Figure 1, will contain the database schema update scripts.

There are two possible ways to modify database objects: a partial update and a full update. A partial update means that the objects which are no longer needed will be dropped, objects which need changes will be modified, and the newly created objects will be added. In my opinion this way is more appropriate for hot fixes and patches issued between main database versions rather than for performing a full scale database update.

When modifying the database using the full update, all of the original database objects will be removed completely and the new objects will replace them. This approach is better for updating the database objects, since it does not require keeping track of the database objects history.

All scripts that are needed for the deletion and creation of the database objects are stored in the "drop" and "create" folders respectively. The source code of the various database objects is stored in special directories: folder named "uddt" contains the source code for the user-defined data types, folder "udf" is used for user-defined functions, folder "view" contains view definitions, folder "sp" is for stored procedures, and folder "trigger" is for triggers.

The next thing to update is the data itself. Usually there are several tables that contain the data influencing the application's functionality. As an example, a database can store the application menu and submenu items, sets of report samples, standard finance information, some geographical data, etc. This information should be either completely or partially refreshed during database update. Thus a folder named "data" contains the data from all the tables that should be copied into the customer database and folder named "copydata" contains all the necessary scripts to do it. Folder "patch" contains the scripts to fix inconsistent data – if any.

Folder "job" contains source code for all the jobs that should be run on the database server. For example, if you need to run a report on a regular basis you can create a job to do that. Also, you can create a job that will monitor particular database tables and execute necessary procedures upon the specified data change.

Having discussed all things that have to be changed during the database update, let's now take a look at how this update works. Before you start the update I would strongly recommend to make a full database backup and to ensure that the backup is good.

To start database update you have to execute the "run_update_db.bat" batch file (see Figure 1) with no parameters. This file is just a convenience to call another batch file with a lot of preset parameters:

```
update_db.bat server1 pubs sa_password %CD% customer1 > update_result.txt
```

You can modify the parameters by changing server name and sa user password, save the file and double-click its name in Windows Explorer to start the update. The output log file update_result.txt will show up in the current directory.

While update is running, let's review the "update_db.bat" file (see Listing 1a). The first part of this script checks all passed parameters:

```
rem Check parameters

rem Server\Instance
if "%1" == "" goto usage
if "%1" == "/?" goto usage
if "%1" == "help" goto usage
rem Database
if "%2" == "" goto usage
rem sa password
if "%3" == "" goto usage
rem Scripts Directory
if "%4" == "" goto usage
rem Insert Data
if "%5" == "" goto usage
date /T
time /T
```

The first three parameters are setting the connection to the database:

- Instance name. If you need to update database on the default instance, this parameter can be the server name, alias name or server IP address. If the database is on the named instance, the instance name should be added after back slash.
- Database name
- Password for sa login

The fourth parameter is the root path to our scripts - the directory where the batch file is stored and where the output log file will be created. It could be a full path like "C:\Build\pubs20\db", or if you run the script from the current directory, it could be the operating system variable %CD%.

The fifth parameter lets you add specific customer or customer group name in case some data should be updated in slightly different way for different customers. We will discuss this parameter later.

The first two script commands generate the run start timestamp; the two similar commands at the end of the script generate the run end timestamp and allow us to calculate the run time. These calculations can help us schedule the update for the most appropriate time.

The second part of this script updates database schema and recreates the database objects. All of the database objects depend on each other, thus it is very important to modify them in the required order.

First of all we should create new User Defined Data Types that could be used in the table's DDL:

```
rem Create new data types
osql  -S%1 -d%2 -Usa -P%3 -i%4\uddt\uddt_zip.SQL -n -b
if %ERRORLEVEL%==1 GOTO end
```

After that, the database structure should be modified. All modification scripts should be ran in the order in which they have been released by developers:

```
rem Run AlterTable scripts
osql  -S%1 -d%2 -Usa -P%3 -i%4\schema\pubs_2_0_01.SQL -n -b
if %ERRORLEVEL%==1 GOTO end
osql  -S%1 -d%2 -Usa -P%3 -i%4\schema\pubs_2_0_02.SQL -n -b
if %ERRORLEVEL%==1 GOTO end
```

Then the following commands delete all other existing database objects:

```
rem Run Delete Database Objects Scripts
osql  -S%1 -d%2 -Usa -P%3 -i%4\drop\drop_tr.sql -n
osql  -S%1 -d%2 -Usa -P%3 -i%4\drop\drop_sp.sql -n
osql  -S%1 -d%2 -Usa -P%3 -i%4\drop\drop_view.sql -n
osql  -S%1 -d%2 -Usa -P%3 -i%4\drop\drop_udf.sql -n
```

After these objects have been deleted they must be recreated in the following order: User Defined Functions, Views, Stored Procedures, and finally Triggers. Keeping this order is very important because every new group of created objects may need the previous groups of objects to already exist. For example, some views can use UDF's, and stored procedures can use both UDF's and views, and so on. The following code will recreate the database objects in the described order:

```
rem Run Create Database Objects Scripts
call create\create_udf.bat %1 %2 %3 %4
call create\create_view.bat %1 %2 %3 %4
call create\create_sp.bat %1 %2 %3 %4
call create\create_tr.bat %1 %2 %3 %4
```

The third part of this script processes the data that needs to be re-created. In this example we will completely change data in the "stores" and "jobs" tables, and change the user-defined error messages in the *sysmessages* table in the *master* database. Also, we will add certain data into the new "app_modules" table which contains customer-related data chosen based on the fifth parameter. Here are the commands that do all of this:

```
rem Truncate Tables
osql  -S%1 -d%2 -Usa -P%3 -i%4\copydata\remove_data.sql -n
rem Insert Data
if "%5" == "customer1" call copydata\bcpin_customer1.bat %1 %2 %3 %4
if "%5" == "customer2" call copydata\bcpin_customer2.bat %1 %2 %3 %4
rem Restore Constraints
osql  -S%1 -d%2 -Usa -P%3 -i%4\copydata\restore_constraints.sql -n
```

Let's assume that during software development process some errors were made and, as a result, some of the data needs to be fixed. In given example we fix data in the discounts table:

```
rem Run Patches
osql  -S%1 -d%2 -Usa -P%3 -i%4\patch\patch_discounts.sql -n
```

You can also create jobs that can assist your application. In the example below the job will generate a daily report:

```
rem Create Jobs
osql -S%1 -d%2 -Usa -P%3 -i%4\job\ytd_report.sql -n
```

Finally, the script refreshes database version information:

```
rem Update ver_history table
osql  -S%1 -d%2 -Usa -P%3 -i%4\copydata\ins_ver_history.sql -n
```

Now we know what happens when "run_update_db.bat" executes. When the update is done, we can review "update_result.txt" log file (see <u>Listing 1b</u>). It contains results of all the commands that the script called. It also contains all warning, error, and failure messages. The size of this log file depends on the number of the scripts we ran, and can become really big. To automate the tedious process of finding the typical warnings or errors in the text, you can write a simple program searching for the following keywords: 'Msg', 'Level', 'SQLState', and 'NativeError'. Below I describe the most typical messages.

A warning message is logged if the stored procedure being generated is calling another procedure that cannot be found:

```
C:\Build\pubs20\db >osql -Sserver1 -dpubs -Usa -Psa_password -i"
C:\Build\pubs20\db\sp\aubyroyalty.SQL" -n
Cannot add rows to sysdepends for the current stored procedure because it
depends on the missing object 'byroyalty'. The stored procedure will still be
created.
```

If the update script is correct, a warning can only appear in case the stored procedure being generated is recursive. An error message is logged in case the creation of a database object failed for any reason; the specific failure reason, object name, and the code line number are listed in the message:

```
C:\Build\pubs20\db>osql -Sserver1 -dpubs -Usa -Psa_password - C:\Build\pubs20\db\uddt\zip.SQL -n -b
Msg 15180, Level 16, State 1, Server server1, Procedure sp_droptype, Line 32
Cannot drop. The data type is being used.
```

The next example is a typical error message occurring when the data is being copied into a table:

```
C:\Build\pubs20\db >bcp "pubs.dbo.stores" in
"C:\Build\pubs20\db\data\stores.dat" -c -t"|" -Usa -Psa_password -Sserver1
Starting copy...
SQLState = 23000, NativeError = 515
Error = [Microsoft][ODBC SQL Server Driver][SQL Server]Cannot insert the value NULL into column
'stor_id', table 'pubs.dbo.stores'; column does not allow nulls. INSERT fails.
SQLState = 01000, NativeError = 3621
Warning = [Microsoft][ODBC SQL Server Driver][SQL Server]The statement has been terminated.

BCP copy in failed
```

The log file can be very helpful during update script development. Also, if the errors occur during the actual update of the customer's database, this log file can help you identify the possible problems in the target database, or find errors in the scripts, which were overlooked.

In case of a serious error, you can restore the database from the backup, fix the scripts, and run the process again. Now we are ready to prepare the update package.

Preparing Update Package

Developers usually store their source code in source code control systems, such as Microsoft Visual Source Safe, CVS, etc. The folder structure in such a system should be the same or very similar to the structure shown on the Figure 1. All source code should be stored in the corresponding folders. Only "create" folder should be empty at this moment. We will discuss how to prepare all database object creation scripts later in this chapter.

Let's look at examples of source code from each folder. Folder "uddt" contains the "zip.sql" script which creates a new user-defined data type called "zip". Since the script shown in Listing 1a does not delete UDDT, the script in Listing 2 includes a drop section to avoid an error message, if such data type already exists.

```
/* zip.SQL */
if exists (select * from dbo.systypes where name = N'zip')
exec sp_droptype N'zip'
GO
setuser
GO
EXEC sp_addtype N'zip', N'char (5)', N'null'
GO
setuser
GO
```

Listing 2. Create new user defined data type.

Folder "schema" contains two scripts: "pubs_2_0_01.SQL" which modifies existing tables, and "pubs_2_0_02.SQL" which creates two new tables. Because the pubs database has no specific users, permission for each database object should be granted to public role only. This way we can add the Grant section after the Create section for each created object (see Listing 3).

```
/* pubs_2_0_01.SQL */
ALTER TABLE publishers ADD zip zip
GO
ALTER TABLE employee
ADD manager_id         empid
        CONSTRAINT CK_manager_id CHECK (manager_id LIKE
            '[A-Z][A-Z][A-Z][1-9][0-9][0-9][0-9][0-9][FM]' or
            manager_id LIKE '[A-Z]-[A-Z][1-9][0-9][0-9][0-9][0-9][FM]')
GO
ALTER TABLE employee ADD
        FOREIGN KEY (manager_id) REFERENCES employee (emp_id)
GO
/* pubs_2_0_02.SQL */
CREATE TABLE ver_history (
        time_stamp            datetime               NOT NULL DEFAULT (getdate()),
        applied_to_ver  varchar(50)           NULL,
        package               varchar(255)    NULL)
GO
GRANT ALL ON ver_history TO public
GO
CREATE TABLE app_modules (
        mod_id        id        CONSTRAINT UPKCL_appmod PRIMARY KEY CLUSTERED,
        mod_title     varchar(50)     NOT NULL,
        mod_file      varchar(50) NOT NULL,
        install_key bit              NOT NULL)
GO
GRANT ALL ON app_modules TO public
GO
```
Listing 3. Schema modification scripts.

Folder "drop" contains scripts that delete all existing database objects: triggers, stored procedures, views, and UDF.

```
/* drop_tr.sql */ -- drop all triggers
declare @trigger_name    varchar(255)
        ,@SQLString NVARCHAR(1000)

DECLARE Trigger_list CURSOR forward_only static for
select [name]
   from sysobjects
   where xtype = 'TR'       -- Trigger
   and status >= 0
for read only

OPEN Trigger_list
FETCH NEXT FROM Trigger_list into @trigger_name
WHILE @@FETCH_STATUS = 0
BEGIN
    set @SQLString = N'if exists (select * from dbo.sysobjects
                    where id = object_id(N''[dbo].['+@trigger_name+']'')
                    and OBJECTPROPERTY(id, N''IsTrigger'') = 1)
drop trigger [dbo].['+@trigger_name+']'
        exec sp_executesql @SQLString
    FETCH NEXT FROM Trigger_list
        into @trigger_name
END
CLOSE Trigger_list
DEALLOCATE Trigger_list
/* drop_sp.sql */ -- drop all stored procedures
declare @sp_name         varchar(255)
        ,@SQLString NVARCHAR(1000)

DECLARE sp_list CURSOR forward_only static for
select [name]
   from sysobjects
  where xtype = 'P'         -- stored procedures
  and status >= 0
for read only
OPEN sp_list
FETCH NEXT FROM sp_list into @sp_name
WHILE @@FETCH_STATUS = 0
BEGIN
    set @SQLString = N'if exists (select * from dbo.sysobjects
                    where id = object_id(N''[dbo].['+@sp_name+']'')
```

```
                          and OBJECTPROPERTY(id, N''IsProcedure'') = 1)
    drop procedure [dbo].['+@sp_name+']'
          exec sp_executesql @SQLString
     FETCH NEXT FROM sp_list           into @sp_name
END
CLOSE sp_list
DEALLOCATE sp_list
/* drop_view.sql */
-- drop all views
declare @view_name        varchar(255)
        ,@SQLString NVARCHAR(1000)

DECLARE view_list CURSOR forward_only static for
select [name]
        from sysobjects
        where xtype = 'V'        -- view
and status >= 0
for read only

OPEN view_list

FETCH NEXT FROM view_list into @view_name
WHILE @@FETCH_STATUS = 0
BEGIN
    set @SQLString = N'if exists (select * from dbo.sysobjects
                     where id = object_id(N''[dbo].['+@view_name+']'')
                     and OBJECTPROPERTY(id, N''IsView'') = 1)
    drop view [dbo].['+@view_name+']'
          exec sp_executesql @SQLString

    FETCH NEXT FROM view_list
        into @view_name
END
CLOSE view_list
DEALLOCATE view_list
/* drop_udf.sql */ -- drop all UDF
declare @udf_name         varchar(255)
        ,@SQLString NVARCHAR(1000)

DECLARE udf_list CURSOR forward_only static for
select [name]
  from sysobjects
  where xtype in (N'FN', N'IF', N'TF')     -- Scalar function,Inlined table-function,Table function
  and status >= 0
for read only
OPEN udf_list
FETCH NEXT FROM udf_list
into @udf_name
WHILE @@FETCH_STATUS = 0
BEGIN
    set @SQLString = N'if exists (select * from dbo.sysobjects
                     where id = object_id(N''[dbo].['+@udf_name+']'')
                     and xtype in (N''FN'', N''IF'', N''TF''))
    drop function [dbo].['+@udf_name+']'
      exec sp_executesql @SQLString
      FETCH NEXT FROM udf_list
        into @udf_name
END
CLOSE udf_list
DEALLOCATE udf_list
```

Listing 4. Drop database object scripts.

Folders "udf", "view", and "sp" contain source code with embedded Grant sections. If actual production database contains more users, and customer business rules require complex database object/user policy, then all Grant statements should be moved to a dedicated script in the "create" folder and a new command should be added to "update_db.bat" in the "Create Database Objects" section. The command will call this script.

File "areacode.SQL" in the "udf" folder is an example of a user-defined function returning the area code of a phone number (see Listing 5).

```
/* UDF areacode */
CREATE FUNCTION areacode
-- input phone number
   (@PhoneNumber char(12))
RETURNS char(3) -- output area code
AS
BEGIN
```

```
    RETURN (left(@PhoneNumber,3))
END
GO
GRANT execute ON areacode TO public
GO
```

Listing 5. New UDF areacode.

Folder "view" contains source code for the old "titleview" view, and two files with source code for new views – "aupubview" and "empjobview". Please notice that "aupubview" view is based on "titleview" view.

```
/* view empjobview */
CREATE VIEW empjobview
AS
SELECT e.fname+' '+e.lname AS emp_name, j.job_desc
FROM employee e, jobs j
WHERE e.job_id=j.job_id
GO
GRANT ALL ON empjobview TO public
GO


/* view aupubview */
CREATE VIEW aupubview
AS
SELECT DISTINCT tv.au_lname, p.pub_name
FROM titleview tv, publishers p
WHERE tv.pub_id = p.pub_id
GO
GRANT ALL ON aupubview TO public
GO
```

Listing 6. New views for pubs database.

Folder "sp" includes four old procedures: "byroyalty", "reptq1", "reptq2", "reptq3", and the new procedure "aubyroyalty" which uses "areacode" function and "byroyalty" procedure.

```
/* proc aubyroyalty */
CREATE PROCEDURE aubyroyalty @pct int
AS
CREATE TABLE #au (au_id varchar(11))
INSERT INTO #au EXEC byroyalty @percentage=@pct
SELECT au_fname, au_lname, dbo.areacode(phone) AS area_code
FROM authors a, #au
WHERE a.au_id = #au.au_id
DROP TABLE #au
GO

GRANT execute ON aubyroyalty TO public
GO
```

Listing 7. New stored procedure "aubyroyalty".

There is nothing new in the "trigger" folder, just the old "employee_insupd" trigger.

The "data" folder contains the following pipe-delimited data files:

- stores.dat - contains the sample records to be inserted into STORES table that has no IDENTITY column; some records are new and some are copies of already existing records;
- jobs.dat - contains the sample records to be inserted into JOBS table that does have an IDENTITY column; here also, some records are new and some are copies of already existing records;
- app_modules_cust1.dat and app_modules_cust2.dat - contain application data for two different customers or customer groups;
- sysmessages.dat - contains three user-defined error messages.

Script "remove_data.sql" in the "copydata" folder demonstrates both ways of removing data: truncation and deletion, and contains examples of how to prepare the tables for data purge - unchecking or dropping constraints, disabling triggers, allowing system tables modification, etc. While, script "restore_constrains.sql" rolls back all these changes after the data has been replaced.

If new table with data has been created or data in the existing table has been significantly changed the UPDATE STATISTICS command for such tables can be added into the "restore_constrains.sql" script.

Two batch files: "bcpin_customer1.bat" and "bcpin_customer2.bat" show how to use BCP utility to copy data into the tables that do not have an IDENTITY column, and how to use BULK INSERT command with osql utility to insert data into the table which does have an IDENTITY column.

```
/* remove_data.sql */
-- truncate table without constraints
TRUNCATE TABLE app_modules
GO
-- drop constraints and then truncate table
ALTER TABLE employee DROP CONSTRAINT FK__employee__job_id__1BFD2C07
GO
TRUNCATE TABLE jobs
GO
-- disable constraints and then delete table
ALTER TABLE sales NOCHECK CONSTRAINT FK__sales__stor_id__0AD2A005
ALTER TABLE discounts NOCHECK CONSTRAINT FK__discounts__stor___0F975522
GO
DELETE stores
GO
-- enable system tables update
EXEC sp_sqlexec 'sp_configure "allow updates", 1'
EXEC sp_sqlexec 'reconfigure with override'
GO
DELETE master..sysmessages
WHERE error > 50000
GO
```
Listing 8. Remove data from tables.

```
/* restore_constraints.sql */
-- restore constraints
ALTER TABLE employee ADD CONSTRAINT FK__employee__job_id__1BFD2C07
        FOREIGN KEY (job_id) REFERENCES jobs (job_id)
GO
-- enable constraints
ALTER TABLE sales CHECK CONSTRAINT FK__sales__stor_id__0AD2A005
ALTER TABLE discounts CHECK CONSTRAINT FK__discounts__stor___0F975522
GO
-- disable system tables update
EXEC sp_sqlexec 'sp_configure "allow updates", 0'
GO
EXEC sp_sqlexec 'reconfigure with override'
GO
```
Listing 9. Roll back all changes.

```
rem bcpin_customer1.bat
rem bulk copy data from data files to database
rem Server\Instance
if "%1" == "" goto usage
if "%1" == "/?" goto usage
if "%1" == "help" goto usage
rem Database
if "%2" == "" goto usage
rem sa password
if "%3" == "" goto usage
rem Data Directory
if "%4" == "" goto usage
rem Insert data into the tables without IDENTITY column
bcp "%2.dbo.app_modules" in "%4\data\app_modules_cust1.dat" -c -t"|" -Usa -P%3 -S%1
bcp "%2.dbo.stores" in "%4\data\stores.dat" -c -t"|" -Usa -P%3 -S%1
rem Insert data into the tables with IDENTITY column
osql -S%1 -d%2 -Usa -P%3 -Q"BULK INSERT jobs FROM '%4\data\jobs.dat' WITH (FIELDTERMINATOR = '
|',ROWTERMINATOR = '\n',KEEPIDENTITY)" -n
rem Insert data into the system table
bcp "master.dbo.sysmessages" in "%4\data\sysmessages.dat" -c -t"|" -Usa -P%3 -S%1
goto end
:usage
echo usage: bcpin_customer1.bat Server\Instance Database sa_password ScriptsDirectory
echo Example usage: bcpin_customer1.bat server1 pubs sa_password C:\Build\pubs20\db
:end
```
Listing 10. Copy data into the tables.

The "patch_discount.sql" script in the "patch" directory (Listing 11) provides an example of how to fix data if necessary.

```
/* patch_discount.sql */
-- Fixed data in the discounts table
UPDATE discounts
SET lowqty=10, highqty=100
```

```
WHERE discounttype='Initial Customer'
GO
```
Listing 11. Script to fix the data.

The "job" folder contains the <u>source code</u> of the "ytd_reports" job, that executes the "reptq1" procedure daily at 11:00 PM and saves the report at location "C:\pubs\report\ytd_report.txt".

If all previous commands have completed successfully, the "ins_ver_history.sql" script refreshes the database version information (see Listing 12).

```
/* ins_ver_history.sql */
INSERT ver_history (applied_to_ver,package)
VALUES('pubs2000.2.0','UpdatePubs2.0_200603071632')
GO
```
Listing 12. Refresh database version information.

By now all the folders but one are filled with scripts and data files. Folder "create" still remains empty. We will generate and store in this folder the following four scripts, that create the database objects:

- create_udf.bat
- create_view.bat
- create_sp.bat
- create_tr.bat

Since triggers cannot be nested they can be generated in any order. However, functions, views, and procedures can be nested and therefore must be created in the reverse order of referencing. In the case that the referenced objects are not found the following happens for each type of database object:

- functions are created successfully but will produce run-time errors;
- stored procedures are created with warnings;
- views fail to generate and return an error message.

To generate all those objects in the proper order I use simple C# program that assumes that all required source code modules are already in the proper folders, and the names of the source files correspond to the names of the database objects; there are other ways of code parsing, but using the file name convention seems to be easy and reliable. Another advantage of this approach is that it does not depend on any source code management tool.

The size of this article does not allow providing the full program listing but we list the key function (see Listing 13). This function is a member function of the DatabaseObjectCollection class. It creates dependency trees for a set (collection) of database objects. Each collection object has a name, SQL source code (script), and the list of dependencies where we will store references to the other collection objects it depends on.

To create the dependency trees this function uses two nested FOR loops, both iterating over the whole objects collection. The outer loop treats each object as a parent and the inner loop tries to find its children – the objects this parent depends on. To do it the function takes the name of the object and searches for that name in the parent's script. If the name is found, the object is added to the parent's collection of dependencies.

When searching for a name, the function looks for the first valid appearance of this name in the parent's script. A valid appearance means that the name is either enclosed in double quotes or brackets, or is bordered by a space or tab on the left and by a space, tab, comma, or EOL on the right. For the sake of simplicity we do not analyze the script for comments.

After the dependencies have been created, generating the batch script becomes simple, since each collection object has its own collection of dependencies. To generate the batch script, recursively traverse the dependency tree of each object. At each step of the traversal, if the current object hasn't been already added to the batch file, we recursively process it, traversing its children before writing the current object to the batch script.

```
public void BuildObjectDependancies()
{
    string up; //string that stores the name of a potential child
    string script; //string that stores the script of a parent
```

```
Console.Write("["+DateTime.Now.ToString()+"] Analyzing dependencies... ");
foreach(DatabaseObject parent in this) //traverse each parent
  {
   script = parent.Script.ToUpper(); //get the sql source, of the parent
   foreach(DatabaseObject child in this) //traverse each potential child
    {
     up = child.Name.ToUpper(); //get the name of the child's script
     int length = child.Name.Length; //length of the name
     char first, last; //the characters that border the name found in the script
     int index=1; //start searching at 1, because the name of sp can't be in the begining
     bool done = false; //indicates when the search is over

     while (!done && index<script.Length) //search for the name in the parent's script
       {
        if ((index = script.IndexOf(up,index)) != -1)
          { //found another instance of the name in the script
           first = script[index - 1]; //get the bordering char on the left
           index += length; //update the starting index
           if (index >= script.Length) last = '\n'; //get the bordering char on the right
            else last = script[index];

           //check if the appearance is valid
           if (((first == ' ' || first == '\t' || first == '.') && //bordered by space ?
              (last == ' ' || last == '\t' || last == '\n' || last=='\r' || last==',')) ||
              (first=='\"' && last=='\"') || //bordered by quotes ?
              (first=='[' && last==']')) //bordered by brackets ?
             { //valid appearance of the name found
              parent.DependsOn.Add(child); //set this object as the child of the parent
              done=true; //search is over
             }
          }
         else done = true; //if no instance found, then search is over
       }
    }
  }
}
}
```
Listing 13. The dependency building function.

The examples of the generated batch scripts are below (see Listing 14). Please note that since view "aupubview" references view "titleview" (see Listing 6), the "titleview.SQL" file will be run before "aupubview.SQL" file; for the same reason stored procedure "byroyalty" will be generated before stored procedure "aubyroyalty" (see Listing 7):

```
rem create_udf.bat
osql -S%1 -d%2 -Usa -P%3 -i"%4\udf\areacode.SQL" -n
rem create_view.bat
osql -S%1 -d%2 -Usa -P%3 -i"%4\view\titleview.SQL" -n
osql -S%1 -d%2 -Usa -P%3 -i"%4\view\aupubview.SQL" -n
osql -S%1 -d%2 -Usa -P%3 -i"%4\view\empjobview.SQL" -n
rem create_sp.bat
osql -S%1 -d%2 -Usa -P%3 -i"%4\sp\byroyalty.SQL" -n
osql -S%1 -d%2 -Usa -P%3 -i"%4\sp\aubyroyalty.SQL" -n
osql -S%1 -d%2 -Usa -P%3 -i"%4\sp\reptq1.SQL" -n
osql -S%1 -d%2 -Usa -P%3 -i"%4\sp\reptq2.SQL" -n
osql -S%1 -d%2 -Usa -P%3 -i"%4\sp\reptq3.SQL" -n
```
Listing 14. Generating the database objects.

Now we are ready to package the database update scripts into a zip file (like the "pubs20.zip" mentioned in the beginning) and ship it to the customer. The scripts can be run against either local or remote servers. Please note that there are two restrictions that will prevent running the scripts on the remote server:

- if you have to create a job on the server;
- if you use BULK INSERT command in the osql utility to insert the data into the table with an IDENTITY column.

Conclusion

Based on the provided scripts and material, it is easy to customize and automate the update scripts preparation process, and write your own program that creates required folders, checks out source code from a source control system to those folders, and generates all the scripts described in this article. I used such scripts, for the past 2 years, to successfully update various customer versions of the database which contained more than 300 tables, 900 views and 3,000 stored procedures.

Code:

Outer Join Mystery

By Grant Fritchey

There's an old joke that goes, "Doctor, doctor. It hurts when I do this" as a man swings his arm up and down, to which the doctor sagely responds, "Don't do that." When presented with this little mystery by a co-worker, my response was, "Don't do that." But then I became very concerned, one could even say, obsessed, with why this particular query "hurt." Fair warning, I couldn't find an answer beyond the Microsoft statement that "In some cases, this syntax results in an ambiguous query that can be interpreted in more than one way."

We have two tables, represented for this article by these simple scripts:

```
CREATE TABLE [IIAFeedTransaction] (
        [IIATransactionId] [uniqueidentifier] NOT NULL ,
        [TransactionStatusId] [smallint] NOT NULL ,
                              )
```

and

```
CREATE TABLE [RATSIIAFeedTransaction] (
        [RATS_FILENAME] [varchar] (100) COLLATE SQL_Latin1_General_CP1_CI_AS NOT NULL ,
        [DATE_ENTERED] [datetime] NULL
)
```

The data that goes into the tables is also quite simple:

```
INSERT INTO IIAFeedTransaction VALUES ('{365A0FD8-5042-4297-A082-8F5B11450AF4}',1)
INSERT INTO IIAFeedTransaction VALUES ('{16706611-C94D-4FBC-8F4E-9077C3B9E697}',1)
INSERT INTO IIAFeedTransaction VALUES ('{55DD6703-9693-45E2-A339-987066EA2864}',2)
INSERT INTO IIAFeedTransaction VALUES ('{F4849137-6454-46E5-9811-A6985A189249}',1)
INSERT INTO IIAFeedTransaction VALUES ('{9B33A776-408B-4928-AE2A-0FF43995DE12}',1)
INSERT INTO IIAFeedTransaction VALUES ('{8EEA51CE-D87A-4F76-B9C1-7AD11532D444}',0)
INSERT INTO IIAFeedTransaction VALUES ('{5D31FD56-7C0B-408B-83A5-864B7BD35ADC}',1)
INSERT INTO IIAFeedTransaction VALUES ('{A721BD38-9C76-4C3A-A7C5-9CC0227F90F4}',0)
GO
INSERT INTO RATSIIAFeedTransaction VALUES ('CISF-{260021}-{365A0FD8-5042-4297-A082-8F5B11450AF4}-
{7A050246-59F3-4E72-BFD2-40EB183B7D3C}',GETDATE())
INSERT INTO RATSIIAFeedTransaction VALUES ('CISF-{260346}-{16706611-C94D-4FBC-8F4E-9077C3B9E697}-
{73916523-EC71-4989-BE99-1EDB507D67DF}',GETDATE())
INSERT INTO RATSIIAFeedTransaction VALUES ('RA-1-{259590}-{55DD6703-9693-45E2-A339-987066EA2864}-
{EF41CFCE-20BA-4D2D-A4C8-121BFC7DAEE3}',GETDATE())
INSERT INTO RATSIIAFeedTransaction VALUES ('RA-2-{219960}-{F4849137-6454-46E5-9811-A6985A189249}-
{F7267BD6-62CB-4379-8533-C413DD5EA402}',GETDATE())
GO
```

My co-worker is a very strong DBA who works in both Oracle and SQL Server, whereas I only work in SQL Server. He has been writing Oracle queries as often as he writes SQL Server queries, so he tends to use the old style join syntax of:

```
SELECT ...
FROM Table1 t1, Table2 t2 WHERE t1.Id *= t2.Id
```

He was working on a query to determine records missing between the two tables outlined above. In order to do that, he wrote this query:

```
SELECT S.IIATransactionId
      ,substring(rats_filename,1 +
      patindex('%{_____-____-____-____-_____}%',rats_filename),36) AS OracleTransactionId
 FROM iiafeedtransaction S, ratsiiafeedtransaction o
WHERE S.IIATransactionId *= substring(rats_filename,1 +
           patindex('%{_____-____-____-____-_____}%',rats_filename),36)
 AND  o.Rats_filename IS NOT NULL
 ORDER BY S.IIATransactionId
```

The results that came back were not what he expected, at all:

```
IIATransactionId                    OracleTransactionId
------------------------------------ ------------------------------------
9B33A776-408B-4928-AE2A-0FF43995DE12 NULL
8EEA51CE-D87A-4F76-B9C1-7AD11532D444 NULL
```

```
5D31FD56-7C0B-408B-83A5-864B7BD35ADC NULL
365A0FD8-5042-4297-A082-8F5B11450AF4 365A0FD8-5042-4297-A082-8F5B11450AF4
16706611-C94D-4FBC-8F4E-9077C3B9E697 16706611-C94D-4FBC-8F4E-9077C3B9E697
55DD6703-9693-45E2-A339-987066EA2864 55DD6703-9693-45E2-A339-987066EA2864
A721BD38-9C76-4C3A-A7C5-9CC0227F90F4 NULL
F4849137-6454-46E5-9811-A6985A189249 F4849137-6454-46E5-9811-A6985A189249
```

In theory, with the left outer join and the 'IS NOT NULL' in the WHERE clause, he should have only seen four rows come back, not eight. He was confused. So, he tried switching the 'IS NOT NULL' to 'IS NULL' in order to see what comes back that way. The results did not settle his mind at all:

```
IIATransactionId                     OracleTransactionId
------------------------------------ ------------------------------------
9B33A776-408B-4928-AE2A-0FF43995DE12 NULL
8EEA51CE-D87A-4F76-B9C1-7AD11532D444 NULL
5D31FD56-7C0B-408B-83A5-864B7BD35ADC NULL
365A0FD8-5042-4297-A082-8F5B11450AF4 NULL
16706611-C94D-4FBC-8F4E-9077C3B9E697 NULL
55DD6703-9693-45E2-A339-987066EA2864 NULL
A721BD38-9C76-4C3A-A7C5-9CC0227F90F4 NULL
F4849137-6454-46E5-9811-A6985A189249 NULL
```

Now he not only doesn't have four rows instead of eight, but with the second column showing NULL values, but he's completely lost the data that was there and now has nothing but NULL values. At this point he called me over to see what the problem was.

Since I've pretty much exclusively in SQL Server for the last eight years, I long ago learned to write my syntax following the ANSI-92 standards. When I walked through what he had discovered, my first thought was to simply verify the behavior by changing the query syntax. I re-wrote the procedure to this:

```
SELECT S.IIATransactionId
       ,substring(rats_filename,1+patindex('%{_____-____-____-____-_____}%',rats_filename),
36) AS OracleTransactionId
FROM iiafeedtransaction S
LEFT OUTER JOIN ratsiiafeedtransaction o
ON S.IIATransactionId = substring(rats_filename,1+patindex('%{_____-____-____-____-
_____}%',rats_filename),36)
WHERE o.Rats_filename IS  NULL
ORDER BY S.IIATransactionId
```

Which, I was a little surprised to see, worked without flaw and returned the appropriate data set:

```
IIATransactionId                     OracleTransactionId
------------------------------------ ------------------------------------
9B33A776-408B-4928-AE2A-0FF43995DE12 NULL
8EEA51CE-D87A-4F76-B9C1-7AD11532D444 NULL
5D31FD56-7C0B-408B-83A5-864B7BD35ADC NULL
A721BD38-9C76-4C3A-A7C5-9CC0227F90F4 NULL
```

Now, it begins to get good. We messed with this for quite a while. Rearranging the WHERE clause on the queries that used the old syntax, putting in parenthesis to try to change the query plan that the engine created. Nothing worked. Then we started looking at the query plan. Here, things were really weird. The first query showed the join between the tables, but, for some reason, just completely ignored the WHERE clause and didn't filter the data in any way. Additionally, it added a transform to set all the values for the second field to NULL.

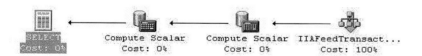

Running the query that simply changed the WHERE clause from 'NOT IN' to 'IN', the join actually occurs, which corresponds to the fact that the data gets returned.

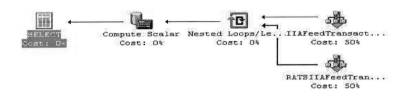

Neither of which corresponds to the accurate query plan represented by the ANSI syntax that shows both the join and a filter to remove the unwanted records.

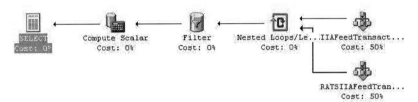

Then, I had an epiphany, a false one as it turned out. It's the substring function! So, I added a column to the table of datatype UNIQUEIDENTIFIER and updated all the columns. This allowed me write a much more simplified query:

```
SELECT S.IIATransactionId
       ,o.Fixed
FROM iiafeedtransaction S,
ratsiiafeedtransaction o
WHERE S.IIATransactionId *= o.fixed
AND  o.fixed IS  NULL
ORDER BY S.IIATransactionId
```

Which promptly returned exactly the same data.

We went on to experiment with changes to the connection settings, database settings, server settings. Nothing made a difference. We ran the same queries in Oracle and got the correct data sets back. I showed the queries to our in house Microsoft consultant who said, "Old syntax? Don't do that." At that point, having come full circle, I stopped worrying about the problem and decided to write it up as an article to see if anyone else has any insight.

Complex Computed Columns

By Tim Chapman

The Mighty, Mighty Computed Column

I've been working with SQL Server for several years now, and I am always searching for new ways to do things. A few days ago, I was experimenting with computed columns in SQL Server 2000, and came across something really, well...neat! It is actually a very simple concept, but one I had never thought of before, and one that I think could be very powerful if used carefully.

We've probably all used a computed column before at some point, whether just experimenting or in production use and I think we can all agree that they can be pretty useful, but also somewhat limited. Most likely, most of us have used a computed column similar to the following context:

```
CREATE TABLE TestComputedColumn
(      TestColID TINYINT IDENTITY(1,1) PRIMARY KEY,
       Value1 MONEY,
       Value2 MONEY,
       Multiplier INT,
       ComputedColumn AS (Value1+Value2)*(Multiplier)
)
```

Nothing new here, just create a simple table and assign a simple statement to the computed column. Now, lets add some values.

```
INSERT INTO TestComputedColumn(Value1, Value2, Multiplier) VALUES(2,2,2)
INSERT INTO TestComputedColumn(Value1, Value2, Multiplier) VALUES(3,3,2)
INSERT INTO TestComputedColumn(Value1, Value2, Multiplier) VALUES(4,5,3)
INSERT INTO TestComputedColumn(Value1, Value2, Multiplier) VALUES(2,7,3)
INSERT INTO TestComputedColumn(Value1, Value2, Multiplier) VALUES(2,2,7)
```

If we run a select statement on the TestComputedColumn table, it looks something like this:

	TestColID	Value1	Value2	Multiplier	ComputedColumn
1	1	2.0000	2.0000	2	8.0000
2	2	3.0000	3.0000	2	12.0000
3	3	4.0000	5.0000	3	27.0000
4	4	2.0000	7.0000	3	27.0000
5	5	2.0000	2.0000	7	28.0000

Looks like our computed columns is working as intended. Now, we are faced with somewhat of an issue. The issue is that if we want to use some complex logic, not only do we have to hard-code the field names into our expressions in the table, but we also have to duplicate the code in different tables if we want to use the same logic on different tables. This can become very cumbersome. Also, in our expression we cannot reference any other tables. It would be very, very nice if we could encapsulate our code into some sort of module, and reference other tables if needed. The solution to our problem is the use of a user-defined function.

In SQL 2000, we can use a user-defined function as the value for a computed column (and as default values for columns in a table if we want to). This is a very powerful tool. This allows us not only to encapsulate our code, but also to reference other tables.

In our above example, we used the expression:

```
ComputedColumn AS (Value1+Value2)*(Multiplier)
```

to define our computed column. But, we can create a user defined function to do the same thing and tie that function to the table.

```
CREATE FUNCTION dbo.udf_FunctionForComputedColumn
(       @ValueField1 MONEY,
        @ValueField2 MONEY,
        @MultiplierField INT
) RETURNS MONEY
AS
BEGIN
        RETURN((@ValueField1+@ValueField2)*(@MultiplierField))
END
```

Now, we can run the following statements to alter the table to tie the new function to the computed column.

```
ALTER TABLE TestComputedColumn DROP COLUMN ComputedColumn
ALTER TABLE TestComputedColumn
    ADD ComputedColumn AS dbo.udf_FunctionForComputedColumn(Value1, Value2, Multiplier)
```

Sure enough, if we do a select on our table, we get the same result as before.

	TestColID	Value1	Value2	Multiplier	ComputedColumn
1	1	2.0000	2.0000	2	8.0000
2	2	3.0000	3.0000	2	12.0000
3	3	4.0000	5.0000	3	27.0000
4	4	2.0000	7.0000	3	27.0000
5	5	2.0000	2.0000	7	28.0000

So, we've solved our problem for code reuse. We can now tie this same function to any table we need to. It must be noted that if we want to change our function after we have tied it to a computed column (or a column default), we cannot alter or delete our function because the field is now dependent on it. We can view this in the database by using the simple query:

```
SELECT OBJECT_NAME(depid) AS Name
```

```
FROM sysdepends
WHERE
        id = OBJECT_ID('TestComputedColumn') AND
        id <> depid AND
        depid >0
```

Which returns the resultset:

	Name
1	udf_FunctionForComputedColumn

Lets take the easy route, and just delete our computed column again.

```
ALTER TABLE TestComputedColumn DROP COLUMN ComputedColumn
```

Now, what if we want to change the way in which we use our Multiplier in our computed column expression. What if we want to pull this value from a constants table in our database, one that can be changed at any point in time, and that will allow our computed columns to reflect this value. We can tie a user-defined function to a table that references another table, and anytime we do a select on this table, it can reference another table (or N number of tables if needed). But, as Spiderman says, "with great power comes great responsibility". The thing is that for every row returned in the result set for our select statement, that user-defined function will get called. Depending our function, this could seriously degrade performance for functions that require a lot of I/O. We can see that this function gets returned for every row in our resultset if we run SQL Profiler. The output is below:

SQL:StmtStarting	select * from TestComputedColumn	SQL Query A...
SQL:StmtStarting	-- udf_FunctionForComputedColumn RETURN((@ValueField1+@...	SQL Query A...
SQL:StmtStarting	-- udf_FunctionForComputedColumn RETURN((@ValueField1+@...	SQL Query A...
SQL:StmtStarting	-- udf_FunctionForComputedColumn RETURN((@ValueField1+@...	SQL Query A...
SQL:StmtStarting	-- udf_FunctionForComputedColumn RETURN((@ValueField1+@...	SQL Query A...
SQL:StmtStarting	-- udf_FunctionForComputedColumn RETURN((@ValueField1+@...	SQL Query A...

We know that have 5 records in our table, and we see that Profiler returns 5 records referencing the user-defined function after our SELECT * FROM TestComputedColumn. The main idea here is to be very careful with these computed columns, especially if you plan to add complex logic in them or have them query other tables, which may take precious I/O in a production environment.

So, back the example. Lets create a SystemConstants table that we can use to store our Multiplier value.

```
CREATE TABLE SystemConstants
(       SystemConstantID TINYINT IDENTITY(1,1),
        LookupValue VARCHAR(15),
        ConstantValue VARCHAR(10),
        ValueDescription VARCHAR(50)
)
GO
INSERT INTO SystemConstants(ConstantValue, LookupValue, ValueDescription)
VALUES('9', 'Multiplier', 'Muliplier value we plan to use.')
GO
```

Now, we have a value in our SystemConstants table that we can use in our user-defined function to return our computed column value. We can alter the function we defined before to look something like this:

```
ALTER FUNCTION udf_FunctionForComputedColumn
(       @ValueField1 MONEY,
        @ValueField2 MONEY
) RETURNS MONEY
AS
BEGIN
        DECLARE @Multiplier INT
        SELECT @Multiplier = CAST(ConstantValue AS INT)
        FROM    SystemConstants
        WHERE
                LookupValue = 'Multiplier'
        RETURN((@ValueField1+@ValueField2)*(@Multiplier))
END
```

Now, if we select the rows from the TestComputedColumn table, the records returned will look like this:

	TestColID	Value1	Value2	Multiplier	ComputedColumn
1	1	2.0000	2.0000	2	36.0000
2	2	3.0000	3.0000	2	54.0000
3	3	4.0000	5.0000	3	81.0000
4	4	2.0000	7.0000	3	81.0000
5	5	2.0000	2.0000	7	36.0000

We can see that the Value1 and Value2 fields are added together and multiplied by the value in our SystemConstants table, which happens to be the value 9.

It is also definitely worth noting that because the use of our user-defined function is labeled as "non-deterministic" because it references another table, we cannot create an index on our computed column. This is just another trade-off in the use of the UDF.

Conclusions

I hope I have outlined something in SQL Server 2000 (haven't tested it yet in 2005) that you can use to be more productive and efficient. There are limitless ways to use computed columns with the use of user-defined functions, and they are especially handy if you look to avoid computing the same data continuously. However, the rule is to be careful when you do use them because misuse can lead to performance degradation. If you use a User-Defined Function for your computed column then every record returned in any select query on the table which includes that computed column, the UDF will be invoked. Just something to think about if you decide to try it out, because calling a UDF which queries other tables for each row of the parent table in a production environment could potentially cripple the system.

I'd love to hear comments about this article. I can be contacted directly at chapman.tim@gmail.com.

Aggregate Queries

By Kathi Kellenberger

The use of aggregate functions in queries is a popular and powerful feature of the SQL language. It takes some practice to become proficient in their use. Query writers are frequently confused about the difference between the WHERE clause and the HAVING clause or have trouble figuring out which columns to include in the GROUP BY clause. This article will explain how to write queries using aggregates and, hopefully, clear up the confusion. It is intended to cover the basics of using aggregate expressions and does not cover the advanced features.

What are aggregate functions?

Aggregate functions are used to summarize data in queries. They usually work on groups of data, however, in some cases they will work on the entire table. The most commonly used aggregate functions are AVG, COUNT, MIN, MAX and SUM. Keep the following in mind when working with these aggregate functions.

- The functions AVG and SUM will only operate on numeric columns.
- The functions MIN and MAX will work on numeric, character and date columns.
- The COUNT function can operate on any column except for text, ntext or image columns.
- COUNT can be used with an asterisk (*) to give the count of the rows by group or entire set of results.
- The aggregate functions ignore NULL values.
- The DISTINCT argument, when used within an aggregate expression, will cause it to operate on non-null unique values.

The following query from the Northwind database finds the count of orders and the maximum freight grouped by EmployeeID. Rows are filtered out of the results if the maximum freight of a group is less than 800 or the ShippedDate of an order IS NULL.

```
SELECT COUNT(*), MAX(Freight), EmployeeID
```

```
FROM Orders
WHERE ShippedDate IS NOT NULL
GROUP BY  EmployeeID
HAVING MAX(Freight) >= 800
ORDER BY EmployeeID
```

The building blocks

Let's take a look at the parts, known as *clauses*, of an aggregate query. I have always found it is easier to write the query if I figure out each clause before moving on to the next one. This step-by-step approach may work for you, too.

The first part of the statement is the SELECT clause. It lists the columns and aggregate expressions that are returned to the client application. Make sure you only include columns that you really need in the results, because the SELECT clause directly affects which columns will be required in the GROUP BY clause. Keep these facts in mind when building the SELECT clause.

- You can use columns, literal values, aggregate expressions and other expressions in the SELECT clause.
- Any columns listed that are not part of an aggregate expression will be used to group the results when you get to the GROUP BY clause.

The next part of the statement is the FROM clause. This clause specifies the tables and or views from which the data is queried. The tables and views are joined using the usual JOIN syntax that is used for any other T-SQL statement. Refer to Books Online if you need to learn more about how to join tables.

The WHERE clause is a very important part of an aggregate query. By using the WHERE clause you can eliminate some of the rows *before* the rows are grouped and the aggregate functions do their work. You can specify any of the available columns from the tables or views in the WHERE clause even if they haven't been used. Notice that the sample query above is filtering on ShippedDate which is not used anywhere else in the query. You are, however, restricted from including any aggregates in the WHERE clause. This makes sense when you consider that the WHERE clause is processed by SQL before the aggregate functions. Remember these rules when building the WHERE clause:

- Any column can be used in the WHERE clause.
- Nonaggregate expressions can be used in the WHERE clause.

The GROUP BY clause is one that query writers struggle with quite often. As its name suggest, it is used to group the data. The aggregate functions are applied to the groups. If a GROUP BY is not used in the query, then the aggregate functions are applied to the entire set of rows returned. Remember, the WHERE clause may be used to filter out some of the rows from the table first. You must include all columns in the GROUP BY clause that are used in the SELECT clause unless the column is part of an aggregate expression. One of my college professors insisted that the opposite was true, that you have to include in the SELECT clause any columns listed in the GROUP BY clause. While it is true that the columns in the two clauses usually match, it is possible to list a column in the GROUP BY clause without listing it in the SELECT clause. I can't think of any good reason to do this, however. I will include an example query demonstrating this technique and a better way to write the same query later in the article.

If you don't want to group on a column, don't list it in the SELECT clause. In the example query above, you can not list information about individual orders since you are grouping the orders by EmployeeID. If you included the OrderID column in the SELECT clause, for example, you would then have to list the column in the GROUP BY clause. Your summary information would no longer apply to EmployeeID but to the individual orders, which wouldn't be a summary at all. There are cases where you will need to list the details about the row that satisfies certain criteria based on an aggregate function, for example, the last order placed by each customer. An sample query later in the article will show how to do this using a derived table.

Remember these rules when writing the GROUP BY clause:

- The results will be grouped by the columns listed in the GROUP BY clause.
- All columns found in the SELECT clause, including those used in nonaggregate expressions, must be listed in the GROUP BY clause.

The GROUP BY clause also has some optional arguments: ALL, WITH ROLLUP and WITH CUBE. These will not be covered in this article.

The HAVING clause is used to filter rows after the grouping has been applied, but before the results are returned to the client. You can only include aggregate expressions and columns that are listed in the GROUP BY clause. It is possible to include different aggregate functions than those in the SELECT clause. In the example query above, you could write a query using the HAVING clause to include only employees whose orders' average freight was above a certain amount. You could also include the EmployeeID column in the HAVING clause since it is listed in the GROUP BY clause. Chances are, though, that it would make more sense to filter the EmployeeID column in the WHERE clause instead.

- Any column or expression listed in the GROUP BY clause may be included in the HAVING clause.
- Filter aggregate results using the HAVING clause, not the WHERE clause.

The last clause is the ORDER BY clause. You might think that the ORDER BY clause would not be necessary -- that SQL would order the results according to the GROUP BY columns, but this is not the case. If you want the results to sort according to the groups, the columns must be specified in the ORDER BY clause. The ORDER BY clause has the same rules as the SELECT clause, only aggregates and columns listed in the GROUP BY are allowed.

- Any column or expression listed in the GROUP BY clause may be included in the ORDER BY clause.
- The ORDER BY is required if you want ordered results.

Sample queries using Northwind

This query joins two tables, orders and order details. It returns the OrderID column along with the count of line items in each order if they were shipped via method 3 and if they have at least two line items. Finally, the results are ordered by the OrderID column:

```
SELECT o.OrderID, COUNT(*) AS Lines
FROM orders o JOIN [order details] od
ON o.OrderID = od.OrderID
WHERE ShipVia = 3
GROUP BY o.OrderID
HAVING COUNT(*) > 1
ORDER BY o.OrderID
```

You can't update a column using an aggregate function directly, but you can use a derived table to product the desired results.

First, run this statement to add a column to the Employees table in Northwind:

```
ALTER TABLE Employees ADD ORDER_COUNT INT NULL
```

The following query will generate an error:

```
UPDATE e
SET ORDER_COUNT = COUNT(*)
FROM Employees e JOIN Orders o
ON e.EmployeeID = o.EmployeeID
```

This update query using a derived table shown in blue works fine:

```
UPDATE e
SET ORDER_COUNT = ORDERCOUNT
FROM Employees e JOIN
(SELECT COUNT(*) AS ORDERCOUNT, EmployeeID
FROM ORDERS
GROUP BY EmployeeID) o
ON e.EmployeeID = o.EmployeeID
```

This example uses a couple of expressions. Notice that they do not need to be included in the GROUP BY clause because they do not use any of the table's columns:

```
SELECT getDate() as CurrentDate, 1 + 2 as Add1Plus2,
EmployeeID, count(*) as ORDERCOUNT
FROM Orders
GROUP BY EmployeeID
```

The query below will run without error because the column, OrderDate, used in the expressions is listed in the GROUP BY clause. It does not, however, give the expected results:

```
SELECT COUNT(*) AS OrderCount,
    MONTH(OrderDate) AS OrderMonth,
    YEAR(OrderDate) AS OrderYear
FROM Orders
GROUP BY OrderDate
ORDER BY OrderDate
```

To get the correct results, a summary by year and month, the query must be grouped by the actual expressions, not just the column:

```
SELECT COUNT(*) AS OrderCount,
    MONTH(OrderDate) AS OrderMonth,
    YEAR(OrderDate) AS OrderYear
FROM Orders GROUP BY YEAR(OrderDate), MONTH(OrderDate)
ORDER BY YEAR(OrderDate), MONTH(OrderDate)
```

It is possible to list a column in the GROUP BY clause and not in the SELECT clause. Here is a query that runs but doesn't really return any useful information:

```
SELECT MAX(OrderID) AS lastOrder
FROM Orders
GROUP BY CustomerID
```

There may be times when this technique can be used with a sub-query to solve a particular problem. In this example, I am listing more information about the latest order for each customer:

```
SELECT OrderID, CustomerID, OrderDate, EmployeeID,
    ShipVia, Freight, ShipName
FROM Orders
WHERE OrderID in (
    SELECT MAX(OrderID)
    FROM Orders
    GROUP BY CustomerID)
```

The query could be better written with a derived table:

```
SELECT OrderID, o.CustomerID, EmployeeID, OrderDate, ShipVia, Freight, ShipName
FROM Orders o JOIN
    (SELECT MAX(OrderID) as MaxOrder, CustomerID FROM orders GROUP BY CustomerID) m
ON o.CustomeriD = m.CustomerID
WHERE OrderID = MaxOrder
```

Conclusion

Writing aggregate queries just takes a little practice once you understand the rules. Remember to first figure out what you need to see in the results (SELECT) and which tables or views the data will come from (FROM). Filter out any rows you don't want included at all (WHERE). Determine how the results will be grouped (GROUP BY) by looking at the SELECT clause. Decide if you need to filter based on the groups using aggregate functions (HAVING). Finally, sort the results (ORDER BY). Often a derived table will help solve more complex problems.

Stored Procedure Naming Conventions

By Joseph Sack

Discussions of naming conventions can, and usually do get ugly. There are so many ways you can do it. Some people don't give standards any thought, while other database developers are zealous to the point of renaming system generated constraints. How far should one go to implement standards across your databases? Do you apply standards to all database object types or just some (for example just views, tables, columns, stored procedures)? What about third party applications where you can't control or modify their object names and source code? The larger the team of database developers, the harder it is to build consensus. Even if you are able to pound out a standard, enforcing it can be difficult.

Why then, is it worth the effort? The best argument I've seen for establishing and using database object naming conventions is for ongoing **supportability**. Intuitively named database objects can be located more easily when troubleshooting a problem. Consistently named columns communicate their usage and "class" to the developer having to reference them. When it comes to the scope of your standard, I would recommend that any "home grown" code developed in your company should follow a standard. Third party products are outside of your scope, but that doesn't mean the rest of your code need be neglected.

Stored Procedure Naming Conventions

This article specifically discusses stored procedure naming standards. If your application uses stored procedures, defining a naming convention is absolutely critical for future supportability. If all of your Transact-SQL code is embedded in stored procedure, you'll need to know where to find exactly what you are looking for. *This is particularly important for databases that contain procedures from multiple applications.* You need a visual means of defining which procedures belong to what application, and have a general understanding of each procedures purpose.

First off, if I am absolutely positive that a single database will only be used for a single, less complex application, I'll use the following naming conventions:

```
usp_ PredominantAction_TableNameOrBusinessProcess
```

The **usp_** prefix is used to let me know that this is a user stored procedure. Some people don't like this prefix. I prefer it because I can easily identify stored procedure objects when querying system tables. I don't want to be using **sp_**, as SQL Server interprets this as a system stored procedure.

The **PredominantAction** part describes what the stored procedure is intended to do. I've used an array of values over time, and I'm sure they will keep changing once I migrate to SQL Server 2005, but here is the list I've amassed so far:

```
SEL - Select - returns multiple rows
GET - Returns 1 row
UPD - Update
DEL - Delete
INS - Insert
EXT - Extract
IMP - Import
SAV - Combines insert/update
```

The **TableNameOrBusinessProcess** is used to tell me what the procedure references or does. If the procedure just works with a single table, I'll use the table name. If it works with multiple tables to perform some kind of operation, I'll use a brief process description.

Examples of this naming convention:

```
usp_SEL_SaleDetail
usp_UPD_Salesperson
usp_GET_ProcessIndicator
usp_IMP_MainframeFiles
```

If a database is shared across multiple applications or meaningful segments, I usually add a third element to the stored procedure name:

```
usp_NNN_ PredominantAction_TableName or Business Process
```

NNN indicates the project, application, or logical segment abbreviation. For example if you have a project called "Master Shipping Application", you can use MSA as the code, for example:

```
usp_MSA_INS_ShipOrders
```

Or if you would like to segment procedures by areas in your application, you could designate the Sales site as SLS and Employee sit as EMP, for example:

```
usp_SLS_UPD_Budget
usp_EMP_SEL_AnnualReview
```

Making it Work for Your Code

This standard allows for much improvisation based on your company standards and application requirements. No matter what standard you come up with, do at least choose to standardize stored procedures. I'm not talking about perfectionism here, just a general respect for how much time naming conventions will save you and your company down the road.

Manipulating Text Columns

By Raj Vasant

Introduction

Normally, applications which are developed these days contain data which are easily stored using the commonly used data-types like VARCHAR, INTEGER, etc. Very rarely you will come across details which will require you to define a table column of data-type TEXT. For example, if you are storing the write-up of some book or some help text, you might be forced to use TEXT data-type. Also, some large-size XML files which need to be parsed regularly can be stored in such a column.

If such a need arises, you might also sometimes need to do some manipulation for such columns. Traditional querying style for TEXT columns will work, but will degrade the performance for the application.SQL Server has provided some in-built functionality to query TEXT columns through the use of READTEXT, WRITETEXT and UPDATETEXT. All the above functions work with a valid pointer to the TEXT column, which can be obtained using TXTPTR (text_columnname). TEXTPTR returns a pointer to the TEXT column in the specified row or to the TEXT column in the last row returned by the query if more than one row is returned. This function returns pointer in a VARBINARY (16) variable. If a valid address (pointer) is not obtained, NULL is returned.

We will use a simple table with the following structure to show the manipulation of TEXT variables:

```
CREATE TABLE TEST (TEST_ID INT, TEST_DESC TEXT)
```

To see the actual address returned by TEXTPTR, execute the following query:

```
SELECT TEST_IS, TEXTPTR (TEST_DESC) FROM TEST
```

To obtain a valid pointer from this table, you must declare a VARBINARY(16) variable:

```
DECLARE @ptr VARBINARY (16)
SELECT @ptr = TEXTPTR (TEST_DESC) FROM TEST WHERE TEST_ID = 1
```

As NULL is returned when a valid pointer is not obtained, it is better to check for NOT NULL like:

```
IF @ptr IS NOT NULL
        --do something
```

Also, check for a valid pointer returned by TEXTPTR can be done by using TEXTVALID ('*tablename.text_column*', TEXTPTR(*text_column*)). The following query will give 1 and 0 as output for text_column if it is a valid pointer and invalid pointer respectively.

```
SELECT TEST_ID, 'IsValid' = TEXTVALID ('TEST.TEST_DESC', TEXTPTR(TEST_DESC)) FROM TEST
```

Here, TEST_DESC is the column name, whose data-type is TEXT.

READTEXT

After getting the valid pointer for the text column, the use of READTEXT, WRITETEXT and UPDATETEXT is possible. READTEXT is used to read the value from the TEXT column. It is possible to get part of the TEXT data in the column by specifying the starting position and the number of characters to retrieve.

The syntax is:

```
READTEXT tablename.text_columnname @pointer start_position no_of_bytes
```

When the query below is executed,

```
READTEXT TEST.TEST_DESC @ptr 0 100
```

the result set includes the first 100 characters of the TEST_DESC column.

WRITETEXT

WRITETEXT is used to overwrite the contents of the TEXT column. Unlike READTEXT, you cannot specify the start_position and no_of_bytes to read. WRITETEXT is executed one row at a time. You can use it from within a cursor. Also WRITETEXT cannot be used on text, ntext, and image columns in views.

The following query will update the row

```
WRITETEXT TEST.TEST_DESC @ptr 'This is new text-value…'
```

Use WRITETEXT to update and replace an entire text, ntext, or image field.

UPDATETEXT

UPDATETEXT is more powerful as it has all the functionality of WRITETEXT with additional features. You can update part-of data from one TEXT column to another. Use UPDATETEXT to change only a portion of a text, ntext, or image column in place.

The syntax for UPDATETEXT is:

```
UPDATETEXT tablename.dest_text_column @dest_ptr
       Start_position no_of_char_to_delete tablename.src_text_column @srcptr
```

We will add one more column TEST_DESC_NEW in our sample table, with TEXT data-type for testing copy of data using UPDATETEXT. By executing the following set of queries, the TEST_DESC_NEW column data will be updated with the data from TEST_DESC column. As 0 is used as the starting position, the data of TEST_DESC column is added in the beginning. And also, the existing data in TEST_DESC_NEW is also not deleted as 0 is used for number of characters to delete from destination column.

```
DECLARE @srcptr VARBINARY (16)
DECLARE @destptr VARBINARY (16)
SELECT @srcptr = TEXTPTR (TEST_DESC) FROM TEST WHERE TEST_ID = 1
SELECT @destptr = TEXTPTR (TEST_DESC_NEW) FROM TEST WHERE TEST_ID = 1
UPDATETEXT TEST.TEST_DESC_NEW @destptr
    0 0 TEST.TEST_DESC @srcptr
```

Conclusion

Though the use of TEXT columns is very rare, it is very useful to store large data. There are some limitations of using TEXT data-type, which we should be knowing before using it:

- You can only use LIKE operator in the WHERE clause for TEXT columns.
- READTEXT, WRITETEXT and UPDATETEXT cannot be used in SELECT statements.
- You cannot declare or manipulate a variable of TEXT data-type in a function or stored-procedure. But you can have a TEXT variable as parameter.

The GO Command and the Semicolon Terminator

By Ken Powers

One of the new syntax requirements for SQL Server 2005 is the use of semicolons in certain situations. Many T-SQL programmers are unfamiliar with how to use semicolons since they were never used in earlier editions of SQL Server. This article is a brief overview of how to use semicolons and how their use differs from the GO command most T-SQL programmers have used.

The GO Command

"GO" is a batch terminator. Technically speaking, the GO command is not even a part of the Transact-SQL language. It is really a command used by the SQLCMD, OSQL and ISQL utilities that can also be used within Query Analyzer and the Query Editor window.

NOTE: A batch should not be confused with a script. A batch is a set of T-SQL statements that are submitted for execution as a group. A script is simply a file containing set of T-SQL statements. One script can contain many batches.

The Semicolon

The semicolon character is a statement terminator. It is a part of the ANSI SQL-92 standard, but was never used within Transact-SQL. Indeed, it was possible to code T-SQL for years without ever encountering a semicolon.

Usage

There are two situations in which you must use the semicolon. The first situation is where you use a Common Table Expression (CTE), and the CTE is not the first statement in the batch. The second is where you issue a Service Broker statement and the Service Broker statement is not the first statement in the batch.

Here is an example of a Service Broker command:

```
USE SQLExamples
DECLARE @ConversationHandle uniqueidentifier;
BEGIN TRANSACTION;
BEGIN DIALOG CONVERSATION @ConversationHandle
FROM SERVICE [ResponseService]
TO SERVICE 'RequestService'
ON CONTRACT [Contract]
WITH LIFETIME = 600, ENCRYPTION = ON
;  -- I must use the semicolon terminator here so that the following SEND command will be the first
word in the command
-- Using GO here would destroy the variable I am using to pass a value to the statement
SEND ON CONVERSATION @ConversationHandle
MESSAGE TYPE [GetRecord]
(<123456789>);
COMMIT;
```

There are also situations in which the GO command is required. Consider a script used to create a stored procedure:

```
SET QUOTED_IDENTIFIER ON
GO
SET ANSI_NULLS ON
GO
CREATE PROCEDURE dbo.uspTestProc1
AS
BEGIN
        SELECT *
        FROM INFORMATION_SCHEMA.TABLES
END
-- The stored procedure is created
/*
Command(s) completed successfully.
*/
SET QUOTED_IDENTIFIER OFF
GO
```

What would happen if I substituted semicolons for the GO commands in this script?

```
SET QUOTED_IDENTIFIER ON;
SET ANSI_NULLS ON;
CREATE PROCEDURE dbo.uspTestProc1
AS
BEGIN
        SELECT *
        FROM INFORMATION_SCHEMA.TABLES
END
-- The attempt to create the stored procedure fails
/*
Msg 111, Level 15, State 1, Procedure uspTestProc1, Line 12
'CREATE/ALTER PROCEDURE' must be the first statement in a query batch
*/
SET QUOTED_IDENTIFIER OFF;
```

Sometimes, it is unclear whether the GO command or semicolon is the better choice for a script.

Consider this example:

```
/* Example 1: Using semicolons */
USE AdventureWorks;
DECLARE @StartProductID int
DECLARE @CheckDate datetime
SELECT @StartProductID = 972
SELECT @CheckDate = '2004-04-04'
```

```
EXEC dbo.uspGetBillOfMaterials @StartProductID, @CheckDate;
-- Now I'll switch databases ...
USE model;
-- ... and then switch back to the AdventureWorks database
USE AdventureWorks;
-- Now I'll change the values of the variables
-- still working within the same batch, so I can assign new values to the variables Created earlier
SELECT @StartProductID = 400
SELECT @CheckDate = '2000-08-08'
EXEC dbo.uspGetBillOfMaterials @StartProductID, @CheckDate;
```

Notice how I switched back and forth between two different databases and yet I was still able to assign new values to the variables I created at the beginning of the script.

Now let's try the same script with the GO command substituted for the semicolons:

```
/* Example 2: Using GO command */
USE AdventureWorks
GO
DECLARE @StartProductID int
DECLARE @CheckDate datetime
SELECT @StartProductID = 972
SELECT @CheckDate = '2004-04-04'
EXEC dbo.uspGetBillOfMaterials @StartProductID, @CheckDate
GO
-- By executing a GO command, I have ended the batch.  The variables I created have been destroyed.
-- Now I'll switch databases ...
USE model
GO
-- ... and then switch back to the AdventureWorks database
USE AdventureWorks
GO
-- Now I'll change the values of the variables
SELECT @StartProductID = 400
SELECT @CheckDate = '2000-08-08'
-- The variables no longer exist, so my attempt to assign values fails with the following messages:
/*Msg
137, Level 15, State 1, Line 3
Must declare the scalar variable "@StartProductID".
Msg 137, Level 15, State 1, Line 4
Must declare the scalar variable "@CheckDate".
*/
EXEC dbo.uspGetBillOfMaterials @StartProductID, @CheckDate
-- The attempt to execute the stored procedure also fails
/*
Msg 137, Level 15, State 2, Line 14
Must declare the scalar variable "@StartProductID".
*/
```

Using semicolons in this script saves me a lot of coding, since I am executing the same commands with different parameter values.

I hope this article has cleared up some of the confusion about the GO command and the semicolon terminator. Feel free to ask me additional questions if you would like more information.

The Dodgy GO Statement

By Subramanyam Krishnamurthy

he 'GO' statement in SQL Server plays very important role. This can be disastrous if you don't know its usage in certain scenario. One of the places where I found it can be useful or create havoc is in its role in stored procedures. The following two examples shows significance of SQL Server 2000 'GO' statements

Tested on SQL version: Microsoft SQL Server 2000, Enterprise Edition with Service Pack 4

```
Create proc MyBoss
as
begin
   select 'My boss is the best'
end

select 'This is a lie'
```

```
go
```

Now to test the output of MyBoss, execute the SP by following command

```
execute MyBoss
```

The output is:

```
-------------------
My boss is the best
------------
This is a lie
```

Say, if you show this SP's output to your boss, then you better have a new job :)

What happened? You were intending only to show him the first line, but the second select outputs also is displayed because the whole code is scripted in syscomments until a go statement is found.

Now, let's see how we can use this for a better purpose?

```
Create proc MagicProcedure
as
begin
    select 'you can not see me next time'
end

drop proc MagicProcedure
go
```

Executing MagicProcedure once, will allow you to execute the SP and then drop the SP permanently. This can be beautifully used in specific needs where you want the client/customer to use code only once to set few things. Try re-writing the same stored procedures, with GO statements like this:

```
Create proc FunnySQLServer
as
begin
    select 'SQL server is funny'
end
go
select 'who said that?'
go
Create proc MagicProcedure
as
begin
    select 'you can not see me next time'
end
go
drop proc MagicProcedure
go
```

You will notice that the query/functions written in the SPs only will be executed. The other queries are no longer part of the Stored Procedure.

SQL Server developers have been forced to use the create statement as the first statement, for the creation of a stored procedure. As such we can add any number of comment statements before the create statement of a stored procedure. But at the same time I don't understand why they allowed any executable statements after the end of stored procedure? This is shown in the below example:

```
select 'who said that?'
Create proc FunnySQLServer
as
begin
    select 'SQL server is funny'
end
go
```

Will raise an error

```
Server: Msg 111, Level 15, State 1,Line 3
'CREATE PROCEDURE' must be the first statement in a query batch.
```

At the same time

```
--'This is to test the use of comment statement before create statement of SP''
Create proc FunnySQLServer
as
begin
```

```
      select 'SQL server is funny'
end
go
```

works just fine.

I hope this article gives you an insight in to SQL server 'GO' statement and potential pitfalls and new uses when creating stored procedures.

Quick Hints for using the RAISERROR Command

By David Poole

Introduction

Sometimes you get a situation where a long-standing stored procedure seems to have started misbehaving. Either unexpected records are returned or expected records are omitted. Perhaps the procedure appears to freeze without completing.

The procedure seems to work correctly using Query Analyser in your test environment but in the live environment with the live application things do not appear to be working correctly.

You quickly establish that:

- The procedure is identical in both environments
- The database schema is identical in both environments
- The data in the tables used by the procedure is as it should be

You suspect that it is the way in which the application calls the stored procedure that is at fault but how do you prove it?

The simple approach

Well my approach would be to watch the parameters going into the procedure and variables flowing through the procedure to make sure that all is as it should be.

In your development environment you may have access to the SQL Query Analyser Debugger but in the live environment you do not thus step through debugging cannot take place. You have to resort to printing out parameters and variables at key stages of the functions in the procedure. There are three ways of doing this.

SELECT statement(s)

This is the simplest way and can print out multiple values of different types at once.

The down side is that other procedures may depend on your problem procedure and tampering with the recordsets that are output could break other parts of your application. For example if you have

```
INSERT INTO dbo.Tbl_MyTable (MyfieldList1....MyFieldListn)
EXEC dbo.usp_GetMyRecords @arg1, @arg2 ...@argn
```
Or you may have used the techniques described in "Reducing round trips to the server" to produce multiple recordsets and therefore having the server return additional recordsets will break application code that makes use of this method.

PRINT statement(s)

These do not break the two dependencies described above but they are somewhat cumbersome to use. If you have an integer your cannot say PRINT 'The integer =' + @myIntVariable without casting the variable first. This makes printing multiple values a laborious job.

In addition the print statements will wait until the batch completes before returning any information. If you are trying to PRINT messages to see how far the procedure actually gets then not getting any messages until the batch completes is going to put a bit of a damper on things.

Of course the problem with both PRINT and SELECT is that your calling application has to be able to trap the message and log it. In large environments retrospectively adding logging code would constitute a new release and therefore instigate a whole new test cycle.

Although such testing is necessary in mission critical software all we want to do is establish some simple message logging.

RAISERROR statement(s)

Again, like the PRINT statement, these do not break the to dependencies described under SELECT statement(s) and they allow multiple values of different types to be printed. They can also echo values into the Windows Event Log which is also a boon to the developer as message logging is shifted out of the application and into the stored procedure. The example script below will write a message directly to the Windows Event Log.

```
DECLARE @sStringVar VARCHAR(440) ,
        @lInteger       Int ,
        @fFloat         decimal(6,2) ,
        @byUnsignedInt  tinyint ,
SELECT @sStringVar='A string' ,
        @lInteger=44 ,
        @fFloat=3.14 ,
        @byUnsignedInt = 56 ,
RAISERROR('The string variable contains %s, the int contains %d, the float contains %d, the uint
contains %d',
        10 - Informational severity only.
        ,1
        ,@sStringVar,
        @lInteger,
        @fFloat,
        @byUnsignedInt
), WITH LOG, NOWAIT
```

The crucial statements are in the WITH clause.

LOG	Causes the message to be echoed into the WINDOWS Event Log as well as to the calling application.
	If you ran the example script in SQL Query Analyser then you will have seen the message appear in the Messages window.
NOWAIT	Causes the message to be echoed when the statement is run as opposed to when the batch completes.
	As discussed earlier trying to track how far a procedure gets before freezing is no good if the messages only appear on completion.

Downsides to the RAISERROR statement

Message size is 440 characters, hardly a major concern.

REAL,Float and DATETIME values not allowed but they may be cast to strings using either CAST or CONVERT statements.

According to books online decimal values can be printed and you can specify the precision however I have never managed to get the statement to return anything other than strings and integers.

Number and type of arguments must match the number and type of place holders. Again, this is hardly a problem.

Tricks with RAISERROR placeholders

%+d will display the integer with the correct sign + or -.
10 will appear as +10, -10 will appear as -10.

%6d creates a space 6 wide to hold the value.
10 will appear right justified as 10

%-6d creates a space 6 wide but left justifies the value.

%x will render the value in hexadecimal and in lower case
%X will render the value in hexadecimal and in upper case.

%#x will render hexadecimal in lower case i.e. 0x8f
%#X will render hexadecimal in upper case. 0X8F

%u will display int values of 0 to 2147483647 as is , -1 to -21474748348 will display as 4294967295 to 21474748348. In other words it displays the 2's complement value.

Real word example

The stored procedure I was trying to debug contained several SQL statements and although the procedure was locking solid there was no indication as to which statement block was causing the lock. All statement blocks contained the same tables/views albeit performing different tasks so sp_lock gave no clues.

What I did was to DECLARE a variable for my message at the head of the procedure.

```
DECLARE @sMessage VARCHAR(440)  ,-- The maximum possible message size
```

Then around each statement block I placed the following commands

```
@dtStart DATETIME ,
@dtEnd DATETIME ,
@lDuration
SET @dtStart=GETDATE()
SET @sMessage = CONVERT(CHAR(19),@dtEnd,120) + ' <proc name>:<block description> started'
RAISERROR(@sMessage,10,1) WITH LOG,NOWAIT
<statement block start>
...
<statement block end>
SET @dtEnd=GETDATE()
SET @lduration = DATEDIFF(ms,@dtStart,@dtEnd)
SET @sMessage = CONVERT(CHAR(19),@dtEnd,120) + ' : completed in %d milliseconds'
RAISERROR(@sMessage,10,1,@lDuration) WITH LOG,NOWAIT
```

The net result was an event log with paired messages confirming that:

- A particular block within the stored procedure had started and at what time.
- A particular block had completed at what time and had taken 'n' milliseconds.

As a side effect to confirming that certain blocks of code were running correctly I also gained a good impression of which blocks were taking the longest to run and were potentially consuming the most resources.

The Array in SQL Server

By Alex Grinberg

On a number of occasions that I have regretted the fact that there is no such thing as Array in Microsoft SQL Server's Transact-SQL. Lots of other SQL programmers would mention the same thing. The array is one of the most common and highly used programming structures. Indeed, T-SQL does not provide for the fully functional array structure. However, SQL 2000 introduced the new feature called a variable of type table, which allows for mimicking an array and/or using it instead of SQL Server cursor.

In this article I will elaborate on the way I am using this 'array' in stored procedures which has drastically increased the functional capabilities of SQL programming.

I have broken my techniques down into three sections.

1. Creating array in stored procedures.
2. Passing and receiving table variables in stored procedures
3. Using 'Array' in place of cursors.

My techniques are primarily based on using table type variables, which have become available starting with SQL Server 2000. If you are still working in SQL Server versions 6.5 or 7, sections 1 and 3 of this article may still be useful to you. However, you will have to use a Temporary Table (declared with # sign) instead of a table variable.

Section 2 is dedicated to using XML, which is why it may not be useful in any development environment other than SQL 2000. TT (temporary tables) can be used in version 2000 as well, but using temporary table you are increasing disk activity since TV (Table Variable) is created in memory as opposed to Temp tables (created in TempDb). In other words, stored procedures incorporating temp tables are slower than the ones using TVs. In order for SQL Server to create TT, the system must

1. Create table in the TempDb system database
2. Enter data into a table (insert)
3. Return data (select)
4. Remove table (Drop)

A similar process is required for TV, but all operations are conducted 100% in memory. I have recently experimented with these alternatives, and found out that the exact same stored procedure using TV is executed twice as fast compared to another stored procedure which used temp tables.

To create a simulated array (TV), we need a structure similar to array as it is known in most programming environments. Declaration of a table variable looks like this:

```
Declare @tbl table (  )
```

The above statement creates an equivalent of an Array. Type of this 'Array' depends on the data type of column. For example,

```
Declare @tbl table (FirstName varchar(20), LastName varchar(20))
```

Creates a string type array. Other data types can be used as well, such as int, float, datetime, money, etc. One should remember that SQL server does not have an implicit datatype conversion functionality (unlike VB and some other development environments). It means that data which you intend to use to populate an array, must be formatted according to the specification of each declared data type. Such functions as Convert or Cast can be used to format data appropriately.

In order to have a 'complete' array, with its full functionality, we lack an Index. I use an additional column for this, declared as Int data type, using an Identity property. Identity definition requires 2 arguments: Seed and Increment. Thus, we can create a 0 (zero) or 1-based array. The following array enjoys its full functionality:

```
Declare @tbl table (RowId int identity(1,1), ItemName varchar(100))
```

Now we can populate this array (using Northwind database) as follows:

```
Insert @tbl
  Select ProductName
    FROM Products
      WHERE ProductName like 'M%'

Select * from @tbl
GO
-- Result:
RowId  ItemName
-----  ---------------
    1  Mishi Kobe Niku
    2  Mascarpone Fabioli
    3  Maxilaku
    4  Manjimup Dried Apples
    5  Mozzarella di Giovanni
```

[In this example you could see that column RowID is provide index functionality, ItemName stores actual values.] Now it is clear that TV is a programming structure equivalent to ARRAY.

We have demonstrated creating an array programmatically in SQL Server. Our major task is to use an array in stored procedures, including passing TV as an argument. Along with that, I would like to elaborate on one more possibility to pass an entire list of values passed to a stored procedure argument and used within the procedure. I use XML for such purposes. This structure has become available to us starting from SQL Server version 2000 only. When is an operation like this required? For instance, if you intend to pass more than one value to a procedure but not sure how many total values will be there. Consider the query:

```
Select * from customers WHERE Region IN ('OR','CA','WA')
```
IN Operator in WHERE clause can use a variable number of values, and return a result set correspondingly to this multiple criteria.

It can be a challenge to pass such a list of values to a stored procedure. In earlier times I had been using so called "composite queries", or "dynamic SQL". It includes putting together a string to be compiled and executed using EXECUTE statement. For example:

```
CREATE PROCEDURE CustomerByRegion
        @List varchar(100)
AS
declare @sql varchar(1000)
set @sql = 'select * from Customers where Region IN (' + @List + ')'
execute (@sql)

-- call procedure
declare @List varchar(100)
set @List = '''OR'', ''CA'', ''WA'''
execute CustomerByRegion @List
```

This technique has some limitations. Varchar type variable cannot accept more than 8000 chars, and Text/nText type variable are invalid for local variables declaration. Let's re view a scenario when XML is used to deliver a list of values to a stored procedure, from which we can CREATE AN 'ARRAY' (TV), and then use that Array, in this case using IN operator as a part of a WHERE clause of a SQL Statement.

```
Create Procedure ShowOrders
@XMLData text
/* TEXT data type allows us to accept a much larger string, compared to Varchar, which is limited to
8000 characters. */
AS
Set Nocount ON
Declare @hDoe int
/*number needed for system to recognize an XML document */
Declare @tbl table (ProductName varchar(100))
/*declaring a TV ('Array') */
Exec sp_xml_preparedocument @hDoc Output, @XMLdata
/*Preparing an XML String for further processing */
Insert @tbl select XML_Emp.ProductName
From OPENXML(@hdoc,'root/products')
With Products XML_Emp
```

Let's examine the insert block in more detail. We have populated Array, using an XML string. OPENXML and OPENXML WITH statements create ROWSET VIEW, using XML Document. An obtained result can be loaded directly to TV or TT. WITH statement allows using an existing name of the TABLE, or creating a new schema. I would recommend the second option, since it improves readability and maintenance). Additionally, if you are using WHERE clause, the first option may generate an error.

```
-- Option 1
Insert @tbl
 select XML_Emp.ProductName
  From OPENXML(@hdoc,'root/products')
  With Products XML_Emp
-- Option2:
Insert @tbl
 select ProductName
  From OPENXML(@hdoc,'root/products')
  With (ProductName VARCHAR(20))
```

Now, upon passing XML rows to TV, we can use an obtained result in the IN clause.

```
USE NorthWind
CREATE PROC GetRegions_XML
        @empdata text
AS
DECLARE @hDoc int
DECLARE @tbl TABLE(state VARCHAR(20))

exec sp_xml_preparedocument @hDoc OUTPUT, @empdata

INSERT @tbl
SELECT StateName
FROM OPENXML(@hDoc, 'root/States')
        WITH (StateName VARCHAR(20))
EXEC sp_xml_removedocument @hDoc

SELECT * FROM Suppliers
WHERE Region IN (SELECT * FROM @tbl)

/*
declare @s varchar(100)
```

```
set @s = '<root><States StateName = "LA"/>
                  <States StateName = "MI"/>
                  <States StateName = "OR"/></root>'

exec GetRegions_XML @s
*/
```

Using Cursors

Everyone is aware of the fact that Cursors are memory-hungry. That is why it is recommended to use them as the last resort, when there are no other ways to solve a problem. This is true. It has been a while since I last used a cursor in my T-SQL programming practice. And it is understandable, since there is a much better alternative: using TV, which works great, and not nearly as much resource-hungry.

One of the main usages of Cursor is the functionality that allows to work with each particular single row out of a given result set. While coding a similar functionality via TV-Array, we need to have a row identifier, or an ID for each row. Using Identity property is very convenient for such purposes. Identity property can serve as a unique identifier for each row and will allow imitating Fetch functionality on the row-by-row basis.

Below you can find a comparative table of 2 stored procedures, one using a traditional Cursor, and the other – TV. You may notice that a cursor-based stored procedure contains fewer lines of code. Nevertheless, the activity and resources used by SQL server are much higher compared to using TV. Indeed, declaring Cursor and using Fetch statements are compact and straightforward. In the event of using TV, there is definitely more coding involved, but it allows programmer more control, and saves SQL Server resources and processing time, which is by all means a very important issue in a high-volume multi-user transactional application setting.

```
-- Transact SQL Cursor
CREATE PROC SQL_Cursor
AS
/*Local variables */
DECLARE @ContName VARCHAR(100),
        @CompName VARCHAR(50)
/*create the cursor*/
DECLARE MyCursor CURSOR FOR
                SELECT  CompanyName, ContactName
                FROM Suppliers
                WHERE ContactName LIKE 'c%'
/*open the cursor*/
OPEN MyCursor
/*get row values*/
FETCH MyCursor INTO @CompName, @ContName
/*perform oterations with single row*/
PRINT 'T_SQL cursor row  |  ' + @ContName + ' |  ' + @CompName
/*establish loop structure*/
WHILE @@FETCH_STATUS = 0
BEGIN
/*get row values*/
FETCH MyCursor INTO @CompName, @ContName
/*perform operations with single row*/
PRINT 'T_SQL cursor row  |  ' + @ContName + ' |  ' + @CompName
END
/*close the cursor*/
CLOSE MyCursor
/*remove the cursor definition*/
DEALLOCATE MyCursor

-- Cursor Simulator
CREATE PROC CursorSimulator
AS
/*Prepare TABLE variable to take resultset*/
DECLARE @tbl TABLE(
        RowID INT IDENTITY(1, 1),
        CompanyName VARCHAR(100),
        ContactName VARCHAR(50))
/*Local variables */
DECLARE @ContName VARCHAR(100),
        @CompName VARCHAR(50),
        @count int, /*create local @@fetch_status*/
        @iRow int   /*row pointer (index)*/
/* create array simulator */
INSERT @tbl
SELECT CompanyName, ContactName
FROM Suppliers
WHERE ContactName LIKE 'c%'
```

```
/*get array Upper Bound (highest ID number)*/
SET @count = @@ROWCOUNT
/*initialize index counter*/
SET @iRow = 1
/*establish loop structure*/
WHILE @iRow <= @count
BEGIN
/*get row values*/
SELECT @ContName = CompanyName, @CompName = ContactName
FROM @tbl
WHERE RowID = @iRow
/*perform operations with single row*/
PRINT 'My cursor row  |  ' + @ContName + '  |  ' + @CompName
/*go to next row*/
        SET @iRow = @iRow + 1
END
```

Despite of the fact that there may be more ways to solve the problem, methods and techniques that I suggested could can obviously broaden our possibilities in using new programming structures of SQL Server 2000.

Think Twice Before You Convert

By Aries Manlig

T-SQL comes with quite effective functions that help convert from one data type to another. But these can be ineffective if one lacks the knowledge of the results of these functions.

I was adding a debugging mechanism to my sproc by capturing the values of all the parameters. All the values are, by default, converted to varchar data type. When I started evaluating the values of the parameters in my sproc, I noticed that one of them, which has a data type of varchar(999), has its length truncated to a size of 30 characters. Then in my code I saw the following conversion:

```
Declare @newValue varchar(999)
Declare @oldValue varchar(999)
Set @newValue = Convert(varchar, @oldValue)
```

After troubleshooting my code above, I've later found out that it truncates the length of my initial varchar (999) type variable to a size of 30. Of course, I was not pleased.

To correct the problem, I had to specify the size of the new varchar data type, as in the following code:

```
Declare @newValue varchar(999)
Declare @oldValue varchar(999)
Set @newValue = Convert(varchar(999), @oldValue)
-- MUST SPECIFY SIZE AS IN THE ORIGINAL DECLARATION
```

Furthermore, I did my research over the Internet, and I googled the following: default varchar size sql. It turns out that according to this site from MSDN, http://msdn2.microsoft.com/en-us/library/ms176089.aspx, if the size is not specified when converting to varchar using Cast or Convert function, the default is 30. These codes were run against SQL 2000 and SQL 2005, and the default on both version is the same.

This is a valuable experience for me. And, I hope other coders who are not aware of the case as I described here will also learn from it.

© 2005 Aries J. Manlig
Absolute Software Corp

The Zero to N Parameter Problem

By Sloan Holliday

Specifying 0 to N parameters for Stored Procedures with XML

While the topic has been discussed before, here is another look at the "Multiple but Optional Parameters" issue, when using TSQL. Sometimes you want to write a stored procedure which returns ResultSet(s), but you may or may not want to pass in some parameters. A common delimited list just does not seem to cut it anymore. And dynamic sql doesn't cut the mustard either.

All of us have been faced at times with a problems like these:
   What if you want to ~sometimes pass in a parameter?
   How do you handle multiple parameters?

I call this the "0:N Parameter" problem. If I pass in a parameter, I want the TSQL to consider it. If I don't pass it in, I want TSQL to ignore it. And of course, sometimes I want to have more flexibility than just 'no parameters or 1 parameter', or said another way, I want to specify N parameters, where N is 1 through infinity.

The below example uses the Northwind database to return Orders. It actually will get 3 ResultSets : Customer, Order, and Order Detail information. The example allows you to specify filters such as: By OrderID , By Customer, an OrderDate before a certain Date, an OrderDate after a Certain Date, and/or by Customer-Country (~any combination of these filters you can think of). The "How to Use" shows how you can set 0 parameters, 1 parameter, or N number of parameters.

This method is not a "cure all" method. There is a performance penalty for using this method. If you have a procedure where performance is the main goal, and you have a lot of records to go through, this solution may not be the answer.

I typically use this procedure for Report Generation, where the User may or may not specify input parameters.

If you're a DotNet developer, and like to create a strongly typed DataSets, you can create one and fill in values that way (And send in the .GetXml() of the DataSet as the parameter). You'll notice my syntax of "ParametersDS", that is not an accident.

Good luck. The method is useful ~at times. Please be aware of possible scalability issues, since there is a performance hit by making the procedure so flexible. I learned this method from a previous colleague. The example is an original one coded against the Northwind database.

Download the code from SQLServerCentral.com

Conclusions

This is my preferred method of handling 0:N parameters. As I said, this is a good approach for needs like Reporting, where you know up front the 0:N parameter need. Pease heed my warning about scalability, and do not consider this a cure-all.

Using SQL-DMO and Excel to Quickly Create Reports for Authors

By Chad Miller

As DBAs, we often wear many hats. Sometimes we focus on administration, sometimes architecture, and sometimes development. Recently I've found myself answering questions for Sarbanes-Oxley (SOX) auditors. These questions typically start with an email from an auditor asking for information about the production SQL Server environment. Some of the questions I've received include:

- Can you provide a list of all production logins including databases they have access to?
- Do you have log backups for all production databases?
- Which logins have create or alter object privileges?

Answering any of these questions is easier when you have just one server, but when you have a couple dozen servers with a few hundred databases, it's a little more challenging. So the first thing I thought about was how can I automate these tasks and iterate through multiple servers. Although I kicked around the idea of rewriting the utility I created a few years ago, SQLDumpSec, ultimately I ended up taking a simpler approach using Excel and SQL-DMO VBA macros to pull security and configuration data from multiple SQL Servers. The SQLDMO_Macros spreadsheet contains five macros which have been tested against SQL 2000 and strictly use Excel VBA and SQL-DMO to get security/configuration information.

GenDropLoginScript	Generates a drop login script with user database drops
getDBRecovery	Reports Database recovery model settings
getLinkSrvLogins	Reports linked server login mappings
getLogins	Reports logins and database DB access of logins
getPriv	Reports logins which have create object privileges

Let's look at one of the SQL-DMO macros, getLinkSrvLogins as an example.

```
Option Explicit
Option Compare Text
Public intCount As Integer
Public Sub getLinkedSrvLogins()
Dim ws As Worksheet
Dim cn As Range
Dim strServer As String
Dim c1 As Range
Call Utility.AddSheetIfNotExists("LinkedServerLogins")
Set ws = Worksheets("LinkedServerLogins")
ws.Cells.Clear
 With Worksheets("LinkedServerLogins").Rows(1)
 .Font.Bold = True
 .Cells(1, 1).Value = "Server"
 .Cells(1, 1).Font.Bold = True
 .Cells(1, 1).Interior.ColorIndex = 6
 .Cells(1, 2).Value = "LinkedServer"
 .Cells(1, 2).Font.Bold = True
 .Cells(1, 2).Interior.ColorIndex = 6
 .Cells(1, 3).Value = "DataSource"
 .Cells(1, 3).Font.Bold = True
 .Cells(1, 3).Interior.ColorIndex = 6
 .Cells(1, 4).Value = "LocalLogin"
 .Cells(1, 4).Font.Bold = True
 .Cells(1, 4).Interior.ColorIndex = 6
 .Cells(1, 5).Value = "RemoteUser"
 .Cells(1, 5).Font.Bold = True
 .Cells(1, 5).Interior.ColorIndex = 6
 .Cells(1, 6).Value = "Impersonate"
 .Cells(1, 6).Font.Bold = True
 .Cells(1, 6).Interior.ColorIndex = 6
End With
' Initialize pub counter
intCount = 1

Set ws = Worksheets("Config")
For Each c1 In ws.Range("Server")
Set cn = c1.Offset(0, 1)
If c1 = "" Then
Exit For
End If
strServer = c1
strServer = Trim(strServer)
Call ListLinkSrvLogins(strServer)
Next
With Worksheets("LinkedServerLogins").Columns("A:F")
.AutoFit
End With
End Sub
Public Function ListLinkSrvLogins(strServer As String)
' SQLDMO variables
Dim dmoServer As SQLServer2
Dim dmoLinkSrv As SQLDMO.LinkedServer2
Dim dmoLinkSrvLogin As SQLDMO.LinkedServerLogin
' Counter variables
Dim intLogin As Integer

' String variables
Dim strLinkSrv As String
```

```
Dim strSrc As String
Dim strLocalLogin As String
Dim strRemoteUser As String
Dim bnImpersonate As Boolean

Set dmoServer = New SQLDMO.SQLServer2
dmoServer.LoginSecure = True

dmoServer.Connect strServer

For Each dmoLinkSrv In dmoServer.LinkedServers

'strServer = dmoServer.Name
strLinkSrv = dmoLinkSrv.Name
strSrc = dmoLinkSrv.DataSource
For Each dmoLinkSrvLogin In dmoLinkSrv.LinkedServerLogins
'For intLogin = 1 To dmoLinkSrv.LinkedServerLogins.Count
strLocalLogin = dmoLinkSrvLogin.LocalLogin
strRemoteUser = dmoLinkSrvLogin.RemoteUser
bnImpersonate = dmoLinkSrvLogin.Impersonate

' Increment line number
intCount = intCount + 1
Call AddToSheet(intCount, strServer, strLinkSrv, strSrc, strLocalLogin, strRemoteUser, bnImpersonate)
'Next
Next
Next


' Cleanup objects
Set dmoLinkSrvLogin = Nothing
Set dmoLinkSrv = Nothing
dmoServer.Close
Set dmoServer = Nothing

End Function
Public Function AddToSheet(intCount As Integer, strServer As String, strLinkSrv As String, _
 strSrc As String, strLocalLogin As String, strRemoteUser As String, bnImpersonate As Boolean)
 With Worksheets("LinkedServerLogins").Rows(intCount)
 .Cells(1, 1).Value = strServer
 .Cells(1, 2).Value = strLinkSrv
 .Cells(1, 3).Value = strSrc
 .Cells(1, 4).Value = strLocalLogin
 .Cells(1, 5).Value = strRemoteUser
 .Cells(1, 6).Value = bnImpersonate
 End With
End Function
```

Looking at the code, first a worksheet called "LinkedServerLogins" is added if it doesn't already exits. Next the header row is created. The code then iterates through the list of servers specified in *Config* tab, *Servers* range calling the SQL-DMO function "ListLinkSrvLogins." And here's why I love SQL-DMO only 11 lines of simple code in the "ListLinkSrvLogins" function gives me all the linked server login mappings. Finally the last function "AddToSheet" outputs the line to Excel. The other SQL-DMO macros follow the same pattern, iterate through the list of SQL Servers, call the SQL-DMO function, and write the output to Excel.

The VBA code requires SQL Server client tools and Microsoft Excel to be installed on the machine you are using. To use the macros, setup your server names in the *Config* tab and follow the instructions in the *Help* tab of the Excel spreadsheet. By using a little SQL-DMO and Excel VBA code you can quickly create SOX reports, eliminating the need for writing a bunch of SQL scripts and manually piecing together the output.

Finding the Next Business Day Recursively

By Rob Scholl

Overview

The other day I found myself needing to come up with a way to calculate the next business day including taking into account holidays. A recursive function turned out to be just the thing to use.

Another challenge was handling different @@DATEFIRST settings. The problem was that in a user defined function you cannot use SET DATEFIRST. To get around this I used the Modulo function. I'll show you the scripts first and then go into the details.

Scripts

To start with, you'll need to create a table to hold the holidays:

```
CREATE TABLE [holiday] (
        [holidayDate] [smalldatetime] NOT NULL ,
        CONSTRAINT [PK_holidayDate] PRIMARY KEY  CLUSTERED
        (    [holidayDate]
        )
)
```

Next you'll need to create the function:

```
create function fnGetNextBusinessDay (@startDate smalldatetime,@numDays int)
returns smalldatetime as
Begin
      Declare @nextBusDay smalldatetime
      Declare @weekDay tinyInt
      set @nextBusDay = @startDate
      Declare @dayLoop int
      set @dayLoop = 0
      while @dayLoop < @numDays
       Begin
          set @nextBusDay = dateAdd(d,1,@nextBusDay)   -- first get the raw next day
          SET @weekDay =((@@dateFirst+datePart(dw,@nextBusDay)-2) % 7) + 1
          -- always returns Mon=1 - can't use set datefirst in UDF
          -- % is the Modulo operator which gives the remainder
          -- of the dividend divided by the divisor (7)
          -- this allows you to create repeating
          -- sequences of numbers which go from 0 to 6
          -- the -2 and +1 adjust the sequence start point (Monday) and initial value (1)
          if @weekDay = 6 set @nextBusDay = @nextBusDay + 2
          -- since day by day Saturday = jump to Monday
            -- Holidays  - function calls itself to find the next business day
            select @nextBusDay = dbo.fnGetNextBusinessDay(@nextBusDay,1)
            where exists (select holidayDate from Holiday where holidayDate=@nextBusDay)
             -- next day
               set @dayLoop = @dayLoop + 1
      End
    return @nextBusDay
End
GO
```

Details

The first interesting thing about this script is the use of Modulo to make sure the function works no matter what @@DATEFIRST is set at. For those of you not familiar with Modulo, it gives the remainder of one number divided by another. So for example: 7 % 7 = 0, 9 % 7 = 2, 15 % 7 = 1 etc. I use this function all the time with Crystal reports to create a greenbar effect. If you take the record number modulo 2 you'll get 0 when it's even and 1 when it's odd. In this case, if you added the @@DATEFIRST value to the weekday value, it resulted in a sequence of numbers that was ripe to have modulo 7 applied to it.

Here's a chart of the numbers:

@@DATEFIRST plus Weekday	1	2	3	4	5	6	7
Monday	2	9	9	9	9	9	9
Tuesday	3	3	10	10	10	10	10
Wednesday	4	4	4	11	11	11	11
Thursday	5	5	5	5	12	12	12
Friday	6	6	6	6	6	13	13
Saturday	7	7	7	7	7	7	14
Sunday	8	8	8	8	8	8	8

Taking (@@DATEFIRST + the weekday value) % 7 always returns the following sequence:

Monday   2
Tuesday   3

Wednesday	4
Thursday	5
Friday	6
Saturday	0
Sunday	1

From there, the next thing to do was subtract 2 from the @@DATEFIRST + the weekday value to start the sequence with 0 on Monday and finally add 1 to that value so that Monday was always 1. If you would like to explore modulo sequences, it's very easy to do using the MOD function in Microsoft Excel (this is what I did).

Now to the recursive part of this procedure. I had taken care of calculating the next business day accounting for weekends and began to work on the holidays part of the procedure. The first step was to check if the next business day was a holiday and therefore had an entry in the holiday table. If there was one, then I had to go to the next day. However it couldn't simply be the next day since the next day could also be a weekend or a holiday. It had to be the next business day. That's when the light went off. Have the function call itself! I just hard coded 1 as the number of days to look forward and then called the function.

Summary

The magic question with recursive functions is : "Do I have to do a calculation and then do the same calculation on the result?" If you ever find yourself asking that question, you've got a great candidate for a recursive function. The magic question with Modulo is "Do I have a repeating series of numbers?" If so, Modulo may be the answer. I hope you found this little piece interesting.

Printing in .NET

By Jereme Guenther

Introduction

A quick summary for those who just want the code and don't want to read the history... I have searched all over the web for good printing code and was unable to find it. I have created a printing class which allows text to be formatted at the character level. It has taken me about a week to get what I have working correctly and I thought it would be nice to save others the time.

The Long Version

Now for those who would like the longer version of the story... I was recently tasked with created a web application which would allow printing to be initiated without the irritation of having to respond to successive prompts. I chose ASP.NET for this project, not only because it is replacing traditional ASP but also because I had had experience with printing in prior versions of MS VB, which is one of the languages that ASP.NET supports. So I started browsing the Internet looking for a printing solution that would fit my needs, unfortunately I didn't find one. While I did find multiple solutions which allowed me to print a large block of text, I couldn't find anything that allowed me to control the formatting at the character level as I needed.

Finally I found a tutorial on how to format each paragraph by placing them separately on the page before it was sent to the printer. Combining this latest find with some of the other tutorials I went to work to make a class which would let me bold a single character if I chose. From the start I realized that this class should be as separate from the rest of the program as possible so I could use it in future projects with similar requirements, this resulted in the creation of variables which could be changed through properties of the class object; it also prompted me to use formatting tags in the text to be printed. I choose the HTML style of tags because I work a lot with them and I figured they would be easier for me and others to remember and use than proprietary tags. Also HTML tags seemed uniquely suited for my purpose because people rarely use them when creating an everyday document which means that my printing class wouldn't pick up a tag where one wasn't meant to be. I do suggest, however, that when utilizing this class you check for the <'s and >'s signifying HTML tags and flag them so the user knows they could be a source of problems.

Through this process I learned a lot, here are some of what I consider to be the more important or obscure. First, when using the OnPrintPage sub of the PrintDocument class, I had trouble understanding how multiple pages were printed since I couldn't find a sendpagetoprinter command. I learned that the

PrintDocument class essentially puts the OnPrintPage sub into a while loop as long as e.HasMorePages=True, this means that as soon as your code is finished executing and the sub is done, then the sub will start back over again if the HasMorePages value is true. There is no magical sustaining of where in the print job I am or what my variable values are which means that I have to be sure that my variables scope is set correctly. The other big problem I was having was figuring out the coordinates to start each character at considering they will be different if the char is bolded or not, this was resolved when one of the tutorials I looked up showed me how to use the MeasureString function from the Graphics object.

My final challenge came when I needed to make sure that words were not chopped off at the end of a line. To overcome this issue I ended up putting a kind of memory in my program which allowed it to collect one words worth of characters before printing them out. To make sure that this word still got printed I implemented a rollback feature so the code would move to the next line or page and start printing at the position it was rolled back to.

Code and Description

My code is easily modified and shouldn't be too hard to understand. It is well commented. It recognizes the HTML bold tag and a special tag which I created to take the place of what tables do in HTML. Paragraphs are separated using vbCrLf and lines will wrap correctly without chopping off a word. The checkBold function is used to parse the incoming text and format the characters correctly; this is the function where you could add support for Italicizing and other features.

Here is the block of code to instantiate and use the class:

```
' Create object, passing in text
Dim MyPrintObject As New TextPrint("<B>this will be bold</B>" + vbCrLf + "<ST=400>this will
start at 400 pixels")
' Set font, defaults to times new roman, 12 if omitted
MyPrintObject.Font = New Font("Tahoma", 8)
' Issue print command
MyPrintObject.Print()
```

Here is the actual printing class which does the work:

```
This can be downloaded from http://www.sqlservercentral.com/bestof
```

Conclusion

Obviously there are many enhancements which can be done to this code, however, it should be a great start for most programmers.

For those who are interested in my research and the tutorials I found that helped me with this project, here are the two articles I used:
http://www.vb-helper.com/howto_net_print_long_text.html
http://www.d eveloper.com/net/asp/article.php/3102381

Get Away From Confusing Code

By Sean McCown

Quite often we're forced to write dynamic SQL for some specific process. One of the things I've always hated is how confusing it is to troubleshoot syntax errors when you start playing with single and double quotes. Is it three quotes here, or four, or is it two? You always have to reason it out and play with the code, and maybe it's not even in the spot you're working on.

What you're trying to avoid is code like this. This statement actually inserts the defrag statement itself into a #Table.

```
insert #Defrag
    select 'DBCC DBReIndex(' + @Table + ',' + '''' + '''' + ', 80)'
```
This statement just has to have so many quotes because of the spaces in the col names. It could be done with [] also, but this is an example so just take it for what it's worth. I also just sketched this code out real quick, and I have no idea if it's actually correct… too many single quotes for me.

```
@sql = ('select col1 as ' + '''Hello Kitty''' + ',
        col2 as  ' + '''Today is Today''' + ',
        col3 as ' + '''War is hell''' +
'from table1')
```

OK, so we've all seen code like this, and even worse. Here's a simple solution that will make your live a lot easier when writing dynamic SQL. Use the ASCII chars instead. You can easily tell where your quotes are supposed to be and you won't have a problem. Here's what I mean. I'll rewrite the statements above with the ASCII chars instead and you'll see what I mean.

```
Declare @SQ char(1)
Set @SQ = char(39)
insert #Defrag
 select 'DBCC DBReIndex(' + @Table + ',' + @SQ + @SQ + ', 80)'
```

Char(39) is the ASCII code for a single quote. Therefore, whenever you need to use a single quote, instead of using the escape method, simply put in the var '@SQ' instead.

Here's the other statement.

```
@sql = ('select col1 as ' + @SQ + 'Hello Kitty' + @SQ + ',
        col2 as  ' + @SQ + 'Today is Today' + @SQ + ',
        col3 as ' + @SQ + 'War is hell' + @SQ +
'from table1')
```

Another couple examples:

```
... ' where LastName = ' + @SQ + @LName + @SQ
... 'where TDate = ' + @SQ + GetDate() + @SQ
... 'where LDate = ' + @SQ + GetDate() - 100 + @SQ
```

Anyway, you get the idea. The thing is, this can be done with anything, even in protecting against SQL injection, so it's good to know. But how are you supposed to know what the ASCII chars are for the entire char set? Well, I've written a small loop that you can run to find the char you're looking for and use it wherever you like. You can see it's very simple code, but very handy to have around if you write a lot of dynamic code.

```
/*
Author: Sean McCown
Date: 06/05/2003
Lists all char codes so you can find the code for the char you're looking for.
Tells that char(39) is ', etc.  Very nice to have around.
*/
Declare @Chars Table
        ( Code varchar(10),
          Char varchar(4)
        )
Declare @i int
Set @i = 0
While @i < 256
  BEGIN
    Insert @Chars
    Select 'Char(' + cast(@i as varchar(4)) + ')', char(@i)
    Set @i = @i + 1
  END
Select * from @Chars
```

Enjoy and I'd welcome comments if you have any.

SQL Server 2005 for SQL2K Developers

By M. Choirul Amri

SQL Server 2005 comes with many enhancements for database developer. There are not only T-SQL enhancements, but also there are brand new features such as Service Broker. Reporting Services also has many improvements that make the database and business intelligence developer more productive. This article is the first in a series on SQL Server 2005 enhancements for developers. The main objective is providing guidance for the SQL Server 2000 developer for dealing with the 2005 changes.

PIVOT and UNPIVOT

This operator provides the capability to transform rows into columns. Developers are already familiar with this task in Analysis Services or Excel Pivot tables. In the past, you should use the CASE function to do this. Dealing with CASE in many rows and columns can be a painful task, so it is why PIVOT comes to make it easier.

Let's build the sample data in a SalesSummarry table, that taken from AdventureWorks database sample:

```
Use AdventureWorks
CREATE TABLE Sales.SalesSummarry
(       OrderYear int NOT NULL,
        SalesPersonID int NOT NULL,
        SubTotal money NOT NULL
)
GO
INSERT INTO Sales.SalesSummarry
SELECT Year(OrderDate), SalesPersonID, SubTotal FROM Sales.SalesOrderHeader
WHERE SalesPersonID IS NOT NULL
```

After the table is build you will have the following data:

```
OrderYear   SalesPersonID SubTotal
----------- ------------- --------------------
2001        279           24643.9362
2001        279           1553.1035
2001        282           39422.1198
2001        282           34689.5578
2001        276           503.3507
```

In the past, you get the cross tab style result with the following script:

```
SELECT SalesPersonID,
        SUM(CASE when OrderYear = 2001 then SubTotal ELSE 0 end) as '2002',
        SUM(CASE when OrderYear = 2003 then SubTotal ELSE 0 end) as '2003',
        SUM(CASE when OrderYear = 2004 then SubTotal ELSE 0 end) as '2004'
FROM Sales.SalesSummarry
GROUP BY SalesPersonID
```

It will return a cross tab result that compares SalesPersonID sales for every years. Using CASE function can be a daunting task when you have many rows to be classified and transformed to columns. But you can do it with the following PIVOT operator automatically:

```
SELECT * FROM Sales.SalesSummarry
PIVOT(SUM(SubTotal) FOR OrderYear IN
([2002],[2003],[2004])) as SalesPivot
```

Maybe you are wonder why should use * in SELECT, don't worry because you can mention the columns as follows:

```
SELECT SalesPersonID, [2002],[2003],[2004] FROM Sales.SalesSummarry
PIVOT(SUM(SubTotal) FOR OrderYear IN
([2002],[2003],[2004])) as SalesPivot
ORDER BY SalesPersonID
```

The basic idea of this operation is sum up the measurement (which is SubTotal) for each changes of OrderYear.

You can also do UNPIVOT to extract the data that has been summarized. Run this script to make a table and sample data to be extrated:

```
Use AdventureWorks
CREATE TABLE SalesByPerson
(       SalesPersonID int NOT NULL,
        [2002] int NULL,
        [2003] int NULL,
        [2004] int NULL
)
INSERT INTO SalesByPerson
SELECT SalesPersonID, [2002],[2003],[2004] FROM Sales.SalesSummarry
PIVOT(SUM(SubTotal) FOR OrderYear IN ([2002],[2003],[2004])) as SalesPivot
```

It's clearly straight forward that after make the sample table, then load it with the summarized data with PIVOT operator. Then you can do UNPIVOT with the following operation:

```
SELECT * FROM SalesByPerson
UNPIVOT(SubTotal FOR OrderYear IN
([2002],[2003],[2004])) as A
```

Using Table Variable for PIVOT Operation

You have another option to make the PIVOT operation without making additional table to store raw data before processing it with PIVOT. The table variable can be used to store temporary data, and then clean up after PIVOT operation is finished.

This script is a modification of the PIVOT operation above:

```
USE AdventureWorks
GO
DECLARE @SummarrySales TABLE
(       OrderYear int NOT NULL,
        SalesPersonID int NOT NULL,
        SubTotal money NOT NULL
);
INSERT INTO @SummarrySales
SELECT Year(OrderDate), SalesPersonID, SubTotal FROM Sales.SalesOrderHeader
WHERE SalesPersonID IS NOT NULL;
SELECT * FROM @SummarrySales PIVOT(SUM(SubTotal) FOR OrderYear
    IN ([2002],[2003],[2004])) as SalesPivot
```

You do it in one batch, create table variable, load it with raw data, then do PIVOT operation on it.

Happy SQLing :)

Generating Permutations in T-SQL

By Eli Leiba

This article describes how to dynamically generate all possible permutations for a given set of values. In a T-SQL stored procedure, the set of values is coded directly (as a fixed derived table) inside the Procedure's code to gain optimal performance

In many cases, specifically in QA units , programs need to be tested for all possible input values. The parameters all possible combinations can be considered as a set of values. The process I show here is a method for generating all possible permutations for a fixed and known set of values. The integer parameter n for the procedure is a number <= number of set elements that will limit the permutations calculation for first n elements in the set. The number of permutations will result in n! = P(n)

The T-SQL stored procedure

The stored procedure assumes that the given set of values is given in the following format

```
SELECT 0 as X , v1 as Y    union all
            1 ,            v2  union all
            2,             v3  union all
            . . .
        N-1 ,       vn
```

where X is an alias for a running index and Y is the actual set value. I'll refer to this query as S for the next explanation

The procedure takes this SELECT as a base "table" and generates a dynamic SQL statement in the following format

```
SELECT    T1.Y, T2.Y, T3.Y,.....................Tn.Y
FROM S T1, S T2,          .........., S Tn
where   T1.X < n AND
        T2.X < n AND
        . . .
        Tn.X < n AND
        Ti.X <> Tj.X    (FOR all i <> j , i,j <=n, all possible clauses)
```

This query will give all permutation combinations for the first n Y values in S because the Cartesian product of all Si is constrained to be less than n and all X values are not equal to one another. Note that there are n Ti.X < n where clause and n!/ [(n-2)!*2] = (n/2)* (n-1) Ti.X <> Tj.X clauses (all possible i,j selections where i<>j, i,j <=n)

The procedure's code

(I coded A,B,C,D,.....J as the set values without losing the generality of the program - replace the values for your needs)

You can download this code from www.sqlservercentral.com/bestof

Conclusion

The TSQL code that I presented here can be a generic tool for generating permutations for a fixed and known set of values a generated SQL that constraints the Cartesian product for N buffers for the given set S with all the needed constraints to produce the permutations This process can be very useful for automating the generations of permutations for program unit checks and QA tests.

Notes :

- **exec sp_permutate 7** will produce the 7! = 5040 all possible permutations for A,B,C,D,E,F,G
- Note that if you try to replace the base SELECT with a pre-defined view and try to run the procedure , the MSSQL optimizer can fail because a plan cannot be generated. I the code is coded directly in the procedure code, this problem will not occur.

Download the code

Eli Leiba works at Israel Electric Company as a Senior Application DBA in Oracle and MS SQL Server. He also has certifications from Microsoft and BrainBench in Oracle and SQL Server database administration and implementation. Mr. Leiba holds a B.S. in Computer Science since 1991 and has 14 years' experience working in the databases field. Additionally Mr. Leiba teaches SQL Server DBA and Development courses at Microsoft CTEC and also serves as a senior database consultant for several Israeli start-up companies. (e-mail: Eli.Leiba@2cher.com)

Practical Uses of PATINDEX

By Robert Davis

Practical Uses of PatIndex() ... Or Why CharIndex() is not enough

One question that I am frequently asked by developers new to T-SQL is whether they should use CharIndex () or PatIndex() and what the difference between the two is. *SQL Server Books Online* explains that the difference between the two is that PatIndex can use wildcard characters. This is often unclear to many developers because they associate the term wildcard with the percent sign (%) only. What *Books Online* does not make clear is that PatIndex() can make use of the full spectrum of wildcard characters. This gives it power well beyond that of CharIndex().

PatIndex **is Like Like**

To really see the full capability of PatIndex(), you must take a look at the Like command in *SQL Server Books Online*. *Books Online* describes the available wildcards characters as follows:

Wildcard character	Description	Example
%	Any string of zero or more characters.	WHERE title LIKE '%computer%' finds all book titles with the word 'computer' anywhere in the book title.

_ (underscore)	Any single character.	WHERE au_fname LIKE '_ean' finds all four-letter first names that end with ean (Dean, Sean, and so on).
[ ]	Any single character within the specified range ([a-f]) or set ([abcdef]).	WHERE au_lname LIKE '[C-P]arsen' finds author last names ending with arsen and beginning with any single character between C and P, for example Carsen, Larsen, Karsen, and so on.
[^]	Any single character not within the specified range ([^a-f]) or set ([^abcdef]).	WHERE au_lname LIKE 'de[^l]%' all author last names beginning with de and where the following letter is not l.

If we adapt this table for PatIndex(), it would look something like this:

Wildcard character	Description	Example
%	Any string of zero or more characters.	WHERE PatIndex('%computer%', title) > 0 finds all book titles with the word 'computer' anywhere in the book title.
_ (underscore)	Any single character.	WHERE PatIndex('_ean', au_fname) > 0 finds all four-letter first names that end with ean (Dean, Sean, and so on).
[ ]	Any single character within the specified range ([a-f]) or set ([abcdef]).	WHERE PatIndex('[C-P]arsen', au_lname) > 0 finds author last names ending with arsen and beginning with any single character between C and P (Carsen, Larsen, Karsen, and so on).
[^]	Any single character not within the specified range ([^a-f]) or set ([^abcdef]).	WHERE PatIndex('de[^l]%', au_lname) > 0 finds all author last names beginning with de and where the following letter is not l (finds Derry but not Delton).

Let's Get Practical

Let's take a real world example. If we have a varchar field that may contain non-numeric data and we want to Select the records and include the data in this field if it contains numbers only and nothing else, we can use PatIndex().

Background:
As the DBA for my company, my team supports all database needs for our company's applications including a web application. A key data field within this application is the customer's internal company ID for their employees. Since this ID is defined by the client, we must allow the use of alpha-numeric codes. A separate customer driven project calls for us to export their roster data to send to a third party. One of the requirements of the project is that if an employee's company ID contains data other than a number, we should assume that the value is incorrect and not include it.

Solution:
I decided to use PatIndex() in a Case statement with the *not within a range* wildcards. The range in this case would be 0 to 9 ([0-9]), and I would express *not within this range* by using the expression [^0-9]. My resulting Case statement looks like:

CompanyID = Case When PatIndex('%[^0-9]%', IsNull(CompanyID, '*')) > 0 Then Null Else CompanyID End

Going a little further:
If I want to go a little further with this concept, I could write a User-Defined Function (named fnIsInt()) that accepts a varchar value and returns a 0 or a 1 indicating if the value could be converted to an integer data type as is without any other string manipulation. This function would work much like the built-in IsNumeric() function. The difference between the two functions is that IsNumeric() allows additional characters such as the decimal point, currency symbols, commas.

Since this article is focusing on practical uses of PatIndex, I will only be checking to see if the string value contains digits only with the exception of allowing it to begin with a negative sign. I will not include checking to see if the value is within the allowable range of the Int data type.

```
Create Function dbo.fnIsInt(
        @value varchar(11))
        Returns int
As
Begin
    Declare @IsInt int
    Set @IsInt = 0

    If PatIndex('%[^0-9]%', @value) > 0 Or PatIndex('-%[^0-9]%', @value) > 0
        Begin
            Set @IsInt = 0
        End
    Else
        Begin
            Set @IsInt = 1
        End

    Return @IsInt
End
```

Testing the function:
```
Select IsNumeric('4'), PatIndex('%[^0-9]%', '4'), dbo.fnIsInt('4')
----------- ----------- -----------
1           0           1

Select IsNumeric('4.2'), PatIndex('%[^0-9]%', '4.2'), dbo.fnIsInt('4.2')
----------- ----------- -----------
1           2           0

Select IsNumeric('4-2'), PatIndex('%[^0-9]%', '4-2'), dbo.fnIsInt('4-2')
----------- ----------- -----------
0           2           0

Select IsNumeric('-4'), PatIndex('%[^0-9]%', '-4'), dbo.fnIsInt('-4')
----------- ----------- -----------
1           1           0

Select IsNumeric('4,2'), PatIndex('%[^0-9]%', '4,2'), dbo.fnIsInt('4,2')
----------- ----------- -----------
1           2           0

Select IsNumeric('$42'), PatIndex('%[^0-9]%', '$42'), dbo.fnIsInt('$42')
----------- ----------- -----------
1           1           0
```

The Big Deal?

Okay, I admit that I could have done the above Case statement just as easily using Like commands. Since I did not need to know the position of the offending characters, PatIndex() was more than was needed for that situation. If the project had required that I remove the non-digit characters rather than simply returning Null, PatIndex() would have been the perfect solution.

I can easily leverage the full power of PatIndex() by creating a User-Defined Function that accepts a varchar value and returns a varchar value with all non-digit characters removed.

```
Create Function dbo.fnDigitsOnly(
        @value varchar(50))
        Returns varchar(50)
As
Begin
    If PatIndex('%[^0-9]%', @value) > 0
        Begin
            While PatIndex('%[^0-9]%', @value) > 0
                Begin
                    Set @value = Stuff(@value, PatIndex('%[^0-9]%', @value), 1, '')
                End
        End
    Return @value
End
```

The Big Finish

So, what's the difference between CharIndex() and PatIndex()? Well, like *Books Online* says, PatIndex() can use wildcards. To put it as simple as I can, PatIndex() combines the capabilities of the CharIndex()

function and the Like command. 99.99% of the time, CharIndex() and PatIndex() are used interchangeably. That 0.01% of the time that you need something more, you'll be glad to have PatIndex() in your T-SQL toolbox.

Deduping Data in SQL Server 2005

By Charles Hawkins

Introduction

Recently I read Muthusamy Anantha Kumar's article "Row_NUMBER() function in SQL Server 2005" (http://www.sqlservercentral.com/articles/articlelink.asp?articleid=2239) article. In it, he explored not only the new ROW_NUMBER() function, but, also gave a good example of SQL Server 2005's common table expression.

When I saw his sample, I immediately realized that I could use this to solve one of my more perplexing problems in SQL Server - how to reduce duplicates in a record set to a single row. I will demonstrate how to "de-dupify" a record set in SQL Server 2005 in a single query - a feat I would find myself using a cursor for in earlier versions of SQL Server. Particularly vexing were issues where you didn't just have two copies of a record but might have three or more copies or ragged numbers - two here and three there. My solution below accounts for this hardest case of the ragged numbers of duplicates.

I slightly modified Muthusamy's original example.

First build an EMPLOYEE table in TEMPDB (my scratchpad of choice). I added a reference date to each record so that later when I de-dupify, we'll show you how to keep the earliest or latest duplicate record.

```
USE [TEMPDB]
GO
IF  EXISTS (SELECT * FROM SYS.OBJECTS
    WHERE OBJECT_ID = OBJECT_ID(N'[DBO].[EMPLOYEE]') AND TYPE IN (N'U'))
DROP TABLE [DBO].[EMPLOYEE]
GO
CREATE TABLE EMPLOYEE (EMPID INT, FNAME VARCHAR(50), LNAME VARCHAR(50), REFDATE DATETIME)
GO
```

Next, populate the EMPLOYEE table. Notice how I use the semi-colon to separate my queries while still keeping the context of the @NOW variable relevant. When you use common table expressions (as we'll later do), semi-colons are important.

```
DECLARE @NOW DATETIME
SELECT @NOW = GETDATE()
INSERT INTO EMPLOYEE(EMPID,FNAME,LNAME,REFDATE) VALUES(2021110,'MICHAEL','POLAND',DATEADD(MI,1,@NOW));
INSERT INTO EMPLOYEE(EMPID,FNAME,LNAME,REFDATE)VALUES (2021110,'MICHAEL','POLAND',DATEADD(MI,2,@NOW));
INSERT INTO EMPLOYEE(EMPID,FNAME,LNAME,REFDATE)VALUES (2021115,'JIM','KENNEDY',DATEADD(MI,3,@NOW));
INSERT INTO EMPLOYEE(EMPID,FNAME,LNAME,REFDATE)VALUES (2121000,'JAMES','SMITH',DATEADD(MI,4,@NOW));
INSERT INTO EMPLOYEE(EMPID,FNAME,LNAME,REFDATE)VALUES (2011111,'ADAM','ACKERMAN',DATEADD(MI,5,@NOW));
INSERT INTO EMPLOYEE(EMPID,FNAME,LNAME,REFDATE)VALUES (3015670,'MARTHA','LEDERER',DATEADD(MI,6,@NOW));
INSERT INTO EMPLOYEE(EMPID,FNAME,LNAME,REFDATE)VALUES (1021710,'MARTHA','MANDEZ',DATEADD(MI,7,@NOW));
INSERT INTO EMPLOYEE(EMPID,FNAME,LNAME,REFDATE)VALUES (2021110,'MICHAEL','POLAND',DATEADD(MI,8,@NOW));
INSERT INTO EMPLOYEE(EMPID,FNAME,LNAME,REFDATE)VALUES (2021115,'JIM','KENNEDY',DATEADD(MI,9,@NOW));
INSERT INTO EMPLOYEE(EMPID,FNAME,LNAME,REFDATE)VALUES (2021115,'JAMES','KENNEDY',DATEADD(MI,10,@NOW));
GO
```

Illustration 1.0 shows our EMPLOYEE table. Your reference dates will be different but will maintain the one-minute offsets between rows.

2021110	MICHAEL	POLAND	2006-01-18 09:41:08.297
2021110	MICHAEL	POLAND	2006-01-18 09:42:08.297
2021115	JIM	KENNEDY	2006-01-18 09:43:08.297
2121000	JAMES	SMITH	2006-01-18 09:44:08.297
2011111	ADAM	ACKERMAN	2006-01-18 09:45:08.297
3015670	MARTHA	LEDERER	2006-01-18 09:46:08.297
1021710	MARTHA	MANDEZ	2006-01-18 09:47:08.297

2021110	MICHAEL	POLAND	2006-01-18 09:48:08.297
2021115	JIM	KENNEDY	2006-01-18 09:49:08.297
2021115	JAMES	KENNEDY	2006-01-18 09:50:08.297

Illustration 1.0

You see that EMPID/FNAME 2021110/Michael has three repeats and 2021115/Jim has two, our ragged duplicates.

```
SELECT EMPID, FNAME, LNAME, REFDATE FROM EMPLOYEE
```

Here is Muthusamy's query to show you how to use the ROW_NUMBER() function. I've also added our REFDATE to the ORDER BY clause so that the earliest records come first.

```
SELECT ROW_NUMBER() OVER (ORDER BY EMPID ASC, REFDATE ASC) AS ROWID, * FROM EMPLOYEE
```

The results are seen in illustration 2.0:

1	1021710	MARTHA	MANDEZ	2006-01-18 09:47:08.297
2	2011111	ADAM	ACKERMAN	2006-01-18 09:45:08.297
3	2021110	MICHAEL	POLAND	2006-01-18 09:41:08.297
4	2021110	MICHAEL	POLAND	2006-01-18 09:42:08.297
5	2021110	MICHAEL	POLAND	2006-01-18 09:48:08.297
6	2021115	JIM	KENNEDY	2006-01-18 09:43:08.297
7	2021115	JIM	KENNEDY	2006-01-18 09:49:08.297
8	2021115	JAMES	KENNEDY	2006-01-18 09:50:08.297
9	2121000	JAMES	SMITH	2006-01-18 09:44:08.297
10	3015670	MARTHA	LEDERER	2006-01-18 09:46:08.297

Illustration 2.0

Now here is our common table expression,EMPLOYEE ORDERED BY ROWID, query to de-dupify the record set. I'm wrapping it in a BEGIN TRAN and ROLLBACK TRAN for testing purposes. Later when you get the record set that you want, you can change the ROLLBACK to a COMMIT. I've given you a before and after SELECT of the record set so you can see the change. In this case, we are keeping the earliest record.

```
BEGIN TRAN;
SELECT ROW_NUMBER() OVER (ORDER BY EMPID ASC, REFDATE ASC) AS ROWID, * FROM EMPLOYEE;
WITH [EMPLOYEE ORDERED BY ROWID] AS
(SELECT ROW_NUMBER() OVER (ORDER BY EMPID ASC, REFDATE ASC) AS ROWID, * FROM EMPLOYEE WHERE 1 = 1)
DELETE FROM [EMPLOYEE ORDERED BY ROWID] WHERE ROWID NOT IN
(SELECT MIN(ROWID) FROM [EMPLOYEE ORDERED BY ROWID] GROUP BY EMPID,FNAME,LNAME);
SELECT ROW_NUMBER() OVER (ORDER BY EMPID ASC, REFDATE ASC) AS ROWID, * FROM EMPLOYEE;
ROLLBACK TRAN;
-- COMMIT TRAN;
GO
```

Notice how I terminate the each of the queries above with a semi-colon. In SQL Server 2005, certain queries absolutely must be separated from other queries by a semi-colon. Common table expressions are one such query type. If I had not used the semi-colon in the first SELECT statement, I would have received the following error:

```
Msg 336, Level 15, State 1, Line 3
Incorrect syntax near 'EMPLOYEE ORDERED BY ROWID'. If this is intended to be a common table expression,
you need to explicitly terminate the previous statement with a semi-colon.
```

The results of the SELECT before our DELETE are those of illustration 2 above. Illustration 3 shows the results of the post-DELETE SELECT query:

1	1021710	MARTHA	MANDEZ	2006-01-18 09:47:08.297
2	2011111	ADAM	ACKERMAN	2006-01-18 09:45:08.297
3	2021110	MICHAEL	POLAND	2006-01-18 09:41:08.297

4	2021115	JIM	KENNEDY	2006-01-18 09:43:08.297
5	2021115	JAMES	KENNEDY	2006-01-18 09:50:08.297
6	2121000	JAMES	SMITH	2006-01-18 09:44:08.297
7	3015670	MARTHA	LEDERER	2006-01-18 09:46:08.297

Illustration 3.0

Thus, we've de-dupified the EMPLOYEE table in one DELETE query above.

The DELETE query above using the common table expression is very powerful. You can manipulate the final record set in several different ways.

Notice that I added a "WHERE 1 = 1" clause to my definition of the common table expression. This is unnecessary. I added it just to demonstrate that you can limit the scope of the common table expression [EMPLOYEE ORDERED BY ROWID] by limiting the employee record set returned by the WHERE clause.

If I wanted to retain the later date for the employee record, I could do this in one of two ways. I could sort the population of the common table expression [EMPLOYEE ORDERED BY ROWID] by using REFDATE DESC. Alternatively, I could use the MAX function for ROWID in the subquery of the DELETE statement.

Finally, I specify the uniqueness of the duplication by modifying the GROUP BY clause of the sub-query. Notice that we have two records for EMPID 2021115 remaining in our final record set. We de-dupified the records for Jim Kennedy, but James Kennedy still remains. Removing FNAME from our GROUP BY clause would cause the earlier record for Jim Kennedy to remain. This may or may not be desirable. You would probably want to resolve the disparity between Jim and James with the application owners before proceeding, displaying the usefulness of the earlier discussed ROLLBACK/COMMIT option for testing what you really want your final record set to look like.

I'll leave it to you to try deleting the EMPID and LNAME columns from the GROUP BY clause and see what happens to your record set.

Conclusion

In this article, we have shown how SQL Server 2005 ROW_NUMBER() function and common table expressions allow you to de-dupify record sets in one quick query.

Business Intelligence, Reporting Services, and ETL

Supposedly the hot new area for DBAs. That's been the talk for a few years now, but the BI world of Analysis Services, cubes, and MDX hasn't really taken off. That has now stopped Microsoft from continuing to develop in this area and one of the hot new technologies during the time these articles were written was Reporting Services.

We're bringing you a few articles in each area, designed to help you get started and understand a bit more about the BI world. A short look at DTS along with a couple on Analysis Services, a part of SQL Server that many DBAs have not worked with.

Lastly we have 4 articles on Reporting Services, the newest add-on to SQL Server that Microsoft has given us. A true reporting engine and development tool that competes nicely with Crystal Reports and other report writers at a great price. Free.

DTS Polling

By Andre Quitta

Background

There are a number of SQL Server Data Transformation Services that are the starting point to multi-step processing. For those processes to work, it is assumed that the data downloaded from an outside source is present.

I ran into trouble when the download data was not ready on a consistent basis. Originally we had to run the processes manually, which defeated the purpose of scheduled SQL jobs. Below describes a technique where the SQL job and a DTS are used to poll the data source for an indicator, and when that indicator is found, to proceed with the processing.

Areas Covered in this Document

- Audit trails
- DTS global variables
- DTS branching
- SQL jobs

Audit Trails

I kept a log of events in a table so that performance could be documented. This measures the status of the SQL jobs and also provides a documented history.

```
CREATE TABLE [dbo].[EventAudit] (
        [EventAuditID] [int] IDENTITY (1, 1) NOT NULL ,
        [DateOccurred] [datetime] NULL ,
        [EventClass] [varchar] (20) COLLATE SQL_Latin1_General_CP1_CI_AS NULL ,
        [PackageName] [varchar] (50) COLLATE SQL_Latin1_General_CP1_CI_AS NULL ,
        [PackageStep] [tinyint] NULL ,
        [EventNotes] [varchar] (2000) COLLATE SQL_Latin1_General_CP1_CI_AS NULL
) ON [PRIMARY]
```

DTS Global Variables

The ActiveX Scripting part of DTS allows you to use variables to make decisions. When you click on the Package menu of the DTS, and then Properties, the Global Variables tab opens up **(Figure 1)** a wide range of possibilities. In this case, I use it to hold the test value to determine if my processing can continue.

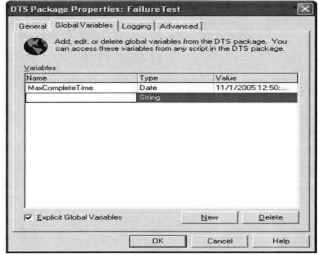

Figure 1

DTS Branching

The ActiveX Scripting gives a default interface like the one below:

```
'****************************************************************
'  Visual Basic ActiveX Script
'****************************************************************
Function Main()
        Main = DTSTaskExecResult_Success
End Function
```

What it doesn't mention is that there is another result that can be returned:

```
Main = DTSTaskExecResult_Failure
```

Because DTS allows three possible workflows, it allows you to direct the program flow. Keep this in mind. A lot of the process depends on this.

SQL Jobs

This job is scheduled to run from 8am to 11:30am every 15 minutes. FailureTest should return a Failure indication until it is ready to run **(Figure 2)**. Once it is running, it will not try to run again until the job is complete.

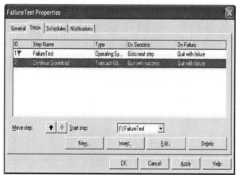

Figure 2

This is an important point. FailureTest should not only test whether the data is ready to download, it should also test whether it had already ran that day.

Create the FailureTest step by scheduling the DTS through Enterprise Manager. This will create a job with the DTS name. The code for that step can be copied into this job step.

Step by Step

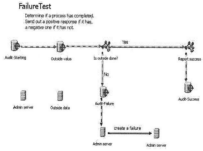

Figure 3

In summary, the process works as follows:

- Write to the log that the DTS has started
- Test the outside data source and put the results of that test in a Global Variable
- If the Test says that the download is ready, set a Success Flag and write to the log. Start the

download in the next SQL job step
- If the Test says the download is not ready, set a Failure Flag, write to the log and set up a failure through a transformation that will fail.

Write to the log that the DTS has started

This is just a SQL Task that has a connection to the EventAudit table.

```
INSERT INTO EventAudit ( DateOccurred, EventClass, PackageName, PackageStep, EventNotes)
VALUES (getdate(), 'DTS', 'ReadyToGo', 0,  'DTS Started' )
```

Test the outside data source and put the results of that test in a Global Variable

This is also a SQL Task that just has some simple SQL to test whether the download is complete. You can put in T-SQL that can test for the existence of a value, or a row count threshold, or any other criteria.

```
select   Completion Time
from     OutsideServer.OutsideTable
where    MarketValue = 'PortlandMarket'
```

What makes this SQL different is the Parameters... button **(Figure 4)**

Figure 4

Because there is only one value being returned by this SQL statement, I can map it to an Output Global Variable **(Figure 5)**

Figure 5

ActiveX Script

```
'*****************************************************************
'  Visual Basic ActiveX Script
'*****************************************************************
Function Main()
        'MsgBox "MaxCompleteTime: " & vbcrlf & FormatDateTime( DTSGlobalVariables
( "MaxCompleteTime" ).Value, VBShortDate )
        'MsgBox FormatDateTime( Date, VBShortDate)
        if  FormatDateTime( _
        DTSGlobalVariables( "MaxCompleteTime" ).Value, VBShortDate ) = _
        FormatDateTime( Date, VBShortDate) then
                ' finished process.  Is running or already ran
                '  so don't run any further
                Main = DTSTaskExecResult_Failure
                exit function
        end if
        Main = DTSTaskExecResult_Success

End Function
```

Failure through Data Transformation Mismapping

```
CREATE TABLE [dbo].[FailureDest] (
       [FailureDestID] [int] IDENTITY (1, 1) NOT NULL ,
       [FailureColumn] [datetime] NULL
) ON [PRIMARY]
```

```
CREATE TABLE [dbo].[FailureSource] (
       [FailureSourceID] [int] IDENTITY (1, 1) NOT NULL ,
       [FailureColumn] [varchar] (50) COLLATE SQL_Latin1_General_CP1_CI_AS NULL
) ON [PRIMARY]
```

One of the easiest ways for a DTS to fail is when there is a transformation from one data type to another.

To force failure, the FailureDest table was created with the important FailureColumn (tinyint) inside, so that when a character string column was transformed into it, it would fail. The Source data was FailureSource, though any table with a VARCHAR data type would work. **(Figure 6)**

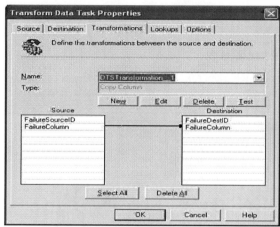

Figure 6

When the initial auto mapping happens, the Transformation screen will prevent it from happening, saying there is a data mismatch. Define the FailureDest.FailureColumn initially as a VARCHAR, do the transformation mapping and then change the definition back to TINYINT.

Cautionary Note

Once the DTS reports success and the download begins, the job will not run again until it's finished. Thereafter, it will try to run again during the next 15 minutes, or whatever interval you've set in your SQL job. You'll need to include another test and branching to determine if the job had already finished in the past to avoid running it again.

SSIS - Code Reuse and Complex Control Flows

by Kristian Wedberg

If you're anything like me, you get a queasy feeling in your stomach when you're copying a piece of code over and over again, reusing it in different places - you just *know* that it will come back and bite you, usually in the shape of an ugly, hairy beast, growling "copies not synchronized, psycho." I sure felt it breathing down my neck when setting up a benchmark recently; this article is all about how to tame that beast - here's my original starting point:

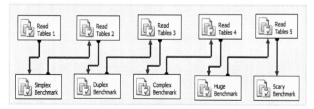

The five tasks at the bottom (*Simplex Benchmark* to *Scary Benchmark*) all produce the same end result, but do it in five different ways (I'll leave the details of *that* to another article.) The five tasks at the top though

(*Read Tables 1* to *Read Tables 5)*, they all do the exact same thing, namely reading the same two tables from start to end - their purpose is to give each benchmark a reasonably consistent initial environment.

> **Tip:** To get reliable results, I need to control not only what happens in the database and on the host *while* the benchmark is running, but also put the whole system in a consistent state *before* starting each benchmark. More on that at a later date.

Copy&paste

Let's not forget, copy&paste *is* the first level of code reuse - the fact that you can so easily select a number of components and duplicate them somewhere else in your package, or even in a *different* package, is a real timesaver, both when creating exact duplicates like in the above screenshot, and when using it as a starting point for creating new functionality.

Right now though, I can't stop glancing over my shoulders, I *really* want to get rid of all but one of those *Read Tables* tasks; it's time to *refactor* the solution by extracting the duplicated functionality, and put it in a single spot, making it easy to maintain.

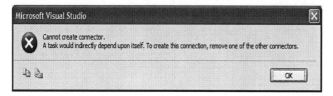

I remember that the precedence constraints between tasks in the control flow does not allow circular paths - a task can not be linked to itself, not even indirectly via another task, so that's out.

Let's check out the

Simple for loop

It's instructive to think about *for loops* and *for each loops* as not just being very useful iterators of numbers, files etc., but also as being very (common and) useful ways of reusing code:

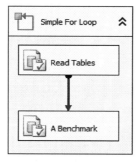

If I configure my for loop to do five iterations, I will have reused the *Read Tables* and *A Benchmark* tasks five times, just perfect! Except that in my particular case, I need five *different* benchmarks, which leads us to create a

Not so simple for loop

My for loop is configured to set the variable *Step* to {1, 2, 3, 4, 5}, in that order. This will be the clock tick that makes our construct work, changing the control flow each time.

For Loop Properties	
InitExpression	@Step = 1
EvalExpression	@Step <= 5
AssignExpression	@Step = @Step + 1

We use a single copy of *Read Tables*, and five different benchmark tasks. I've also numbered the benchmark tasks from 1 to 5 to match up with the for loop *Step* values - this visual aid makes it easier to see in which order tasks will execute, even after moving them around in the layout pane.

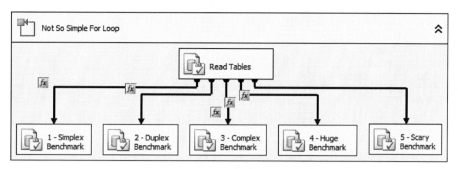

The final part is to drag the precedence constraints from *Read Tables* to each of the benchmark tasks, and then double click each link (or right click and "Edit...", or use the properties window to set the corresponding values) and configure them like this, changing the number to "1" through "5" for the five links:

When we run this, the execution order will be:

- *Read Tables*
- *1. Simplex Benchmark*
- *Read Tables*
- *2. Duplex Benchmark*
- *Read Tables*
- *3. Complex Benchmark*
- *Read Tables*
- *4. Huge Benchmark*
- *Read Tables*
- *5. Scary Benchmark*

Now this seems like a perfect fit for my problem in terms of functionality and complexity, so as long as I only need this simple sequence, this is what I'll use.

> **Tip:** In the Precedence Constraint Editor above we specified Evaluation operation = "**Expression**". This has the side effect of allowing the benchmark tasks to run *even if the* Read Tables *task fails!* An alternative is to set Evaluation operation = "**Expression and Constraint**" - this will stop the precedence from triggering unless *Read Tables* actually succeeds.
>
> **Tip:** You can only set a precedence constraint if you have a preceding task! For instance, if you needed to run *Read Tables* **after** each benchmark, you would still need a preceding task to set the constraints against - simply use a no-op as a preceding task, such as a Sequence Container with nothing in it.

But requirements change! What if I need to run three benchmark tasks in a more complex sequence? Let's investigate the

Downright complex and best avoided for loop

Can it handle this?

1. *Complex Benchmark*
2. *Duplex Benchmark*
3. *Simplex Benchmark* **in parallel with** *Duplex Benchmark*

4. *Simplex Benchmark* **in parallel with** *Complex Benchmark*
5. *Duplex Benchmark* **in parallel with** *Complex Benchmark*
6. *Complex Benchmark*
7. *Duplex Benchmark*

Here we have both repeating sequences of tasks, and tasks that sometimes run sequentially, and sometimes in parallel.

One way to do this is to start with the *Not so simple for loop*, and add more complex precedence expressions:

- We have seven steps, so make the loop variable *Step* go from 1 to 7
- For every benchmark, check which steps it should run in, i.e. *Complex Benchmark* runs in step 1, 4, 5, 6
- For every benchmark, set the precedence expression to evaluate to true for the identified steps, i.e. "@Step==1 || @Step>=4 || @Step<=6"

Are we having fun yet??? Depending on your answer, feel free to impress me greatly (and get weird looks from your spouse I bet) by having that table driven <u>Finite State Machine</u> on my desk by Monday, 9am sharp! To implement it though, instead of *Downright complex...* I suggest you use the

Getting silly for loop

In the previous *Downright complex...* for loop we had our control logic spread out across many precedence expressions. That's much too easy to get wrong, so let's *refactor* again. Now we have centralized all the logic in the single script called *Logic,* where we can configure arbitrary control flows:

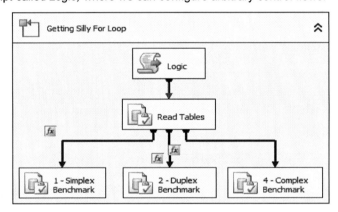

To handle the <u>complex sequence</u>, construct it thusly:

1. Configure the for loop to iterate *Step* from 1 to 7, corresponding to our seven steps in the sequence. Also add an integer variable *BitMask* to the for loop.
2. Name the benchmark tasks as 1, 2, 4 (continuing with 8, 16, 32, 64 etc. for any additional tasks)
3. Add code to the *Logic* script to set the bits in *BitMask* according to which step in the sequence is executing - a set bit means the corresponding benchmark task will execute in the current step:

```
Enum Bits
   SimplexBenchmark = 1
   DuplexBenchmark = 2
   ComplexBenchmark = 4
End Enum
Select Case CType(Dts.Variables("Step").Value, Integer)
  Case 1
    Dts.Variables("BitMask").Value = Bits.ComplexBenchmark
  Case 2
    Dts.Variables("BitMask").Value = Bits.DuplexBenchmark
  Case 3
    Dts.Variables("BitMask").Value = Bits.SimplexBenchmark + Bits.DuplexBenchmark
  Case 4
    Dts.Variables("BitMask").Value = Bits.SimplexBenchmark + Bits.ComplexBenchmark
  Case 5
    Dts.Variables("BitMask").Value = Bits.DuplexBenchmark + Bits.ComplexBenchmark
```

```
      Case 6
        Dts.Variables("BitMask").Value = Bits.ComplexBenchmark
      Case 7
        Dts.Variables("BitMask").Value = Bits.DuplexBenchmark
    End Select
```

4. Set the precedence expressions for the three benchmark tasks to trigger when their corresponding bit in *BitMask* is set:
    *   (@BitMask & 1) != 0
    *   (@BitMask & 2) != 0
    *   (@BitMask & 4) != 0

> **Tip:** Remember that we can have other tasks and containers running in parallel with our for loop - they can signal external events to our *Logic* script via variables for instance. Just don't go overboard with this unless it really is for a good cause...
>
> **Tip:** Instead of using the for loop AssignExpression to change *Step*, you might want to use the *Logic* script to update it - that's especially useful when you want to 'jump around' in the sequence, say "Go from step 5 to step 2 if today is Saturday or Sunday", and when the sequence should 'run forever'.

No downloadable package today, I've left that as an exercise to you the reader (I *really* hate it when writers use cop outs like that. Which is exactly why I *did* say that, just now. Don't get mad, get even.-)

All in all, it *is* a bit silly, but in an irresistible kind of way - just like my <u>wife</u> actually, and we had Love At First Sight! So don't be surprised if this thingumajig pops up again.

Stop, I'm gagging!

I'll give that poor loop a rest for a while. As a heads up though, here are some more ways to implement reuse:

*   Using the loop counter to effect different behavior *inside* a task
*   Putting SQL code in variables and external files
*   Calling child packages
*   Using event handlers
*   Writing .NET assemblies
*   Creating custom components

These are all pretty hefty subjects in their own right; we'll save them for another day.

Ergo sum

*   Precedence constraints can not have circular paths
*   For loops are very useful for implementing reuse as well as for implementing simple and complex control flows
*   Understand the various ways of doing reuse - which technique and what level of complexity is appropriate in your case, taking the foreseeable future of your implementation into account?
*   The *Getting silly for loop* is one way to implement Finite State Machines in SSIS

There is truly an enormous amount of functionality packed inside Integration Services, to the extent that it feels more like a 2.7 version than the 1.0 it really is. As we've seen, there are many ways to accomplish code reuse, which is lucky indeed, 'cause as you know, I *sure* don't like the sound of that growling beast...

Handling Zero Byte Files in DTS

By James Greaves

Zero byte file handling in DTS

This article outlines how to handle the possibility of a zero byte file of any format that your DTS package most likely relies upon for import for a data pump task. Furthermore, when a zero byte file is encountered, an option to bypass or stop the DTS step/package is possible as well as sending an e-mail via CDO as I will illustrate in my example.

The first step is to setup your source and destination data with a data transformation between them. Right click on the data transformation and you will see the menu in Figure 1.

Figure 1: Workflow Properties transformation dialog

Choose the "**Workflow Properties**" option and the dialog box in Figure 2 will appear on the precedence tab by default. Click on the "options" tab and bring up the dialog box as seen in Figure 2 below.

Figure 2: Workflow Properties Options tab

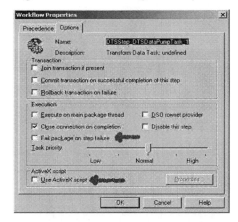

If you wish the package to fail on the step in the event of a zero byte file, click the checkbox "**Fail package on step failure**". If you only desire for the DTS package to bypass the file import if a zero byte file is encountered, leave this checkbox blank and enable "*Option 1*" in the VB script below that will be used to handle the detailed transformation property.

Check the "**Use ActiveX script**" checkbox and then click the "**Properties**" button to open a VBScript window to insert the code that will handle the zero byte file:

```
'**********************************************************************
' Visual Basic ActiveX Script
'**********************************************************************

Function Main()

Dim oFSO
Dim oFile
Dim FileNm
' File you are verifying. Using UNC path name if SQL Agent has domain privileges on share
FileNm = <File Name here> 'A global variable could be used here as well
```

```
Set oFSO =    CreateObject("Scripting.FileSystemObject")
Set oFile = oFSO.GetFile(FileNm)
'  If then statement to check import file. If it is zero bytes and send e-mail using CDO
' notifying of zero byte file and either bypass or fail the     DTS package
If oFile.Size = 0 Then
'Code for sending e-mail to the desired recipient using CDO
Dim objMail
Set objMail = CreateObject("CDO.Message")
objMail.From = <insert e-mail address here>
objMail.To = <insert e-mail address here>
objMail.Subject= <insert subject here>
objMail.TextBody = <insert body text here>
objMail.Send
Set objMail = nothing
'Option1: (Disabled below with comment tick.) Choosing this option will stop the data import
' from taking place but your DTS task will continue
'Main = DTSStepScriptResult_DontExecuteTask
'Option 2: (Enabled below) Choosing this option will fail the DTS package if the "Fail Package
' on Step Failure" is turned on in the package properties
Main = DTSTaskExecResult_Failure
Else
        Main = DTSStepScriptResult_ExecuteTask
End If
Set oFile = Nothing
Set oFSO = Nothing
End Function
```

Conclusions

Once the VB script is in place for the transformation, I suggest making a zero byte file with and testing the transformation by right clicking and choosing "Execute step" within the DTS package. Keep in mind that how you wish to handle zero byte files can be done inside the IF/THEN statement as you wish. I used the CDO mail as an example so I could illustrate how I use it in my work environment. Further modifications of this process could include the use of global variables for the file name and e-mail parameters.

Clustering Reporting Services

By Zach Mattson and Tom Lodermeier

Introduction

Installing SQL Reporting Services on a single machine is a relatively easy task. There are several excellent articles that take you step-by-step through the process of installing Reporting Services on a single machine. However, what happens when that reporting server picks a work day to call in sick? Will you be there to setup a new machine and get your reports up and running? This is the reason that Microsoft has provided us with a failover cluster.

Setting up RS to handle failure is a bit more complicated than a single machine install. The generally accepted and documented method for handling failure is to utilize a load balanced web farm to house the reporting service (IIS and ASP.NET) and keep the reporting databases on a failover cluster. The beauty of the generally accepted solution is that you have to buy additional SQL licenses for your web farm servers (it's beautiful if you are a Microsoft stockholder). Note: Microsoft licensing can be complex, the reporting services licensing is explained here. Given our division's tightening budget, and our desire to forge new frontiers in undocumented processes, we wanted to install the reporting services (IIS, ASP.NET) and the databases on the same cluster. I don't recommend this approach if you are using URL access to your reports from the internet, as your database could be exposed. We are using SOAP to get our reports in PDF format to our application server so the cluster is protected from the outside world.

Tools and Setup

- SQL Server 2000 SP4
- Windows 2003 Server
- SQL Reporting Services 2000
- Windows 2003 Enterprise Cluster
- SAN space for the cluster

- MSDTS service must be started
- MDAC 2.8 SP2 (installed with Windows 2003 SP1)
- IIS with ASP.NET (for the reporting service)
- .Net Framework 1.1 (installed with Windows 2003 SP1)

The Install

Installation procedures for the cluster are well documented. Essentially you install the OS on the active and passive nodes; then setup the cluster administrator on the virtual server. After this has been completed, install SQL Server and get your database files setup on the SAN. Once your SQL Server has been installed, go to the active node and start up the Reporting Services installation executable. The installation is straightforward on the active node. Be sure to put the databases on your clustered SQL Server and files on the SAN drive.

Note: For clarity, the "active node" is the first node you install on the cluster, the subsequent node, is referred to as the "passive node". Typically, in a clustered environment, the node that is handling the work is the active node, and the node standing by is the passive node.

To install the passive node's reporting service, first fail the cluster (simply rebooting the active node will initiate the failover by the cluster) so the passive node becomes the active node (thus allowing the node to see the SQL Server and SAN drives). The passive node's installation is pretty much the same as the active node. The caveat is upon pointing the reporting databases to the clustered SQL Server, the Web Farm Setup screen appears (figure 1 below). The key to making this installation successful is entering the active node's machine name (the first node you installed in the cluster) where it says Report Server. The reason why you need the name of the active node is due to the encryption of the DSN name in the RSReportServer.config and the matching key that resides in the ReportServer database. By giving the active node's name, the passive node can recognize the reporting databases located on the clustered SQL Server. The rest of the installation is normal.

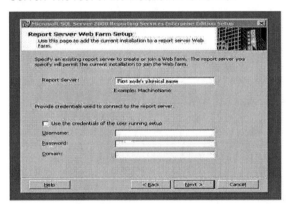

Figure 1

Conclusions

The benefits of this installation are that you have failover built into your reporting solution and do not have to incur the costs of additional licenses setup in the web farm method. In our tests, the failover only took about 15 seconds to bring up the passive node and start serving reports. It sure beats hurrying an installation of Reporting Services under heavy pressure from management and users!

There are a few downfalls of our method. First, you won't see the performance or scalability of a load balanced web farm. Second, the time delay that it takes for the failover to switch will also not exist in a web farm solution and finally, your database cluster will have additional workload serving the reports so database performance could decrease.

The failover cluster all-in-one solution may be just the ticket for the small to mid-size shops that have a reasonable number of reports and users.

Happy "no failure" Reporting!

Upgrading SQL Server 2000 DTS Packages to SSIS

By Brian Knight

If you're like me and most companies, you probably have dozens if not hundreds of SQL Server 2000 DTS packages in you SQL Server environment. The idea of upgrading those packages to SQL Server 2005 SSIS can be daunting. The packages probably drive production loads and you've spent years stabilizing them and don't want that 4AM call. This article shows you your options for upgrading the packages automatically and what components won't be upgraded.

The Server and Workstation Upgrade

After you upgrade your SQL Server to SQL Server 2005, the packages carry over in place and are not upgraded as part of the process. All of your production jobs that call the packages are also carried over without change. Without touching the packages, you can continue to run the 2000 packages since the DTS runtime environment comes over. You'll be able to find your 2000 packages in the Microsoft SQL Server Management Studio under the Management node then Legacy -> Data Transformation Services. The problem is going to be that you'll need to install the SQL Server 2005 Feature Pack (specifically, the Package Designer for 2000) to modify the package after the upgrade. This was not installed by default to give you a smaller surface area in your install. After you upgrade the last node on your SQL Server, the SQL Server 2000 tools are completely removed.

Note: *Support for the Metadata Repository has been removed in SQL Server 2005 so those packages will not come over. You will need to save those packages into a different storage area like MSDB or the file structure before upgrading your instance.*

You can also use the SQL Server 2005 tools to connect to SQL Server 2000 databases to manage the server and packages. I've been using the 2005 tools since an early CTP to manage my entire SQL Server 2000 environment and have encountered very few issues even in beta. The problem will lie in if you chose not to upgrade your tools. You cannot manage or design against a SQL Server 2005 environment with the 2000 tools. In other words, the 2000 tools aren't forward compatible as in past releases of SQL Server.

Package Upgrade Options

The first step that I would recommend in your upgrade path is to run the SQL Server 2005 Upgrade Advisor. The Upgrade Advisor will report also against DTS packages. It will give you warnings and errors and identify specific packages that will cause you grief in the upgrade.

In SQL Server 2005 SSIS packages, you have a new task called Execute SQL Server 2000 Package task. Another way to inch into an upgrade is to create a SQL Server 2005 SSIS package with a single Execute SQL Server 2000 Package task that executes the old package until you can execute have time to upgrade each component. The task has the option to embed the 2000 package into the task itself so as you move the SSIS package, the DTS package comes with it. This tactic will be used later by the Upgrade Wizard for complex logic.

The best way to upgrade your packages is with the Package Upgrade Wizard. The wizard will leave the old package and calling jobs in place but clone the package with no job. The wizard isn't perfect though. It was developed to perfectly upgrade simple workflow and transforms written with the Import/Export Wizard or similar logic. If you have customized transforms like one that does a upper case transform, it will not be ported over exactly as is. If you have any complex transforms or tasks, a small 2000 DTS package that contains that step will be created and a Execute SQL Server 2000 Package task will be created to call that package. The package will be embedded in the task and you can modify the 2000 package by clicking Design Package inside that task (it won't show up in your legacy packages node). Using the wizard, I was able to upgrade about 75% of the packages (with simple logic) and 10% upgraded with issues like I just mentioned and the remainder had to have manual intervention.

There are some components that will not be compatible with SQL Server 2005. Just because they're not compatible though, doesn't mean there's not an upgrade path. The areas of special consideraExecute SQL Server 2000 Package tasktion are:

- **Dynamic Properties task** has no 2005 task to port to. A placeholder Script Task will upgrade over but will not have any functionality. Your package will not work as expected until you upgrade the logic using the new Package Configuration option or expressions.
- **Analysis Services tasks** are wrapped in a Execute 2000 Package task.
- **ActiveX Script tasks** that take extensive use of the DTS object model will not be supported. For example, if you used the model to call other packages or loop, this will not port. You will want to implement some of the built-in controls for this like the For Each Loop container.
- **Global Variables** are ported to package variables with no issues.
- **Data Driven Query tasks** are not supported. The upgrade wizard will use a sub-2000 package to make this work.
- **Any custom task** will be wrapped in a subtask as well.

It's important to note that long term support of SQL Server 2000 DTS is not in the cards. You need to spend this release of SQL Server 2005 getting off of DTS because I can't imagine support of DTS existing in the next release (code named Avalon). I hope some useful information to get you start down the path to upgrading your DTS packages to SSIS.

My New Book

In January, my new book comes out on SQL Server 2005 Integration Services from Wrox. You can pre-order it today on http://www.wiley.com or go to Amazon to get the better price :). This book will help you get past the initial learning curve quickly so that you can get started using SSIS to transform data, create a workflow, or maintain your SQL Server. Offering you hands-on guidance, you'll learn a new world of integration possibilities and be able to move away from scripting complex logic to programming tasks using a full-featured language.

What you will learn from this book

- Ways to quickly move and transform data
- How to configure every aspect of SSIS
- How to interface SSIS with web services and XML
- Techniques to scale the SSIS and make it more reliable
- How to migrate DTS packages to SSIS
- How to create your own custom tasks and user interfaces
- How to create an application that interfaces with SSIS to manage the environment
- A detailed usable case study for a complete ETL solution

Reporting Services 2005

By Anubhav Bansal

Introduction

With the launch of the SQL Server 2005, working with reporting services has been simplified to some extent. Thanks to, Business Intelligence Studio (BI). BI Studio once installed with the SQL Server 2005 offers an interface similar to VS 2005.Net.

Assuming the user or developer has created a team reports using VSTS or BI Studio, he might want to carry out modifications in the reports (often referred to Team Reports).

There are two ways in which you can modify the Team Reports(.rdl). We will explain both the mechanisms one at a time as stated below:

1. Using the Business Intelligence Studio.
2. Using the Report site

In this article I'll outline the procedure to modify the team reports using first method i.e. using BI Studio. My next article would walk through the second method.

Assuming the you are having VSTS or VS.Net 2005 installed on team system along with SQL Server 2005.

Modify Reports using Business Intelligence Studio

1. Open the existing report project with the VSTS IDE.

2. Open the report (.rdl file) that you want to modify by clicking on the report name in the solution explorer. You will notice that there are three tabs in the designer.

Data -> Used to create or modify existing query.

Preview -> View the report that is generated.

Layout -> Change the appearance of the cells and to modify the columns.

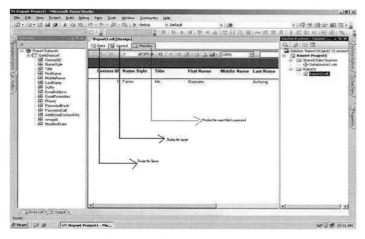

3. Go to the Data Tab. You will notice the data query open up in the designer. Uncheck or check the columns that you do not want to show in the report anymore. I have unchecked first 2 columns for demo. Once you have done this, do execute the query so that changes are reflected. However, if you go to preview tab after this, you will get that report1 is invalid. SO before going to "Preview", Tab, click open the "Layout" Tab

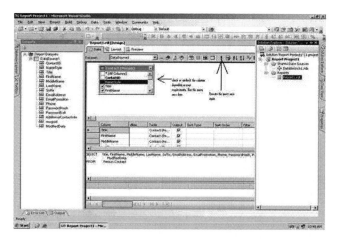

4. Click on the "Layout" Tab. Right click on the column that you wish to remove from the report as shown below and click "Delete Columns" from the context menu. In case, you added columns in your previous operation on the Data Ta, then you will be required to add the columns using "Insert Columns"

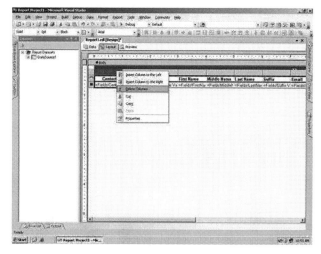

To insert columns back to the report, first include that column in the query on the Data Tab. Changes won't be reflected on the Layout Tab directly. In order to add the column to the table, right click on the existing table in the layout and click Insert Columns. Drag and drop the columns from the dataset at the required position.

You can as well modify the properties by right-clicking on the control (cells, table, etc) and selecting the properties.

5. Now click on the preview the tab. Changes will be reflected in the report that is generated.

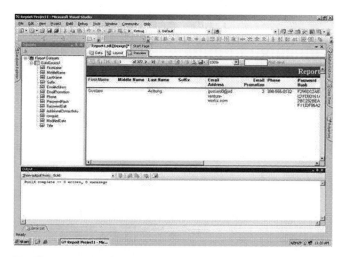

To Modify the reports in VSTS in case the BI Studio in not available on the machine having VSTS

In this case we have the three different layers -> App Tier/ Business Layer/Data Layer.

Data Layer has the SQL Server 2005 running. From the app tier follow the following instructions:-

1. Make sure the SQL Server 2005 in data tier is up and running
2. Open the internet explorer. Type in the url where the reports reside on the data tier. For demo purpose we used :- http://tfsjdata/reports/

You will be re-directed to http://tfsjdata/Reports/Pages/Folder.aspx Similarly, for your case, replace the tfsjdata with the address of your server where SQL Server 2005 with BIS is there. **"This is what I meant by report site"**

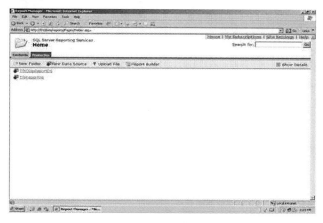

3. On the site you'll have a few templates. Click on the TfsReportsDS. You will find tabs at the top as shown -> Contents/ Properties/Reports.

Click on reports or contents which ever is shown in the tabs. It will list down all the existing reports.

4. Click open one of the reports say→Bug List and bring up the properties. By default, you will have the focus on views. Click on the "properties" Tab.

5. Click on General and there will be two links under Report Definition -> Edit and Update

6. Click on Edit and save the file on the system (i.e. app tier)

7. Then, open the file in the VSTS or note pad and make some changes and save them.

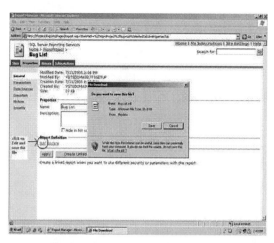

8. Go back to report definition and click on Update as indicated by the arrow in the fugure below.

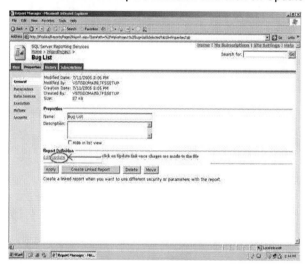

9. Browse to the updated file and Press OK.

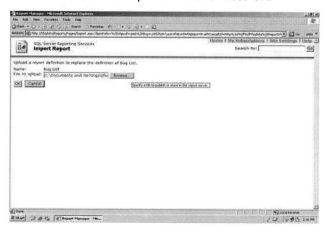

It is likely possible when you add a report to a report project and navigate to the Data Tab, you get a "Connection error – Cannot connect to database. Set and correct the connection settings". To resolve this, please follow the following steps:-

To resolve the same, please follow the following steps:-

1. Once you have added the **Bug List.rdl** to your project, navigate to the Data Tab. You will be prompted for the error as shown above. Once you get this error, click Ok button. Then you need to edit the data set settings. For this, click on the **button ->** next to combo box as depicted in the figure below.

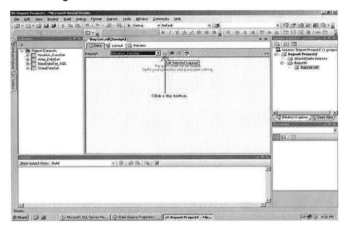

2. Once the Data Set Wizard opens up, click on the Edit button to edit the Data source as indicated by the arrow **(1)**. Then the Data Source wizard would open up.

Once this happen, uncheck the checkbox encircled by blue **(2).** This would enable to edit the connection string

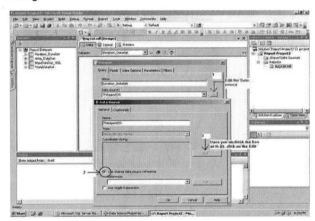

3. Once the Edit button gets enabled click on it the button **(3)** as in above figure. Specify the server name where reports reside in the database server. For this, you can connect to the reporting server in the SQL Server Management Studio and check for the connection string properties of the Data Source. This will tell you the database name that you need to connect to.

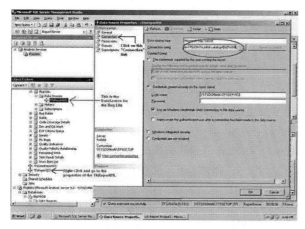

4. Use this connection string to get the Initial Catalog and Data Source. These would be the parameters that would be entered in the connection properties as shown below.

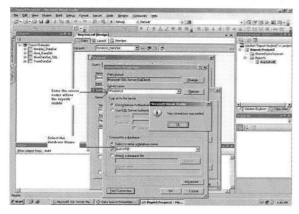

5. Test Connection succeeds. Click **Ok**. On th e Data Source Window, Click Ok once again. And finally on the Data Set window, click **Ok** for the final time. You will be rendered with Data Tab in expected manner with Queries. You can navigate to "Preview" to verify the effects.

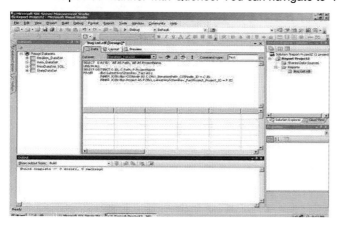

DTS and Global Variables

By Alex Kersha

Summary

I've seen several different articles devoted to using global variables within DTS packages throughout the various SQL Server communities and knowledge bases. What I've never seen is a complete step by step implementation using SQL job, DTS package and some worthwhile utility tied to the process. Here I'll try show you how I've implemented a solution to purge files from my production environment based on a certain number of backup files in a target folder.

Background

The issue many DBAs run into is how to control the amount of data preserved in the local file system of a production server. At **PeopleBusinessNetwork** we have a process that fits each client's data load and open maintenance windows. The most difficult part of the process is figuring out just what type of scenario to use. Do you purge backups based on date in relation to the current day or by the number of the files you currently have in a folder, choosing to keep the most recent X files?

If the scheduling of your data loads is consistent, say every day at 8:00pm, then you're in luck and you can go by date deleting the files say after 14 days or whatever is best for the client, you and the space on your server.   If however you skip weekends or the loads only happen every few days, or even once a month then your purge by date is no longer valid. To resolve this we've decided to come up with a scheme to purge files based on the number of backups that exist in a certain folder. There are various utilities available on the web for this purpose such as *ForFiles.exe* that require install and DLL registration. I specifically wanted to avoid this as well as installing the .Net framework on a production server running SQL 2000 to enable some .Net tool for the job. Keeping the simple things simple, it's pure SQL 2000 job, DTS package and some good ole Vbscript (I know, this is an arguable point).

Requirements

1. SQL job to call DTS package
2. DTS package with global variables defined
3. ActiveX script task to purge files based on number existing in target folder(s)

Implementation

I started with the DTS package and set it up with the thought that it would be called by a scheduled SQL job and that I would want to be able to reuse the same package for every type of file in a target folder. Also, I wanted to be able to update the number of files to keep variable depending on the client it was used for.

The DTS package itself is super simple. It has only 1 ActiveX script task defined in it. No need for connections, Dynamic properties tasks or anything else. We've taken care of everything with the VBScript itself. We have a policy of documenting our DTS packages within the package itself using the annotation tool. Here's a view of the package:

Step by Step (DTS)

1. Open Enterprise Manager
2. Expand the SQL Server Group, local server, Data Transformation Services node
3. Right click on [Local Packages] and choose the New Package menu item.

4. Drag the ActiveX script task icon to the white space of your package (see above)
5. Enter a short description in the field at the top of the scripting window
6. Write your script (I've included my listing at the end of this article)
7. Save your package as type SQL Server or a Structured Storage File depending on how you intend to access the package later. For the purpose of this article, we'll be saving as SQL Server type which makes an entry into the sysdtspackages system table (among others).

Preparing for Global Variables

Now that you have a package saved on your server, we need to make sure that it's ready to accept the global variables that your SQL job will be passing to it.

1. With the package still open, right click on the white space and choose [Package Properties]
2. Click on the [Global Variables] tab
3. Enter the name of each of the global variables that will be passed by your SQL job. My suggestion is to check off "Explicit Global Variables", which forces you to declare each of the variables that will be used. This works very much the same way as the Option Explicit syntax in VBScript.
4. Be careful to specify what each of the variable types are. DO NOT depend on any conversion to take place here.
5. If you're using integers, there must be an integer value placed in the [Value] column. We use 0 for a default.
6. Click [OK] and save and close the package

The SQL job

Now we're ready to create a job to call the package we created and pass to it the variables we need to purge the files.

1. Open the Management, SQL Server Agent node
2. Right click on [Jobs] and choose New Job
3. Define a short, meaningful name for your job
4. Fill out a short description and choose a category for your job. "Database Maintenance" might fit this specific example.
5. Be careful with the owner drop down. For purposes of this example use a local or Domain admin account with rights to the databases or just use "sa" which I would normally tell you is not best practice unless you ABSOLUTELY need to. Security and login rights are beyond the scope of this document.
6. An example of how I filled out the above information is below:

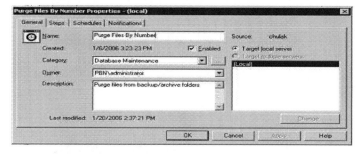

1. Now click on the [Steps] tab
2. Choose [New Step] from the buttons at bottom
3. Fill in a meaningful name for your step
4. Choose [Operating System Command] from the [TYPE] drop down
5. Fill in the command to call your package
6. An example of the step window and the command I'm using is below with an explanation of it's syntax.
7. Click [OK] and then [OK] again to save and close your job. I won't go into the [Advanced] tab as it is beyond the scope of this article and unnecessary for our example.

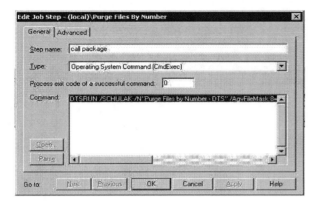

Example Command:

```
DTSRUN /SServerName /N"Purge Files by Number -DTS" /AgvFileMask:8=".bak"
       /AgvFolderPath:8="C:\temp"
               /AgvLogPath:8="C:\Temp\DTSPurgeLog_Number.log" /AgvNumber:3=4 /E
```

The Job Step Syntax

The switches:

1. /S = Server name, can be WINS name or IP Address
2. /N = Package name, put it in double quotes if there are any special chars or spaces
3. /A = global variable, you'll see all the variables we defined in this statement
4. the ":8" denotes a string being passed
5. the ":3" denotes an integer
6. /E = trusted login, this can be replaced with /U and /P for username and Password if you prefer. We have a policy of not putting any security or login information out in plain view.

As you may have already guessed, this command could be easily run from a command line. DTSRUN is an executable available to a "COMMAND" window and will also show the output of the DTS package including any errors. This is very cool and a quick way to keep running a package without needing to open an instance of Enterprise Manager or Query Analyzer.

Getting it Done

Ok, so now we have a DTS package all setup and global variables defined. We also have a SQL job defined passing our globals along. Now we just need a VBScript to fill in the task we dragged to the DTS Designer window. I've included the full listing below complete with comments. In a nutshell, the script does the following:

1. Gets the globals from the SQL job
2. Opens the target folder (gvFolderPath)
3. Creates a collection of all the files there
4. Finds each of the ".bak" files and fills an array with the file objects (gvFileMask)
5. Using a bubble sort, reorders the files most recent on top
6. Deletes all the files in the array (and therefore the folder) except the most recent X number of files (in this case 4). (gvNumber)
7. Logs the variables passed and the files deleted to a text file on the server. (gvLogPath)

This process has been tested over several iterations and works beautifully. I would highly recommend testing on a Development server before letting this loose in Production. The entire process takes about 20 minutes plus testing time to complete. My speciality is not VBScript but I can get things done so if you find a better way to do this, please let us all know. From my experience writing this, I would strongly encourage you to use the Option Explicit syntax at the top of your script to force you to declare all variables. Though a pain at first, it may help save you hours of mindless DEBUG time finding a rogue variable being used or other such errors.

Conclusion

DTS is a very powerful tool in SQL Server. If used to its fullest extent it can easily take the place of some of the more mundane tasks now running under the auspices of windows based scripts on your servers. Using global variables DTS can be extended to do a variety of tasks flexibly and efficiently.

Special thanks to Paul Downing, Engineer, **PeopleBusinessNetwork for his help with the bubble sort in the VBScript used.

Code available for download

DTS Standards

By Jonathan Stokes

If a person familiar with DTS were to go out into the world and audit a sample of DTS packages present in various organisations, I am guessing that half of them would not make any sense other than to the person who created them. Moreover, I doubt many of these will have any consistency and fluctuate in design from package to package, even within the same organisation. The fact that DTS packages are fundamental building blocks to many processes imply that they should be controlled as tightly as any other tool and be subject to the same level of QA.

The purpose of this article is to take a look at what I class as good practice and the attempts I employ to achieve a homogeneous structure. This is, however, not intended to be a definitive guide. The quintessential element here is the need to address these issues and achieve some level of uniformity.

Specifically broken down into the following areas in no particular order of precedence:

a) Layout and presentation

b) Exposing hidden objects

c) Error handling

d) Naming Conventions

Anyone familiar with DTS will have seen the classic package created with the minimum amount of effort, in the minimum amount of time. I'm talking about this sample below:

Microsoft Excel 97...   Microsoft OLE DB ...

Although this example will work if the transform data task is set up correctly, the design is no help to anyone. By allowing DTS to apply the default naming conventions, all the packages will look the same and those with multiple connections will become confusing and prone to error. In this example, all we can tell is that an excel file is being imported into a table in a database. To find out more information, we would have to open both connections and then look at the transformation task.

A better representation of the diagram

srcProdCode   dstProdTable

This diagram is much easier to interpret. Note that the prefix of 'src' is added for source and 'dst' for destination. I apply these naming conventions to establish some uniformity. I do not prefix with the object type nor explain the transform data task as the pictures themselves are a giveaway – After all, I'm writing a package here, not an essay. The only downside here is that there is a limit to the amount of text you can add before it adds those annoying dots at the end. Hence, keep names short.

The next area to deal with is the error handling. It is easy enough to apply logging to a server or a file, but to receive an immediate success/failure message and know exactly how far the package has got, it is a good idea to put some separate failure steps in. We want to import the source spreadsheet before we DTS it in, just in case a user has it open and causes the package to fail.

Success should flow to the right and failure to the left, making it easier to follow the paths. This is not always possible for a package with high volumes of connections, but sticking as close to this method as humanly possible is recommended.

Adding another connection to output to a spreadsheet and then applying an activex script to format that spreadsheet has the effect of making the package harder to follow.

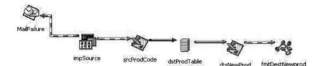

I recommend at this point to start adding some text to the diagram. However, placing help text in and around the objects can also decrease readability. The best place for the text is at the top of the package.

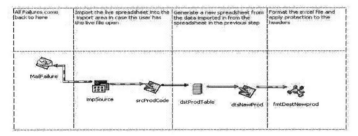

I break the steps into blocks that make the logic easy to follow. If someone who knew nothing about DTS viewed this package, they would have a good idea as to what the package is setting out to accomplish. It is far easier to give a diagram to a user than talk them through a process sans visual aids.

It is worth remembering that not all components of the package are displayed in the diagram. I'm talking specifically about global variables. It's quite easy to miss these when trying to debug packages authored by others. Adding a global variable to supply a filename is noticeable through the Dynamic Properties Task, but again it is needs to be opened and viewed to get an idea of what's going on behind the scenes. Much easier if it is part of the diagram.

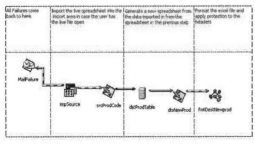

This is the finished product. I am sure you will agree that this package is clear, concise and can be familiarised faster if revisited in months or years time.

As stated in the opening to this article, I would not promote this as being the 'de facto' way of creating packages. The paramount objective in creating packages is to keep them easy to follow, which in turn will make them easier to maintain. Like any pieces of code, you need standards and naming conventions and DTS should be no different.

Overview of DTS Packages

By Rama Nageshwara

Many organizations need to centralize data to improve corporate decision-making. However, their data may be stored in a variety of formats and in different locations. Data Transformation Services (DTS) addresses this vital business need by providing a set of tools that lets you extract, transform, and consolidate data from disparate sources into single or multiple destinations supported by DTS connectivity. By using DTS tools to graphically build DTS packages or by programming a package with the DTS object model, you can create custom data movement solutions tailored to the specialized business needs of your organization.

DTS Basics

Data Transformation Services (DTS) provides a set of tools that lets you extract, transform, and consolidate data from disparate sources into single or multiple destinations. You create a DTS solution as one or more *packages*. Each package may contain an organized set of tasks that define work to be performed, transformations on data and objects, workflow constraints that define task execution, and connections to data sources and destinations. DTS packages also provide services, such as logging package execution details, controlling transactions, and handling global variables.

DTS supplies a number of tasks that are part of the DTS object model that can be accessed graphically, through DTS Designer, or programmatically. These tasks, which can be configured individually, cover a wide variety of data copying, data transformation, and notification situations. For example:

- **Importing and exporting data**
  DTS can import data from a text file or an OLE DB data source (for example, a Microsoft Access 2000 database) into SQL Server. Alternatively, data can be exported from SQL Server to an OLE DB data destination (for example, a Microsoft Excel 2000 spreadsheet). DTS also allows high-speed data loading from text files into SQL Server tables.
- **Transforming data**
  DTS Designer includes a Transform Data task that allows you to select data from a data source connection, map the columns of data to a set of transformations, and send the transformed data to a destination connection. DTS Designer also includes a Data Driven Query task that allows you to map data to parameterized queries.
- **Copying database objects**
  With DTS, you can transfer indexes, views, logins, stored procedures, triggers, rules, defaults, constraints, and user-defined data types in addition to the data. In addition, you can generate the scripts to copy the database objects.
- **Sending and receiving messages to and from other users and packages**
  DTS includes a Send Mail task that allows you to send an e-mail if a package step succeeds or fails. DTS also includes an Execute Package task that allows one package to run another as a package step, and a Message Queue task that allows you to use Message Queuing to send and receive messages between packages.
- **Executing a set of Transact-SQL statements or Microsoft ActiveX® scripts against a data source**
  The Execute SQL and ActiveX Script tasks allow you to write your own SQL statements and scripting code and execute them as a step in a package workflow.

Using DTS Designer

The DTS Designer interface consists of a work area for building packages, toolbars containing package elements that you can drag onto the design sheet, and menus containing workflows and package management commands.

Connections: Accessing and Moving Data

To successfully execute DTS tasks that copy and transform data, a DTS package must establish valid connection(s) to its source and destination data and to any additional data sources, such as lookup tables. When creating a package, you can configure connections by selecting a connection type from a list of available OLE DB providers and ODBC drivers. Table 1 shows the connection details.

Table 1: Connections

	Connection	Description
	Microsoft OLE DB Provider for SQL Server	

Tasks: Defining Steps in a Package

A DTS package usually includes one or more tasks. Each task defines a work item that may be performed during package execution. Table 2 shows some of the tasks generally used.

Table 2: Tasks generally used

	Task	Description
	Transform Data task	Use to move data between a source and destination and to optionally apply column-level transformations to the data.
	ActiveX Script task	Use to write code to perform functions that are not available in the other DTS tasks.
	Send Mail task	Use to send an e-mail message.

Workflows: Setting Task Precedence

When you define a group of tasks, there is usually an order in which the tasks should be performed. When tasks have an order, each task becomes a step of a process. In DTS Designer, you manipulate tasks on the DTS Designer design sheet and use precedence constraints to control the sequence in which the tasks execute. Table 3 shows the workflow precedence and description.

Table 3: Workflow Precedence

Precedence constraint	Description
On Completion (blue arrow)	If you want Task 2 to wait until Task 1 completes, regardless of the outcome, link Task 1 to Task 2 with "On Completion" precedence constraint.
On Success (green arrow)	If you want Task 2 to wait until Task 1 has successfully completed, link Task 1 to Task 2 with "On Success" precedence constraint.
On Failure (red arrow)	If you want Task 2 to begin execution only if Task 1 fails to execute, link Task 1 to Task 2 with an "On Failure" precedence constraint.

Scenario

Assume that you want to transfer data from one table to another table using some parameters (here date is considered as a parameter). One can pass the date values to the query by declaring "Global Variables". Before transferring the data we can check the date values using ActiveX Script. After the data transfer is complete we can send a mail to a person to convey the status of the task as "Success" or "Failure".

Creating a Connection object

To establish a connection, click on "Microsoft OLE DB Provider for SQL Server" from Connection tab. Here you can mention the connection details of the database server. For source and destination database servers you need to create two connection objects. Figure 1 illustrates the steps.

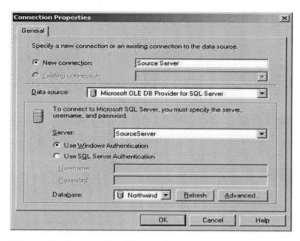

Figure 1: Connection Properties

Creating Global Variables

To pass the variable(s) to a query we need to create global variable(s). These variable(s) can also be used in ActiveX Script also. To create a global variable right click on the DTS Package and select "Package Properties" and select "Global Variables" tab. Click on the "New" button to create a new global variable. Note that global variables won't reset the values to the null after execution of the package i.e., it contains the values before execution of the package. In our scenario we create two global variables: "FromDate" and "ToDate".

Creating ActiveX Script

You can write your own ActiveX Script in VB language. You can run these scripts before or after the required tasks. Here the script is used to validate the date stored in global variables. If the date given in global variables are correct then those dates are considered, if those dates are not in valid format then for FromDate we will consider yesterday's date and for ToDate we will consider today's date. Figure 2 shows the ActiveX Script for this scenario.

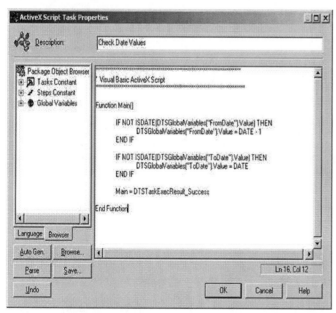

Figure 2: ActiveX Script

Creating a Transform Data Task

You use the Transform Data task to copy data between a source and destination and to optionally apply column-level transformations to the data. The Transform Data task is the most basic implementation of the data pump engine in Data Transformation Services (DTS). Click on "Transform Data Task" from Task tab. Using this task we can mention the table from which the data needs to be transferred or we can go for "SQL Query". In this scenario we will use "SQL Query".

We can configure the properties associated with this task by right-clicking on the relevant Transform Data Task and selecting properties. To log an error select "Options" tab from the "Transform Data Task Properties" and enter the exception file name.

Figure 3 shows the SQL query used in "Transform Data Task Properties".

Figure 3: Transform Data Task Properties (Source Tab)

In the SQL query "?" represents the parameters. To map the parameters click on "Parameters" button.

Clicking on Parameters button will show a window with "Input Global Variables" and "Parameters". Here you can map the global variables to the input parameters.

Managing Transactions between two or more tasks

Transactions play a very important role in database. We can set transactions between two tasks by Right clicking the Transform Data Task and select "Workflow Properties" then select "Options" tab. Here you can select "**Join transaction if present**" option or you can choose "Commit transaction on successful completion of this step" option.

You can also set the transaction at package level by right clicking the package and select "Package Properties" then select "Advanced" tab, check the "Use Transactions" checkbox to enable the transactions at package level. By default it is enabled.

Send Mail Task

The **SendMailTask** object lets you send an e-mail as a task. For example, if you want to notify a database administrator about the success or failure of a particular task (such as a backup), you can link a **SendMailTask** object with a precedence constraint to the previous task. To use a **SendMailTask**, the computer must have the Microsoft messaging API installed with a valid user profile. In this scenario we have created two send mail tasks, one for success and other for failure.

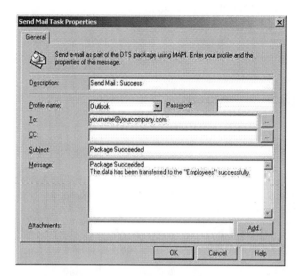

Figure 4: Send Mail Task Properties

Creating Workflow Properties

Using workflow task we can say prioritize which task needs to be executed after task i.e., we can set the precedence of the various tasks. Right click on the task on which you need to define the workflow properties and select "**Workflow**" and then select "**Workflow Properties**". Now click on "New" button to add the precedence. Various precedence available are: Success, Failure and Completion. Select the task as "Source Step" and set the precedence. In this scenario we have created two workflow properties, one for success and other for failure of data transfer task.

Error Logging

Finding if a DTS Package is running

I was stuck at finding a solution to if a DTS Package is executing or not. It could have been started with the scheduler, or started manually. The only solution to this problem which I could come up with without any code changes to the package itself, was to enable Logging to SQL Server, and then checking the state of the package in the **sysdtspackagelog** table by the following query

The various details of the scheduled DTS packages are available in *sysdtspackagelog*, *sysdtssteplog* and *sysdtstasklog* tables in the msdb database. The *sysdtspackagelog* contains the details at package level with columns such as name, lineagefull, start time, end time, computer, operator, logdate, error code, error description etc. The *sysdtssteplog* table contains the details at step level with columns such as lineagefull, step name, start time, end time, error code, error description, etc. The *stsdtstasklog* table contains details at task level. It gives description about the errors occurred in a particular task.

Sample query to get the details of the package from sysdtspackagelog table.

SELECT TOP 1 endtime FROM msdb.sysdtspackagelog WHERE name = 'Your Package Name' ORDER BY starttime DESC

If it returns a date, then the package is not running, and if it returns NULL, then the package is currently in executing stage.

Error Logging in an external file

Using error logging it becomes very easy to track the errors. To achieve this right click "Package Properties" and select "Logging" tab, where we can enter the name of the file in "**Error File**" textbox.

Error log stores the details at package level and at step level also, such as package name, start time, end time, error description, step name, step details, etc.

Logging in Event Viewer

To log the completion of package in the "**Event Viewer**", "Package Properties" and select "Logging" tab, check the "**Write completion status to event log**". To view the event viewer, on the Start menu, point to "Programs/Administrative Tools" and then click on "Event Viewer".

Executing the Package

To execute the package click "Execute" from the Package Menu. The Executing DTS Package dialog box appears, providing step and status information for the two steps. The Package Execution Results dialog box then appears.

Saving DTS Package

To save a DTS package four options are available:

1. Meta Data Services: With this save option, you can maintain historical information about the data manipulated by the package. However, Meta Data Services and the repository database must be installed and operational on your server. You can track the columns and tables that are used by the package as a source or destination. You also can use the data lineage feature to track which version of a package created a particular row. You can use these types of information for decision-support applications.

2. SQL Server: With this default save option, you can store a package as a SQL Server **msdb** table, allowing you to: store packages on any instances of SQL Server on your network; keep a convenient inventory of saved packages in SQL Server Enterprise Manager; and create, delete, and branch multiple package versions during the package development process.

3. Structured Storage File: With this save option, you can copy, move, and send a package across the network without having to store the file in a SQL Server database. The structured storage format allows you to maintain multiple packages and multiple package versions in a single file.

4. Visual Basic File: With this save option, you can programmatically customize a package created in DTS Designer or the DTS Import/Export Wizard. The option scripts out the package as Visual Basic code, and you can later open the Visual Basic file and modify the package definition in your development environment.

DTS Package Passwords

When you save a package to Microsoft® SQL Server™ or as a structured storage file, you can use DTS package passwords. You use DTS passwords in addition to the Windows Authentication or SQL Server Authentication passwords you use to connect to an instance of SQL Server. The following types of DTS package passwords are available:

1. If you set an **owner** password, the package user needs the password to edit or run the package.

2. If you set a **user** password, you also must set an owner password. Package users with access only to the user password can run the package. However, they can neither open nor edit the package unless they have access to the owner password. If global variables are used in the package then they cannot open the package in design mode also.

Loading a DTS Package

You can open an existing package from a .dts file by right clicking "Data Transformation Services" from Enterprise Manager and select "Open Package" option and mention the filename of the DTS to open. Then you can save this file to your server by using "Save As" option from File Menu.

Database Design and Strategy

Spending a few more minutes in design can pay off in a big way when building a system. This is the mantra that we hear and what most people would like to strive for, but it seems that we can never find the time to do detailed design. We don't get what Andy Warren calls "thinking time". So what can you do?

The only real thing that you can do to get better at design is to learn and practice it more. Just as an experienced developer can build things quicker, having that intuition on typing code, an architect of a database system can get better by learning what works and what doesn't.

Below we have a few articles for you that can help with your education and give you some additional insight into design and strategy.

Database Design and Reference Tables

By Ranga Narasimhan

This article is about smart database design. I have been programming in SQL server for more than 8 years. I love the design and analysis phase of a project where you create new tables, views etc... The success of any software project depends on its initial design. Once a poorly designed database hits production, no one will dare to make changes to it!(and if the manager who was in charge is still around, he is not going to agree that it was a badly designed database)

Ok, coming to the point, I am going to talk about Reference tables or Look Up tables. Any database will have some of these, and few database have LOT of lookup tables. In worst cases there are columns in tables with values like 0,1,2,3, etc and with no foreign key reference. You just have to look at the stored procedures which reference these tables and see how these numeric values are interpreted.

I have always used just one lookup table. This works most of the time for me. Let's see some examples of tables which are dependent on LookUp table. Lets see the two tables, Employee and Job from Pubs database:

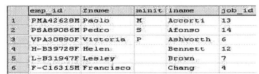

	emp_id	fname	minit	lname	job_id
1	PMA42628M	Paolo	M	Accorti	13
2	PSA89086M	Pedro	S	Afonso	14
3	VPA30890F	Victoria	P	Ashworth	6
4	H-B39728F	Helen		Bennett	12
5	L-B31947F	Lesley		Brown	7
6	F-C16315M	Francisco		Chang	4

Figure 1 - Employee Table

job_id	job_desc
1	New Hire - Job not specified
2	Chief Executive Officer
3	Business Operations Manager
4	Chief Financial Officier
5	Publisher
6	Managing Editor
7	Marketing Manager
8	Public Relations Manager
9	Acquisitions Manager
10	Productions Manager
11	Operations Manager
12	Editor
13	Sales Representative
14	Designer

Figure 2 - Job Table

In the above example, "Employee" table has a column "Job_ID" with integer values. The "Jobs" table has the Job description, usually tables like "Jobs" do not have more than 10 or 15 or at the most 50 records.

Example 2

	ContactName	Address	City	state	zip
1	Howard Snyder	2732 Baker Blvd.	Eugene	OR	97403
2	Yoshi Latimer	City Center Plaza 516 Main St.	Elgin	OR	97827
3	John Steel	12 Orchestra Terrace	Walla Walla	WA	99362
4	Jaime Yorres	87 Polk St. Suite 5	San Francisco	CA	94117
5	Fran Wilson	89 Chiaroscuro Rd.	Portland	OR	97219
6	Rene Phillips	2743 Bering St.	Anchorage	AK	99508
7	Paula Wilson	2817 Milton Dr.	Albuquerque	NM	87110
8	Jose Pavarotti	187 Suffolk Ln.	Boise	ID	83720
9	Art Braunschweiger	P.O. Box 555	Lander	WY	82520
10	Liz Nixon	89 Jefferson Way Suite 2	Portland	OR	97201
11	Liu Wong	55 Grizzly Peak Rd.	Butte	MT	59801
12	Helvetius Nagy	722 DaVinci Blvd.	Kirkland	WA	98034
13	Karl Jablonski	305 - 14th Ave. S. Suite 3B	Seattle	WA	98128

Figure 3 - Customer table

	StateCode	StateName
1	AL	ALABAMA
2	CA	CALIFORNIA
3	TX	Texas
4	FL	Florida
5	NJ	New Jersy
6	NY	New York
7	NV	Nevada
8	NH	New Hampshire
9	GA	Georgia

Figure 4 - State Table

In the above example "state" column in the "Customer" table references "StateCode" column in the "State" table to get the "StateName".

So, there may be several tables in our databases which needs a look up table. For a database with more than 100 tables, there may be atleast 10-20 look up tables, or even more if there are multiple columns in one table which references multiple look up tables.

I came up with a "Generic" lookup table which can be used in most of these scenarios.

intID	strCode	strDescription	strCategory
1	NULL	New Hire - Job not specified	Employee.JobID
2	NULL	Chief Executive Officer	Employee.JobID
3	NULL	Business Operations Manager	Employee.JobID
4	NULL	Chief Financial Officier	Employee.JobID
5	NULL	Publisher	Employee.JobID
6	NULL	Managing Editor	Employee.JobID
7	NULL	Marketing Manager	Employee.JobID
8	NULL	Public Relations Manager	Employee.JobID
9	NULL	Acquisitions Manager	Employee.JobID
10	NULL	Productions Manager	Employee.JobID
11	NULL	Operations Manager	Employee.JobID
12	NULL	Editor	Employee.JobID
13	NULL	Sales Representative	Employee.JobID
14	NULL	Designer	Employee.JobID
15	AL	ALABAMA	Customer.State
16	CA	CALIFORNIA	Customer.State
17	TX	Texas	Customer.State
18	FL	Florida	Customer.State
19	NJ	New Jersy	Customer.State
20	NY	New York	Customer.State
21	NV	Nevada	Customer.State
22	NH	New Hampshire	Customer.State
23	GA	Georgia	Customer.State
1	NULL	Phone	Customer.ModeOfCommunication
2	NULL	Fax	Customer.ModeOfCommunication
3	NULL	Email	Customer.ModeOfCommunication
4	NULL	PostalMail	Customer.ModeOfCommunication
0	NULL	Active	Customer.Status
1	NULL	In-Active	Customer.Status
2	NULL	Pending	Customer.Status
0	NULL	Visa	Customer.CreditCardType
1	NULL	Master Card	Customer.CreditCardType
2	NULL	American Express	Customer.CreditCardType
3	NULL	Discovery	Customer.CreditCardType

Figure 5

From the above data , every distinct category would have replaced a table. Now we do not need "Job" and "State" tables. This is a very simple way to handle multiple small tables and keep the information in one place. Any kind "hardcoding" in stored procedures can be avoided by using this table.

Conclusion

Advantages of "GenericLookUp" Table

1.We can store integer values to most of the data and have the description stored in the "GenericLookUp" table. As we know that performance is always going to be better when we deal with numeric columns than non numeric columns.

2.Easy maintainabilty. Lets say we have 20 LookUp tables in a application. With this "GenericLookUp" table, we just need 3 stored pros(Insert/Update/Delete) to maintain the data.

3.Centralized information in one place. This table would be almost like a data dictionary.

How to retrieve the iformation from "GenericLookUp" table?

Just need one stored procedure to retrieve data from the "GenericLookUp" able. The SP will accept the category as parameter and the code will be something like this:

```
DECLARE @strCategory VARCHAR(100)
SET @strCategory = 'Customer.CreditCardType'
SELECT intID,strCode,strDescription FROM dbo.GenericLookUp (NOLOCK) WHERE strCategory = @strCategory
```

Male,Female, and The Other One (NULL)

By Peter Ward

How do you explain that the sales of Widgets for Widget Inc have been grossly understated for the past six months since the 'new whiz bang going to cost you lots of dollars' reporting systems was implemented. Trying to explain that the reason behind this reporting discrepancy was a misunderstanding by the vendor of the three-value logic concept in ANSI SQL is not the easiest of things to explain to a Chief Financial Officer.

Consider the following example:

```
CREATE TABLE dbo.WidgetSales
(        SaleID INT IDENTITY(1, 1) NOT NULL,
         SalesDate SMALLDATETIME NOT NULL,
         CustomerID INT NOT NULL,
         ProductID  INT NOT NULL,
         Qty SMALLINT NOT NULL,
         TotalAmt NUMERIC(7, 2)
)
INSERT INTO dbo.WidgetSales (SalesDate, CustomerID, ProductID, Qty, TotalAmt)
     VALUES ('2005-11-23 20:20:00', 1, 1, 1, 2.50)
INSERT INTO dbo.WidgetSales (SalesDate, CustomerID, ProductID, Qty, TotalAmt)
     VALUES ('2005-11-23 20:20:40', 1, 2, 2, 5.00)
INSERT INTO dbo.WidgetSales (SalesDate, CustomerID, ProductID, Qty, TotalAmt)
     VALUES ('2005-11-23 22:21:00', 2, 1, 1, 2.50)
INSERT INTO dbo.WidgetSales (SalesDate, CustomerID, ProductID, Qty, TotalAmt)
     VALUES ('2005-11-23 20:22:00', 3, 2, 1, 2.50)
INSERT INTO dbo.WidgetSales (SalesDate, CustomerID, ProductID, Qty, TotalAmt)
     VALUES ('2005-11-23 20:23:00', 4, 2, 2, 5.00)
CREATE TABLE dbo.WidgetCustomers
(        CustomerID INT IDENTITY(1, 1) NOT NULL,
         JoinDate SMALLDATETIME NOT NULL,
         FirstName NVARCHAR(20) NOT NULL,
         LastName NVARCHAR(20) NOT NULL,
         ShipAddress NVARCHAR(200) NOT NULL,
         Gender BIT NULL-- 0 = Male, 1 = Female
)

INSERT INTO dbo.WidgetCustomers (JoinDate, FirstName, LastName, ShipAddress, Gender)
     VALUES ('2005-11-23 20:00:00', 'Peter', 'Ward', 'Where I Live', 0)
INSERT INTO dbo.WidgetCustomers (JoinDate, FirstName, LastName, ShipAddress, Gender)
     VALUES ('2005-11-23 21:00:00', 'David', 'Smith', 'Somewhere Over the Rainbow', 0)
INSERT INTO dbo.WidgetCustomers (JoinDate, FirstName, LastName, ShipAddress, Gender)
     VALUES ('2005-11-23 20:00:00', 'Mary', 'Ward', 'On the Bad Side of Town', 1)
INSERT INTO dbo.WidgetCustomers (JoinDate, FirstName, LastName, ShipAddress, Gender)
     VALUES ('2005-11-23 20:00:00', 'John', 'Doe', 'The Big Building', NULL)
```

To calculate the sales of Widgets you would simply aggregate the TotalAmt column in the WidgetSales table as illustrated below:

```
SELECT SUM(TotalAmt) AS Sales
 FROM dbo.WidgetSales
-------------------------------------
17.50
(1 row(s) affected)
```

To calculate the sales of Widgets bought by Males a query similar to the one below would be written:

```
SELECT SUM(s. TotalAmt) AS Sales
 FROM dbo.WidgetSales s JOIN WidgetCustomers c
   ON s.customerid = c.customerid
 WHERE c.gender = 0  -- Male
```

```
Sales
---------------------------------------
10.00
(1 row(s) affected)
```

To calculate the sales of Widgets bought by Females a query similar to the one below would be written:

```
SELECT SUM(s. TotalAmt) AS Sales
 FROM dbo.WidgetSales s JOIN WidgetCustomers c
    ON s.customerid = c.customerid
 WHERE c.gender = 1  -- Female
```

```
Sales
---------------------------------------
2.50
(1 row(s) affected)
```

So the total sales for Widgets is $12.50. That is the sales of Widgets purchased by Males ($10.00) plus the sales of Widgets for Females ($2.50). But we know from the aggregation of the TotalAmt values in the WidgetsSales table that the total sales is actually $17.50. In this simplified example three-valued logic produced a third unknown gender value that was not catered for.

In most programming languages a logical expression can only return one of two possible values; TRUE or FALSE, Or in the Widgets example, MALE or FEMALE. However, ANSI SQL is unique in the fact that a logical expression can return TRUE, FALSE or UNKNOWN, or in the Widgets example, MALE, FEMALE and NULL. Although NULL is called a value it is simply a marker indicating the complete lack of a value.

Although this issue could be resolved by the Nullability of the gender column being set to FALSE so that NULL values cannot be entered, this is not always an appropriate solution. For example, Widget Inc's privacy policy makes the collection of gender optional so that a person has the ability to not specify their gender when subscribing as a customer of Widget Inc. This could be corrected by using an appropriate encoding scheme for gender. For example the ISO gender codes are 0 = Unknown, 1 = Male , 2 = Female and 9 = Not Applicable. Not Applicable is used for an entity which does not have a gender such as a company. The real issue though in this reporting discrepancy is not the schema design, but the way that NULL values are being handled in logical expressions.

The behavior of NULLS is particularly evident in WHERE clauses where a NULL is involved in the expression. A WHERE clause will only return the expressions that are evaluated to be TRUE. NULL values are always treated as UNKNOWN and as they are not TRUE they are not returned. For example 10 < 20 is always evaluated as TRUE and 10 > 20 is always evaluated as FALSE. However the expression 10 = NULL is UNKNOWN as NULL is an unknown value. It could be 20 or it could be any other value hence it can not be evaluated so a NULL value is evaluated as UNKNOWN. Therefore, 10 = NULL will always return UNKNOWN. So in the gender example UNKNOWN values do not equal MALE or FEMALE and are therefore not returned.

An additional source of confusion with three-valued logic is that NOT(UNKNOWN) is always UNKNOWN. For example, NOT(TRUE) is evaluated as FALSE and NOT(FALE) is evaluated as TRUE. However NOT (UNKNOWN) is evaluated as UNKNOWN. Consider the example below to return all the sales of Widgets that have not been purchased by a Male:

```
SELECT SUM(s.TotalAmt) AS Sales
 FROM dbo.WidgetSales s JOIN WidgetCustomers c
    ON s.customerid = c.customerid
 WHERE  NOT(c.gender) = 0 -- Male
```

Or

```
SELECT  SUM(s.TotalAmt) AS Sales
 FROM  dbo.WidgetSales s JOIN WidgetCustomers c
    ON s.customerid = c.customerid
 WHERE  c.gender <> 0  -- Male
```

Both Queries return the result below:

Returns:

```
Sales
---------------------------------------
2.50
```

The observation made from this example is that UNKNOWN results will not be returned in a WHERE clause, as only those results that are satisfied to be TRUE will be returned. For example, return IF NOT ('male') = 'female' is TRUE where as IF NOT(NULL) = 'female' is UNKNOWN. In order to check if a value equals (=) NULL then the IS NULL expression should be used, and to check that a value does not equal (<>) NULL then the IS NOT NULL expression should be used.

So, in order to calculate the total sales of Widgets by all genders the sales of Males, Females and Unknown genders must be aggregated to ensure that sales from the Unknown gender are considered. ie.

```
SELECT SUM(s.TotalAmt) AS Sales
 FROM   dbo.WidgetSales s JOIN WidgetCustomers c
    ON   s.customerid = c.customerid
 WHERE c.gender IS NULL
```

Returns:

```
Sales
--------------------------------------
5.00
```

By understanding and knowing how NULL values are treated in TSQL the Unknown will no longer be something that you need to worry about as you will be able to anticipate and prepare for NULL values.

The Pitfalls of Foreign Keys

By David Poole

Introduction

I enjoy reading the articles published by Red Gate Software under their Simple talk site.

In particular I enjoy the columns by "Phil Factor" and a paragraph in one in particular caught my eye.

> *Many features that we accept as part of a relational database were put there to defend the integrity of the database against the ham-fisted endeavors of the freelance programmer. Checks on foreign keys and uniqueness are excellent in development but are scarcely necessary if creating, updating and deleting are done through well-tested stored procedures. And, they will certainly slow data throughput in a hard-working production system.*

To see the full article see cursors and embedded SQL

As regular visitors to SQLServerCentral will have observed articles advocating a particular approach are usually hotly debated and so in the context of the quoted paragraph in particular I should like to show you the results of some experimentation I carried out with declared data referential integrity.

The basic scenario

For my experiments I considered a hypothetical Web Content Management System (CMS), based around my favourite commercial CMS, using SQL Server 2005 as the database repository.

The system consisted of a number of user editable objects that could be represented by

- A single table to hold the common properties for all objects within the system such as name, hyperlink, creation date, security context
- A separate table to hold the specific properties for each type of object

The basic layout is a star layout as shown below

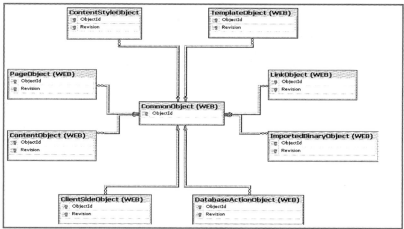

The common properties table has an IDENTITY column as the primary key.

With a high end CMS performance is one of the prime considerations. Direct access to database tables is frowned upon especially as all legitimate tasks can be carried out by an API.

I began to ask myself what would be the difference in performance in the above scenario between the schema with a full set of foreign keys and one with DRI enforced purely in the stored procedures used to control the data layer?

Inserts

To test inserts I set up a straight forward stored procedure that would

- Populate the CommonObject table
- Take the SCOPE_IDENTITY() from the new record and use it to populate one of the specific object tables

Without DRI the execution plan was as follows

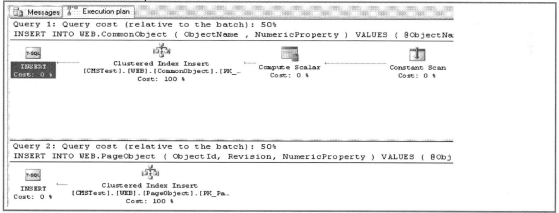

With DRI the execution plan reveals that SQL Server performs an additional index seek to make sure that DRI rules are adhered to.

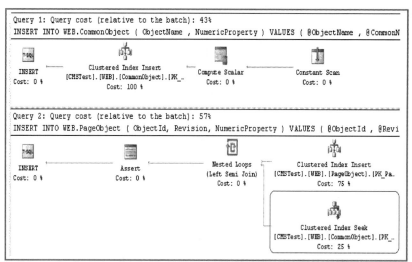

In this particular case the cost of an extra index seek is trivial and in SQL 2005 the cost is slightly less than half that for the same operation on a SQL2000 box.

Let us consider a slightly different scenario where we have a customer table supported by several lookup tables. If we were to add foreign keys to the table then each addition into the customer table would require a check against every supporting lookup table to maintain data referential integrity. In small to medium systems even in this situation the cost will be negligible however in high volume systems small costs soon multiply up to reveal a more significant affect.

Deletes

Again a stored procedure was set up to perform the following action

- Remove a record from one of the specific object tables
- Remove the associated common property record

Without DRI the execution plan for the delete is just a couple of simple Clustered Index Deletes.

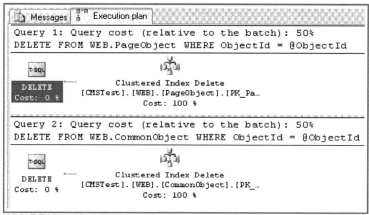

With DRI enabled the execution plan is dramatically more complex.

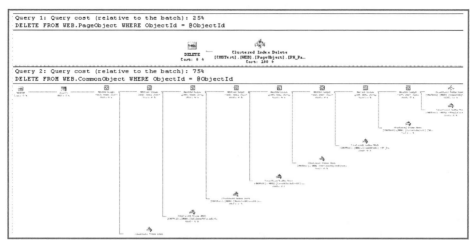

Data referential integrity rules mean that deleting a central CommonObject record requires that all the tables that refer to the CommonObject table must be checked to ensure that DRI is not violated. In our example this means that deleting the CommonObject record is 3 times more expensive than a deleting a specific record.

This raises another important consideration. In our example the one CommonObject record can have many entries in one of the specific object tables. Now consider a Customer table attached to various lookup tables.

If we have to delete an entry from one of those lookup tables the Customer table will have to be checked to ensure that DRI rules are not violated. *This more or less dicates that the referencing column in the Customer table HAS to be indexed!* If it is not indexed then the execution plan will show costly scans or even table scans!

OK my example with a customer table is probably not a good one and lookup tables tend to be fairly static but the point is that your application may never search on the referencing column and therefore you would want to save yourself the overhead of having an index on that column. With DRI enforced you more or less have to place an index on a column to get acceptable performance during a delete.

Updates

In my CMS example update performance was not impacted by DRI. Reverting back to the Customer example, let us suppose that you have a CountyId field and decide that a customer's address has incorrectly been assigned to Lancashire when the customer is clearly a Yorkshireman. The update of the customer record will require a check to be made on the County table to ensure that the new value for the CountyId field is valid. As with INSERTs such operations are trivial until you are dealing with very high volumes of data.

Concluding remarks

It is worth remembering that if a table is referenced by a foreign key constraint you cannot use the TRUNCATE TABLE statement on that table.

Having enforced DRI also affects the order in which inserts and deletes can take place for the various tables. In general this is no bad thing but there are few absolutes in SQL Server. If you are in the habit of archiving data off into history tables the ability to move data in an order not dictated by DRI rules may be desirable. In such a scenario the DRI checking will have been carried out in populating the live tables so it may be possible to get away with little or no DRI checking on the history tables.

Phil Factor's statement that DRI will

> *"slow data throughput in a hard-working production system"*

is true but it will be a hard working system indeed where this becomes apparent, particularly using SQL 2005. The big exception to this is where DELETEs occur.

The over-riding point is that DRI is a design issue. Careful, well thought out design can maximize the advantages of DRI while minimising the disadvantages.

I am in two minds about his comment that DRI is

"scarcely necessary if creating, updating and deleting are done through well-tested stored procedures".

It sounds a perfectly logical statement to make however my experience has been that large projects often become subject to compressed delivery schedules towards their completion. In consequence test cycles are cut in the belief that any serious errors will show up in user acceptance testing. My experience is that this is not always true and large complex systems are able to hide large complex bugs.

In the real version of my hypothetical CMS example there was no declared DRI, but the package did have a suite of specific repository checking and repair routines to cater for orphaned data. The developers had also realised that delete activity was potentially a bottle neck and so their approach was to have a flag to indicate that an object should be considered deleted. True deletion could be carried out at scheduled times to avoid impacting on either the users of the system or the visitors to the site served by the system.

XML

The use of XML is growing in all areas of technology, but especially in SQL Server. The release of SQL Server 2005 has greatly expanded the capabilities, including a native XML data type.

The use of XML is still limited in many enterprises, and the number of articles we've received reflects that. Here is a sampling of the articles that we have received in 2005 and 2006.

Importing XML Files into SQL Server

By Steve Moore

Introduction

So, for whatever reason you are fed up with your marriage to XML and you want to go back to storing your data in (gasp!) a database. This article explains one approach for doing just that. In the example, we are using Windows Scripting Host to iterate through a few thousand XML files that will be imported into a SQL Server table. There is an added level of complexity in that the content of the XML files is formatted in HTML.

The Tools

- SQLXML 3.0, which can be downloaded here
- ActivePerl (optional), which can be downloaded here

The Situation

You are in the situation of working with thousands of XML files used to show FAQs on a web site. The structure of the XML files are as such:

```
<?xml version="1.0" encoding="utf-8" ?>
<FAQ ID="020001" LanguageCode="EN" Priority="1">
<Question><!-- How can I solve my problem? --></Question>
<Summary><!-- Run the hardware utility. --></Summary>
<Content>
    <!--
    <div id="contentcenter">
    <p>Perform a <b>hardware</b> check with the utility to assure the quality of the system driver,
etc., etc.</p>
    </div>
    -->
</Content>
</FAQ>
```

If your content is not stored as HTML or you already have it enclosed in CDATA tags, then you can skip directly to the section titled "Importing the XML Files."

In order to use SQLXML to import the data, you need to get rid of the comment tags. There are probably ways to create an XML Schema that will ignore the comment tags, but I chose instead to find and replace the comment tags with CDATA tags. CDATA is used to tell the XML parser to ignore anything between the tags. For reasons that I won't get into, I chose to use Perl to handle the text manipulation.

(NOTE: I know many developers would suggest using the REPLACE function, or .NET XmlTextReader with an INSERT statement to import to the database. As I mentioned, this is just ONE way to import the data. An example from a guy using VBScript is here.)

Open Notepad and save the code below as a file called Replace.pl. After installing ActivePerl, you open the file from a command prompt and run it. You will be prompted for what you want to replace. The find and replace process is twofold: replacing the beginning comment (<!--) with the beginning CDATA tag (<![CDATA[) and the end comment (-->) with the ending CDATA tag (]]>).

```
#!/usr/bin/perl
#
# NOTE: the find-and-replace IS case-sensitive.

$dir = $ARGV[0] || '.';
$!=1;
chdir($dir) or die $!;
opendir(DIR,$dir) or die $!;
my $changes=0;
print "\n :: find :. ";
$find=<STDIN>; chop($find);
print " :: replace :. ";
$replace=<STDIN>; chop($replace);
$/=undef;
foreach my $file (readdir(DIR))
{
if($file=~/^.+\.xml$/) # adjust pattern to your needs
{
```

```
print "parsing file $file..\n";
open(FILE,"<$file") or die $!;
my $file_data=<FILE>;
close(FILE);
$changes += $file_data =~ s/$find/$replace/gme;
open(FILE,">$file") or die $!;
print FILE $file_data;
close(FILE);
}
}
print "Voila. ($changes changes)\n";
```

The data are now ready to be imported.

Importing the XML Files

You will need to create a table that has the same format as the XML schema used to import the data. The XML Schema is below; the table name is referenced as sql:relation="<tablename>".

The following is saved as a file called FAQschema.xml.

```
<xsd:schema xmlns:xsd="http://www.w3.org/2001/XMLSchema" xmlns:sql="urn:schemas-microsoft-com:mapping-schema">
    <xsd:element name="FAQ" sql:relation="FAQ" >
        <xsd:complexType>
            <xsd:sequence>
            <xsd:element name="Question" type="xsd:string" sql:use-cdata="1" />
            <xsd:element name="Summary" type="xsd:string" sql:use-cdata="1" />
            <xsd:element name="Content" type="xsd:string" sql:use-cdata="1" />
            </xsd:sequence>
            <xsd:attribute name="ID" type="xsd:string" />
            <xsd:attribute name="LanguageCode" type="xsd:string" />
        </xsd:complexType>
    </xsd:element>
</xsd:schema>
```

Once the table and the schema are ready, you can use the SQLXMLBulkLoad object and the File System Object to iterate through each file and insert the data into the table. The following is a VBScript file used to do the import and write success/errors to a file. Save the file with a .vbs extension and run from a command prompt in the same directory as the XML files.

```
set objBL = CreateObject("SQLXMLBulkLoad.SQLXMLBulkload.3.0")
objBL.ConnectionString="provider=SQLOLEDB;datasource=localhost;database=TEST;integrated security=SSPI"
objBL.ErrorLogFile = "C:\FAQImport\error.log"
' Here is the path to your XML files
Const path = "C:\FAQImport\FAQs\"

Dim Text, Title, oFile
Dim fso, oFolder, oFiles, wsh ' Object variables
Text = "Folder "
Title = "XML Files"
Set wsh = WScript.CreateObject("WScript.Shell")
' Create FileSystemObject object to access the file system.
Set fso = CreateObject("Scripting.FileSystemObject")
' Get Folder object.
Set oFolder = fso.GetFolder(wsh.ExpandEnvironmentStrings(path))
' Get All Files
Set oFiles = oFolder.Files
For Each oFile In oFiles
        If oFile.Type = "XML Document" Then
                Text = Text & oFolder & vbCrLf & vbCrLf
                Text = Text & "Name" & vbTab & vbTab & "Size" & vbCrLf
                Text = Text & oFile.Name & vbTab
                Text = Text & FormatNumber(oFile.Size, 0) & vbCrLf
                objBL.Execute "C:\FAQImport\FAQschema.xml", oFile.Name
        End If
Next
Dim IFile
Set IFile = fso.CreateTextFile("C:\FAQImport\results.log", True)
IFile.WriteLine(Text)
IFile.Close
MsgBox "FAQ import successful!", vbOKOnly + vbInformation, Title
Set objBL = Nothing
Set fso = Nothing
```

Conclusions

You can usually find many examples about how to consume XML data in SQL Server or inversely how to import/export a single XML file. This article looks at how to import multiple XML files. Personally, I couldn't find much on this particular topic so I decided to write this up. I hope you find it useful!

Download the code

Credits

1) VBScript: The basis of the file/folder iteration come from a script developed by Günter Born.

2) XSD and SQLXML examples are derived from the Help files in the SQLXML download.

3) Perl Script: This is something I got off of CPAN a few years back and I've found it to be invaluable. If you know the source PLEASE contact me so I can give him or her proper credit.

Simplify the Creation of XML from SQL Server Data

By Hugh Lynch

Introduction

Like many developers, my team and I were enchanted by the possibilities of XML and XSL/XSLT when they emerged a few years ago. It seemed we could describe anything using XML and morph it to our hearts' content using XSL. We wove the new technology deep into our designs, building substantial web applications in which the data is rendered as XML then transformed to HTML and other formats.

While I am content with the decision to embrace XML, there were significant obstacles. Chiefly, how to create XML from our relational data in SQL Server? Existing techniques held early promise, but proved either too simplistic (FOR XML AUTO) or too cumbersome (FOR XML EXPLICIT, XML Views, etc) for widespread adoption.

We wanted something simple and efficient to leverage our existing tools, experience and the capabilities of SQL Server. We invented a simple XML-assembly grammar that we embed in the results returned from stored procedures, utilizing SQL Server's ability to return multiple "chained" result sets from a single command invocation.

Next, we created a general-purpose interpreter (we implemented COM and .NET versions) to parse the embedded XML-assembly instructions and render the returned data accordingly as XML.

Finally, we developed two general-purpose invocation utilities, one for the command line and one for web-based (implemented in .NET and ASP.NET, respectively). These tools provide simple mechanisms to invoke parameterized stored procedures, process the results using the interpreter, and output the resulting XML, either raw or transformed.

The benefits of this approach, which we call "data shapes" or simply "shapes", include:

    a.   *Simplicity*. With the grammar defined and the interpreter written, developers simply write conforming stored procedures to create arbitrarily complex XML documents. Unlike some alternatives, complex documents do not require complex procedures – just select the data to assemble and accompany it with simple text instructions like "RELATE Employee.CompanyID to Company.CompanyID" (more on the grammar later).

    b.   *Efficiency.* Returning all of the data for a document (sometimes dozens of recordsets) from a stored procedure keeps database trips to an absolute minimum. The technique also delegates the assembly of the XML from the database server to the interpreter, which can be distributed across middle- or presentation-layer machines. Writing XML involves conversion and formatting of native data types as text, character escaping, and filtering of child recordsets, all of which consume valuable CPU cycles.

    c.   *Performance and Control.* Writing shapes as stored procedures gives the developer all the benefits of that language: pre-compiled execution plans, caching, parameterization, conditional logic, temporary storage, permission controls, nested calls, etc.

d.   *Familiarity.* While the grammar of shapes is no doubt novel, the tools used to create, edit, test and analyze them are not. Shapes can be developed in Query Analyzer and Visual Studio or any other T-SQL tool. Their performance can be evaluated using SQL Profiler, and dissected by examining execution plans. Because a shape encapsulates both data selection and assembly instruction in a single scriptable procedure, it can be easily migrated between development, test and production environments.

This article provides a complete definition of the shape grammar as well as functional explanations of the shape interpreter and shape invoker utilities. The accompanying download includes the binary and configuration files necessary to experiment with shapes on your own. Installation instructions are listed at the end of the article.

You can also see shapes in action at http://tech.rssgroup.com/shapes.

Let's begin with some examples.

Example 1 – Hello, World!

Tradition dictates that all new programming technologies introduce themselves, so here is a very simple shape listing:

```
create procedure dbo.shpHello
as
    select 'dataset root.Hello' _shp
    select 'Hello, World!' Msg
go
```

which can be invoked through ASP.NET, using the URL:

```
http://.../shpHello.aspx
```

And here are the results it produces:

```
<?xml version="1.0" encoding="utf-8"?>
<Hello Msg="Hello, World!"/>
```

While trivial, there are a couple of things to note. The shape instruction ('dataset root.Hello') tells the interpreter to name the following result set "root" and to represent each record within it as a <Hello> element. By default, the interpreter maps the single column of the data set (Msg) to an attribute of the same name in the <Hello> element.

Example 2 – A Realistic Report

Using Microsoft's standard Northwind database, we will create a shape to return all of the orders created by a specified employee during a specified date range. The data will be organized by customer.

The following URL invokes the stored procedure dbo.shpEmployeeActivity with three parameters: employeeID, startDate and endDate.

```
http://.../shpEmployeeActivity.aspx?ID_Employee=6&startDate=1/1/97&endDate=1/31/97
```

Here's the listing of the stored procedure. The embedded instruction statements are again highlighted in blue. The procedure uses a table variable to store orderIDs.

```
create procedure dbo.shpEmployeeActivity (
  @employeeID  int
, @startDate   smalldatetime
, @endDate     smalldatetime
as
```

```
set nocount on
-- create a table variable to hold the set of filtered orderIDs
declare @nOrders int
declare @tblOrders table (        OrderID int primary key)
insert @tblOrders
select orderID
 from orders
 where employeeID = @employeeID
 and orderDate between @startDate and @endDate
set @nOrders = @@rowcount
set nocount off
select 'dataset root.Employee' _shp
select EmployeeID, LastName, FirstName, Title, ...
 from Employees
 where employeeID=@employeeID
if @nOrders>0
 begin
    select 'dataset Customers.Customer relate to root' _shp
    select *
     from customers
      where customerID in
        (select customerID from orders where orderID in
          (select orderID from @tblOrders))
    select 'dataset Orders.Order relate customerID to Customers.customerID' _shp
    select *
     from orders
      where orderID in (select orderID from @tblOrders)
    select 'dataset OrderDetails.Item relate orderID to Orders.orderID' _shp
    select *
     from [Order Details]
      where orderid in (select orderID from @tblOrders)
 end
go
```

And here are the results (wider date ranges produce a lot more data):

```
<?xml version="1.0" encoding="utf-8"?>
<Employee EmployeeID="6" LastName="Suyama" FirstName="Michael"...>
    <Notes><![CDATA[Michael is a graduate of...]]></Notes>
    <Customer CustomerID="GOURL" CompanyName="Gourmet Lanchonetes"...>
        <Order OrderID="10423" EmployeeID="6" OrderDate="1/23/1997"...>
            <Item ProductID="31" UnitPrice="10.0000" Quantity="14" Discount="0" />
            <Item ProductID="59" UnitPrice="44.0000" Quantity="20" Discount="0" />
        </Order>
    </Customer>
    <Customer CustomerID="LAMAI" CompanyName="La maison d'Asie"...>
        <Order OrderID="10425" EmployeeID="6" OrderDate="1/24/1997"...>
            <Item ProductID="55" UnitPrice="19.2000" Quantity="10" Discount="0.25" />
            <Item ProductID="76" UnitPrice="14.4000" Quantity="20" Discount="0.25" />
        </Order>
    </Customer>
</Employee>
```

As in the prior example, records were mapped to elements and columns were mapped to attributes of the same name, except for the SQL text-typed column "Notes", which was mapped to a CDATA block within a child element in order to preserve whitespace and minimize character escaping.

Let's take a closer look at the embedded instructions.

```
select 'dataset root.Employee' _shp
select ... from employees where ...
select 'dataset Customers.Customer relate to root' _shp
select * from customers where ...
select 'dataset Orders.Order relate customerID to Customers.customerID' _shp
select * from orders where ...
select 'dataset OrderDetails.Item relate orderID to Orders.orderID' _shp
select * from [Order Details] where ...
```

Notice how the selection of each data set (SELECT *[fields]* FROM *[table]*) is preceded by an instruction (SELECT 'dataset...' _shp). These instructions tell the shape interpreter what is coming next and where to put it.

Here's what the instructions mean:

```
select 'dataset root.Employee' _shp
```
Name the following result set "root" and represent each record within it as an <Employee> element.

```
select 'dataset Customers.Customer relate to root' _shp
```
Name the following result set "Customers" and represent each record within it a <Customer> element. Make the <Customer> elements appear as child elements of the <Employee> elements produced by the "root" result set. In this case, there is only one <Employee> element because we are selecting by primary key. If there were more than one, the <Customer> elements would be repeated as child elements of each.

```
select 'dataset Orders.Order relate customerID to Customers.customerID' _shp
```

Name the following result set "Orders" and represent each record within it as an <Order> element. Make the <Order> elements appear as child elements of the <Customer> elements produced by the "Customers" result set. The <Order> elements will be filtered such that only those orders with matching customerID fields appear as children of each <Customer> element. When rendering to XML, the shape interpreter will not render the customerID attribute of the <Order> element, since it is implicit in the XML structure.

```
select 'dataset OrderDetails.Item relate orderID to Orders.orderID' _shp
```

Name the following result set "OrderDetails" and represent each record within it as an <Item> element. Make the <Item> elements appear as child elements of the <Order> elements produced by the "Orders" result set, grouped by orderID.

Note that any Order records that do not match a selected Customer record will not appear in the XML. Nor will any OrderDetails records appear that do not match a selected Order. In other words, if the `where` clauses (in orange) were omitted, the XML produced would be identical, but the amount of data loaded by SQL Server and passed to the interpreter would increase dramatically.

Because this error is not detectable in the output, except through degraded performance, it can be difficult to diagnose. It is always a good idea to test your shapes in Query Analyzer to verify that the data sets are appropriately filtered. It is also possible that a future version of the interpreter could detect this condition and produce a warning.

While this shape is intended to be representative of actual, useful shapes, it does not fully exercise the shape grammar, which provides fine controls over the mapping and formatting of records and columns. Simple options are available to:

a.   wrap record elements in a grouping element. For example, <Customer> elements could be wrapped by a <Customers> element.

b.   render all columns as child elements

c.   render an individual column as an attribute, child element, free text, CDATA block or nested XML

d.   format numeric and date columns using Excel-like formatting strings

e.   omit a column from the XML output

The Shape Interpreter

The shape interpreter analyzes the multiple result sets returned from the stored procedure, parses the instructions according to the grammar defined above, and renders the data accordingly as XML. The implementation of the interpreter may interest developers wanting to customize or simply understand it, but it is not a requirement for its use. In fact, its function is thoroughly wrapped by the URL- and command-line invocation methods described in the next section, so feel free to skip ahead.

Our .NET implementation of the interpreter (included in the download) is encapsulated in a DataShape class derived from System.Data.DataSet. The DataShape class is typically employed in a two-step operation. First, the data and instructions are read from the data source (a SqlCommand or SqlDataReader), populating the DataSet's internal DataTable and DataRelation collections. Then the DataShape is rendered as XML by passing a suitable output (filename, IO.Stream, TextWriter or XmlWriter) to its WriteShapeXml() method.

After writing, the DataShape is typically disposed of, having served its purpose. It is, however, fully serializable and can be written to and restored from a file (or other destination) if its contents are still of interest. For instance, it is fairly straightforward to implement a paging system in this manner, without requiring additional trips to the database.

The DataShape class can also be populated manually or with multiple calls to various stored procedures because it exposes and employs the underlying capabilities of the standard DataSet class.

The Shape Invokers

Having all of information necessary to create an XML document contained in the results of our shape procedures, along with a general-purpose interpreter for converting those results to XML, all that is needed is a mechanism to invoke the store procedure, process the results using the interpreter, and output the results. We created two: one for command line invocations and one for browsers.

Let's begin with the web-based tool, which we created using ASP.NET. Essentially, we wanted a concise URL that identifies a stored procedure and allows for the specification of parameter values and a few options. The two examples above include simple web-based invocation URLs, with and without parameters:

```
http://.../shpHello.aspx
http://.../shpEmployeeActivity.aspx?ID_Employee=6&startDate=1/1/97&endDate=1/31/97
```
The general format of these URLs is:

```
http://.../shapeName.aspx[?paramA=value[&paramB=value..][&o=optionA:value;optionB:value]
```
The first thing to note is that there is actually no .aspx file necessary to process these requests. By adding an entry to the httpHandlers section of the web.config file, all .aspx requests are routed to the ShapeHandler class of the RSSWebShapes assembly, which knows how to interpret the URL.

If shapes need to co-exist with standard .aspx pages, it is a simple matter to register a different extension for shapes and substitute that extension for .aspx in shape URLs. Typically, we use .shp. Changing the extension does require custom configuration of the virtual directory in IIS.

The ShapeHandler class creates a SqlCommand object for executing a stored procedure named *shapeName*. Using a database connection defined in the web.config, the ShapeHandler retrieves the parameter list from the database and populates any command parameters that were provided in the URL.

When passing parameters, note that parameter values should be URL escaped and that parameter names should omit the @ prefix.

The available options are described below:

URL Invoker Options

`x[:xsltFileName]`
> Specifies an XSLT file name that is used to transform the XML. The ShapeHandler will search for templates in paths specified in the "ShapeTemplatePaths" app setting of the web.config file. If an extension is omitted, the default is .xslt. If the entire name is omitted, a file name of shpName.xslt is used. If the x option is specified the content type of the response defaults to text/html; to specify a different type use the m option.

`m:contentType`
> Specifies the contentType of the response. The default is text/xml unless the x option is used, in which case the default is text/html.

`r[:rootName]`
> Specifies an element name in which to wrap the output of the shape procedure. If the option is specified, but no rootName is provided, the default name is "root".

`c:indentChar`
> Specifies a character to use when indenting XML child elements. The default is tab.

`i:indentLevel`
> Specifies the number of indentChars to use when indenting XML child elements. The default is 1. A value of 0 (zero) turns off all XML formatting, including newlines.

`o[:outputFile]`
> Specifies that the output should be directed to a file rather than the browser. The output location is determined by

the "ShapeOutputPath" app setting in the web.config file. If no extension is specified, the default is .xml. If no outputFile is specified, the default is shpName.xml.

The command line invoker, makeShape.exe, supports essentially the same options with the exception of the contentType. Output is written to the console unless an output file is specified. The general format of the command line is:

```
makeShape -s=shapeName [-option[=val]...]] paramA=val paramB=val
```

The available options are described below:

Command Line Invoker Options

`x[=xsltFilePath]`

Specifies the path of an XSLT file that is used to transform the XML. If an extension is omitted, the default is .xslt. If the entire name is omitted, a file name of shpName.xslt is used.

`r[=rootName]`

Specifies an element name in which to wrap the output of the shape procedure. If the option is specified, but no rootName is provided, the default name is "root".

`c=indentChar`

Specifies a character to use when indenting XML child elements. The default is tab.

`i=indentLevel`

Specifies the number of indentChars to use when indenting XML child elements. The default is 1. A value of 0 (zero) turns off all XML formatting, including newlines.

`o[=outputPath]`

Specifies the path of the file to which output should be written rather than the console. If no extension is specified, the default is .xml. If no outputPath is specified, the default is shpName.xml.

Shape Testing

The accompanying distribution includes a general-purpose web page (default.htm) for testing stored procedures in general, and shapes in particular. The page provides three panes: the list pane, the form pane and the results pane. The list pane shows all of the stored procedures defined in a configured database that match a search criterion, such as "shp%".

The form pane presents text boxes for each parameter of a stored procedure selected from the list pane as well as a button to execute it. The form displays default values and data types for each parameter and a checkbox to specify use of the default. The form pane also allows for the specification of invoker options, such as an XSLT transform or output file name. The results pane shows the shape results, typically as XML.

Use of the shape testing web page requires the creation of one stored procedure and one user-defined function within the configured database. See the installation instructions for details.

Conclusion

While there are several documented methods for creating XML from relational data, none offers the combination of simplicity, performance and control that encourages widespread adoption. With shapes, a developer can use familiar tools and language (T-SQL) to create a single, intuitive stored procedure that produces a potentially complex, precisely controlled XML document that is URL- and ommand-line-addressable. Moreover, the data for the document are gathered with optimal efficiency in a single trip to the database, and assembled into XML by client processes that can be distributed across intermediate servers. To see shapes in action without performing any installation, visit http://tech.rssgroup.com/shapes.

Currently, the tools are .NET-based and SQL Server centric. The concept and the grammar, however, are thoroughly portable and could support different databases (notably Oracle) and different middleware (e.g. java). Given sufficient interest, I will establish a project on SourceForge.NET to manage future development.

Installation

To experiment with shapes, I recommend using Microsoft's standard Northwind database (although if you have a test database with existing stored procedures that can be more interesting).

1. The first step is to create a directory to host a simple website, let's say:

   c:\inetpub\wwwroot\shapes

2. Unzip the included files to that directory:

   default.htm   - presents a frameset used to test shapes

   web.config   - configures database access

   bin\RSSWebShapes.dll - the shape interpreter

   _xslt\shpList.xslt   - used by default.htm

3. Edit the properties of the website using Internet Services Manager:

   a.   create a new application for the site if it is using the Default Application

   b.   turn off anonymous access – this means the web user's credentials will be used to establish database connections.

4. Edit the database connection string in web.config:

```
<DatabaseConnectionSets>
  <local        core="server=localhost;database=Northwind;trusted_connection=yes"
  />
</DatabaseConnectionSets>
```

5. Use Query Analyzer to install shpList and some sample shapes.

   _sql\shpList.sql   - T-SQL proc used by default.htm

   _sql\shpSamples.sql   - T-SQL procs for experimentation

6. Open http://localhost/shapes/

   This site is a generic site for listing and executing stored procedures. It is especially useful for testing shapes.

Using OpenXML

By Raj Vasant

Introduction

OPENXML provides an easy way to use an XML document as a data-source for your procedures.

OPENXML allows the data in XML document to be treated just like the columns and rows of your database table i.e., xml tags as columns and the value as rows. Data can be inserted / updated very quickly and efficiently without multiple trips to the database.

For example, if 100 records are to inserted / updated, then the traditional SQL method is using 100 insert / update statements. This means that 100 trips are made to the database, which results in degradation of performance. Using XML, these 100 trips can be reduced to 1 trip. This increases the performance of your application.

In this article, we would look at the basic syntax of OpenXML and end with a simple example.

Basic Syntax

OPENXML (**idoc** int [in],**rowpattern** nvarchar[in],[**flags** byte[in]]) [WITH **SchemaDeclaration | TableName**)]

Arguments
Idoc is the document handle of the internal representation of an XML document.
This handle is obtained by calling the system stored procedure sp_xml_preparedocument, which is

discussed later.

Rowpattern is the XPath query used to identify the nodes to be processed as rows.

Flags indicates the mapping between the XML data and the relational rowset. (optional parameter)

0 - Defaults to attribute-centric mapping.
1 - Attribute-centric mapping. (Combined with XML_ELEMENTS)
2 - Element-centric mapping. (Combined with XML_ATTRIBUTES)
8 - Combined with XML_ATTRIBUTES or XML_ELEMENTS

SchemaDeclaration is the schema definition of the form:

ColName ColType [ColPattern | MetaProperty][, ColName ColType [ColPattern | MetaProperty]...]

Eg: WITH (EMPLOYEENAME VARCHAR(30), EMPLOYEESALARY INTEGER)

TableName is the table name that can be given, instead of Schema Declaration, if a table exists.

The **WITH** clause provides a table format using either **SchemaDeclaration** or specifying an existing **TableName**. If the optional WITH clause is not specified, the results are returned in an **edge table** format. Edge tables represent the fine-grained XML document structure (e.g. element/attribute names, the document hierarchy, the namespaces, PIs etc.) in a single table.

System Stored Procedures for OpenXML

SQL Server provides system stored procedures that are used in conjunction with OPENXML:

- sp_xml_preparedocument
- sp_xml_removedocument

To write queries using OPENXML, you must first create an internal representation of the XML document by calling **sp_xml_preparedocument**. It is similar to LoadXML() function provided in System.XML namespace. The stored procedure returns a handle to the internal representation of the XML document. This handle is then passed to OPENXML, which provides tabular view of the document based on Xpath query.

The internal representation of an XML document can be removed from memory by calling **sp_xml_removedocument** system stored procedure.

About sp_xml_preparedocument

Steps which occurs when this procedure is executed:

1. Reads the XML text provided as input.
2. Parses the text using the XML parser.
3. Provides the parsed document, which is in tree form containing various nodes (elements, attributes, text, comments, and so on) in the XML document.
4. It returns a handle that can be used to access the newly created internal representation of the XML document. This handle is valid for until the connection is reset, or until the execution of sp_xml_removedocument.

Note: A parsed document is stored in the internal cache of SQL Server 2000. The MSXML parser uses one-eighth the total memory available for SQL Server. To avoid running out of memory, run **sp_xml_removedocument** to free up the memory.

The syntax is:

sp_xml_preparedocument **hdoc** OUTPUT [, **xmltext**] [, **xpath_namespaces**]

hdoc is the handle to the newly created document.(Integer value)

[**xmltext**] is the original XML document. The default value is NULL, in which case an internal representation of an empty XML document is created.

[**xpath_namespaces**] Specifies the namespace declarations that are used in row and column XPath expressions in OPENXML.

Returns: 0 (success) or >0 (failure)

About sp_xml_removedocument

Removes the internal representation of the XML document specified by the document handle.

The syntax is: sp_xml_removedocument hdoc

hdoc is the handle to the newly created document.(Integer value)

Returns: 0 (success) or >0 (failure)

Basic structure of stored-procedure(using OPENXML)

```
CREATE PROCEDURE dbo.TestOpenXML
(        @strXML VARCHAR(2000)
)
AS
DECLARE @XMLDocPointer INT
EXEC sp_xml_preparedocument @XMLDocPointer OUTPUT, @strXML
BEGIN TRANSACTION
      ------ Any DML can be used here -------(see examples)
COMMIT
EXEC sp_xml_removedocument @XMLDocPointer
RETURN
```

Examples

Consider two tables: Employees & Departments.
  Employees: EmployeeID, EmployeeName, EmployeeSalary, DeptID.
  Departments: DeptID, DeptName.
  (EmployeeID and DeptID are Identity fileds.)

The XML file will follow the structure.
(XML Type 1)

```
<RECORD>
  <EMPLOYEE>
    <EMPLOYEENAME>Test Name</EMPLOYEENAME>
    <EMPLOYEESALARY>1000</EMPLOYEESALARY>
    <DEPTID>10</DEPTID>
  </EMPLOYEE>
    .
```

```
</RECORD>
```

If 100 employees have been recruited, u can generate a XML file having the following structure with 100 <EMPLOYEE> tags, the query should be:

```
INSERT INTO Employees(EmployeeName, EmployeeSalary, DeptID)
SELECT EMPLOYEENAME, EMPLOYEESALARY, DEPTID
FROM OPENXML(@XMLDocPointer,'/RECORD/EMPLOYEE',2)
WITH (EMPLOYEENAME VARCHAR(30), EMPLOYEESALARY INTEGER, DEPTID INTEGER)
```

If 100 employees are transferred from Production Department to Stores Department, the query should be:

```
UPDATE Employees
SET DeptID = xmlTable.DEPTID
FROM OPENXML(@XMLDocPointer,'/RECORD/EMPLOYEE',2)
WITH (EMPLOYEEID INTEGER, DEPTID INTEGER) XmlTable
WHERE XmlTable.EMPLOYEEID = Employees.EmployeeID
```

Note: use of alias for XML document is required to avoid confusion.

If the XML file contains attributes, there is minor change to the syntax.
(XML Type 2)

```
<RECORD>
<EMPLOYEE DEPTID = '10' NAME = 'Test' SALARY = '10000'/>
<EMPLOYEE DEPTID = '10' NAME = 'Test' SALARY = '10000'/>
<EMPLOYEE DEPTID = '10' NAME = 'Test' SALARY = '10000'/>
.
.
</RECORD>
INSERT INTO Employees(EmployeeName, EmployeeSalary, DeptID)
SELECT NAME, SALARY, DEPTID
FROM OPENXML(@XMLDocPointer,'/RECORD/EMPLOYEE',2)
WITH (NAME VARCHAR(30) '@NAME',
SALARY INT '@SALARY',
DEPTID INT '@DEPTID')
```

Another scenario for attributes (accessing the parent node)
(XML Type 3)

```
<RECORD>
    <DEPT ID='10'>
        <EMPLOYEE NAME = 'Test101' SALARY = '10000'/>
        <EMPLOYEE NAME = 'Test102' SALARY = '10000'/>
    </DEPT>
    <DEPT ID='11'>
        <EMPLOYEE NAME = 'Test111' SALARY = '10000'/>
        <EMPLOYEE NAME = 'Test112' SALARY = '10000'/>
        <EMPLOYEE NAME = 'Test113' SALARY = '10000'/>
        <EMPLOYEE NAME = 'Test114' SALARY = '10000'/>
    </DEPT>
    .
    .
</RECORD>
INSERT INTO Employees (EmployeeName, EmployeeSalary, DeptID)
SELECT NAME, SALARY, DEPTID
FROM OPENXML (@XMLDocPointer,'/RECORD/DEPT/EMPLOYEE',2)
WITH (NAME VARCHAR(30) '@NAME',
SALARY INT '@SALARY',
DEPTID INT '../@ID')
```

Finally, your store procedure should look like (using XML Type 2):

```
CREATE PROCEDURE dbo.TestOpenXML
(       @strXML VARCHAR(2000)
)
AS
DECLARE @XMLDocPointer INT
EXEC sp_xml_preparedocument @XMLDocPointer OUTPUT, @strXML
BEGIN TRANSACTION
        INSERT INTO Employees(EmployeeName, EmployeeSalary, DeptID)
        SELECT NAME, SALARY, DEPTID
```

```
FROM OPENXML(@XMLDocPointer,'/RECORD/EMPLOYEE',2)
        WITH (NAME VARCHAR(30) '@NAME', SALARY INT '@SALARY', DEPTID INT '@DEPTID')

COMMIT
EXEC sp_xml_removedocument @XMLDocPointer

RETURN
```

Conclusion

With SQL Server 2000, there are many ways you can get XML representation of relational data. One simple way is using the FOR XML clause with SELECT statement. A reverse mechanism, which allows turning XML document into tabular, relational rowset format is provided by T-SQL keyword named OPENXML.

The steps for using OPENXML can be simplified as:

1. Call sp_xml_preparedocument. (system stored procedure which loads XML document string into memory, parses it and returns a handle).
2. Use XPath querries for extracting required information from the XML through the handle.
3. Call sp_xml_removedocument. (system stored procedure which frees up the memory allocated to the internal representation of the XML document).

In this article, we studied the OPENXML syntax and options available with it, with simpe examples. Future articles we will discuss other XML features offered by SQL Server 2000.

Using OPENXML Part II

By Raj Vasant

Introduction

OpenXML is a feature of SQL Server 2000, which allows manipulation of XML data in your database. You can get the basics for OpenXML by going through Books online or my previous article Using OpenXML.

Most of the applications use XML as their data carrier for bulk data processing. For example, you can pass a XML string to your stored procedure containing the list of selected ID's of the record and return back or do some processing for that set of ID's. This reduces your database trips.

There might be some instances where one of your procedures is calling another procedure and so on. The procedure is using XML as one of its parameter and some part of that same XML data needs to be processed in other procedures. It is not possible to break your XML data and pass it to other procedure. Surely you can pass the entire XML data again to the other procedure. This way of passing data uses more memory chunk as your XML data will be loaded whenever sp_xml_preparedocument is used in each procedure.

Another way for reusing your XML data is by using the document handle returned from sp_xml_preparedocument in the first procedure, as an argument to the other stored procedures using the same XML data. This document handle points to the internal representation of an XML document.

You do not need to load the XML data again in each procedure as the same document handle is used in each procedure.

Example:

This is the test table used.

```
CREATE TABLE  Test_table (
        Id int IDENTITY (1, 1) NOT NULL ,
        MyName VARCHAR(50) NULL ,
        City VARCHAR(50) NULL
)
(bare with the NULL's in the column definition :>)
```

Code for the main procedure which will have XML data as its parameter:

```
CREATE PROCEDURE Test_OpenXML
(@strXML VARCHAR(8000))
AS
DECLARE @intPointer INT
SET @strXML =
EXEC sp_xml_preparedocument @intPointer output, @strXML
INSERT into Test_Table (MyName, City)
SELECT MYNAME , CITY FROM OpenXML(@intPointer,'/RECORD',2)
WITH (MYNAME VARCHAR(50), CITY VARCHAR(50))
EXEC Test_OpenXML_Child @intPointer
EXEC sp_xml_removedocument @intPointer
GO
```

Code for child procedure which is executed from the main procedure and has parameter of INT type, which will be used as document handle for OpenXML:

```
CREATE PROCEDURE Test_OpenXML_Child
( @Pointer INT )AS
INSERT into Test_Table (City)
SELECT CITY FROM OpenXML(@Pointer,'/RECORD',2)
WITH (CITY VARCHAR(50))
GO
```

In query analyzer use the following:

```
DECLARE @str VARCHAR(8000)
SET @str = '<RECORD><MYNAME>Vasant Raj</MYNAME><CITY>Vadodara</CITY></RECORD>'
EXEC Test_OpenXML @str
```

This query will insert two rows in the Test_table. This was a very simple example.

Conclusion

This logic can be implemented in very complex situations where you have all the details in single XML parameter and part of this XML data is used by different procedures.

Replication

Replication is one of those technologies that isn't widely used, but when someone decides to implement it, it usually becomes an integral part of the enterprise.

Content on the new version of SQL Server has been fairly scarce, probably because most people know there will be changes and are waiting until at least Beta 3 to do any heavy duty writing. The changes from then to the RTM version, if this product follows a similar cycle to those in the past, will be mostly performance related.

So if you haven't seen the product, here's a small sample of what it's like.

Handling Conflicts in Merge Replication

By Satia Madimchetty

Introduction

Merge replication is a bi-directional replication where the data changes that occur on the publisher and the subscriber are merged at the time of synchronization. This article primarily focuses on how merge replication detects conflicts and how they are resolved using the default and custom conflict handlers.

Conflict Detection

Conflict occurs whenever data changes both on the publisher and the subscriber at the time of synchronization. You can specify whether you want merge replication to recognize conflicts at a row-level or at a column-level based on your business requirements. This is illustrated in figure 1. When row-level conflict detection is enabled for the authors table, changes to a particular row in the table on the publisher and the subscriber will be considered a conflict even though the columns changed may be different. However, in the case of column-level conflict detection, the data changes must happen to the same columns in a particular row on both the publisher and the subscriber.

Figure 1. Choosing the conflict detection type

For instance, the last name for the author Michel has changed from DeFrance to Olivier on the publisher, while the phone number has changed from 219- 547-9982 to 340-545-6677 on the subscriber. In this case, merge replication will detect a conflict only if row-level conflict detection has been enabled for the table Authors. If column-level detection is enabled, then the changes will be merged without any conflict. Regardless of the conflict type, when a conflict occurs, the entire row from the publisher will overwrite the one on the subscriber if the default conflict resolver is selected (Figure 2.) and if the publisher wins the conflict.

Figure 2. Choosing the conflict resolver type

In merge replication, all updates and inserts are tracked in the **MSmerge_contents** system table and deletes in **MSmerge_tombstone** system table in the publication and subscription databases. For each row modified in a base table there is only one row created in these two system tables. The **lineage** column in the two system tables plays the role of version tracking for all the changes that have occurred to a row so far. At the time of synchronization, the merge agent compares the lineage values in the system tables on the publisher and the subscribers. If they are different then the row has been updated since the last synchronization.

If conflict detection is enabled at the column level for a table, then **colvl** column (varbinary data type) in MSmerge_contents system table tracks version numbers for all the columns in the base table. Suppose if the lastname column in the authors table is updated, the lineage value for the row changes and the colvl correspondingly gets a new version number to reflect this change. So column-level tracking results in more overhead compared to the row-level as changes to every single column in a table have to be tracked. After the synchronization, the lineage and the colvl values are updated so that the versions values look identical on the publisher and the subscriber.

Conflict Resolution

SQL Server comes with a wide range of conflict resolvers. Let us look at some of the available options

1. Default Resolver

The default resolver is a priority-based resolver, where you can assign different priority values to the subscribers to determine who would win in the case of a conflict.

When setting up a subscriber using the wizard, you will see a screen as illustrated in figure 3 where you can set the subscription priority. There are two options you can choose from. The first one creates a local subscriber, so that the merge agent uses the publisher as a proxy for the subscriber when resolving conflicts. A local subscriber is one whose priority is 0.00. The second option creates a global subscriber with the priority value you assign. You can assign priority values between 0.00 and 99.99 to the global subscribers. Subscribers with higher values win over those with lower values when a conflict occurs.

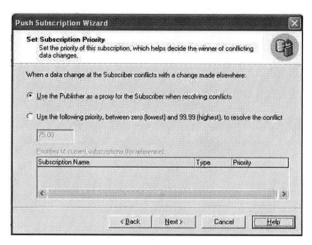

Figure 3. Choosing the subscription priority

When you want all your subscribers to have the same level of priority then, you can create local subscribers. After the first local subscriber synchronizes with the publisher, the changes assume the priority value of the publisher. Since the publisher has the highest priority by default, the first local subscriber's changes at the publisher will always win over any subscriber conflicts during later synchronizations.

When you want different subscribers to have different priorities, you can manually assign the priority values. Let us look at a few examples to understand how conflicts between subscribers with different priority levels are resolved. Let us assume that Company ABC has its headquarters in Dallas (Publisher) with four other office locations as illustrated in the table below. We have couple of local subscribers and couple of global subscribers at Chicago and New York with priority values of 90 and 65 respectively. Data changes made at any location will be merged with the rest.

Location	Priority
Dallas (Publisher)	100.00
Atlanta (Local Subscriber)	0.00
Chicago (Global Subscriber)	90.00
New York (Global Subscriber)	65.00
Phoenix (Local Subscriber)	0.00

Let us assume that a Customer David Smith lives in zip 77523. Initially all the subscribers have the same value.

Location	Zip
Dallas (Publisher)	77523
Atlanta (Local Subscriber)	77523
Chicago (Global Subscriber)	77523
New York (Global Subscriber)	77523
Phoenix (Local Subscriber)	77523

Scenario 1: Publisher and Local Subscriber Conflict on update

Publisher updates the zip for David Smith to 77644 and the Local subscriber at Atlanta changes it to 76222. The next time Atlanta synchronizes with the publisher (Dallas), a conflict is detected. Since the publisher has the highest priority, the changes at the publisher win. The rest of the subscribers subsequently synchronize with the publisher and receive the changes.

Location	Zip
Dallas (Publisher)	77644

Atlanta (Local Subscriber)	77644
Chicago (Global Subscriber)	77644
New York (Global Subscriber)	77644
Phoenix (Local Subscriber)	77644

Scenario 2: Publisher and Global Subscriber Conflict on update

Publisher now updates the zip for David Smith to 72233 and the Global subscriber at Chicago changes it to 72111. The next time Chicago synchronizes with the publisher (Dallas), a conflict is detected. Since the publisher has the highest priority, the changes at the publisher win. The rest of the subscribers subsequently synchronize with the publisher and receive the changes.

Location	Zip
Dallas (Publisher)	72233
Atlanta (Local Subscriber)	72233
Chicago (Global Subscriber)	72233
New York (Global Subscriber)	72233
Phoenix (Local Subscriber)	72233

Scenario 3: Global and Local Subscriber Conflict on update

Suppose the Global Subscriber at New York updates the zip for David Smith to 55223 and the Local subscriber at Phoenix updates it to 43232. There are two possibilities here as to who wins the conflict based on who synchronizes with the Publisher (Dallas) first.

Case 1: Global Subscriber Synchronizes first

Suppose the Global Subscriber at New York synchronizes first with the publisher.

The priority value of 65 for this subscriber is also stored at the publisher. When the local subscriber synchronizes now, it loses since the global subscriber has a higher priority level.

Location	Zip
Dallas (Publisher)	55223
Atlanta (Local Subscriber)	55223
Chicago (Global Subscriber)	55223
New York (Global Subscriber)	55223
Phoenix (Local Subscriber)	55223

Case 2: Local Subscriber Synchronizes first

Suppose the Local Subscriber at Phoenix synchronizes first with the publisher.

The changes take the priority of the publisher. When the global subscriber synchronizes now, it loses since the Publisher has the highest priority level.

Location	Zip
Dallas (Publisher)	43232
Atlanta (Local Subscriber)	43232
Chicago (Global Subscriber)	43232
New York (Global Subscriber)	43232
Phoenix (Local Subscriber)	43232

Scenario 4: Global Subscribers Conflict on update

Suppose the Global Subscriber at New York updates the zip for David Smith to 76063 and the Global subscriber at Chicago updates it to 66345. New York (priority value 65.00) synchronizes first with the publisher. The priority value of 65 is stored at the publisher to resolve any conflicts. When Chicago (priority value of 90.00) synchronizes now, the subscriber with the highest priority value wins the conflict regardless of whether it is the first one to synchronize

Location	City
Dallas (Publisher)	66345
Atlanta (Local Subscriber)	66345
Chicago (Global Subscriber)	66345
New York (Global Subscriber)	66345
Phoenix (Local Subscriber)	66345

2. Custom Resolvers

If the default resolver does not meet your business requirements you can choose to use a custom resolver. Custom Resolvers are specific to a table. If you alter your table, make sure that you modify the resolver accordingly.

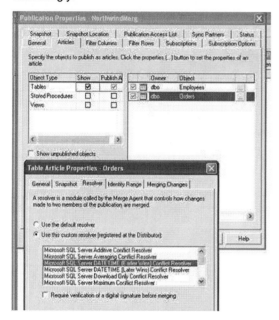

Figure 4. Choosing a Custom Resolver

You can choose a custom resolver by clicking on the Table Properties button (...) and selecting the Resolver tab on the Properties screen as shown in figure 4. You can also use the merge stored procedures sp_addmergearticle and sp_changemergearticle to specify the custom resolvers.

SQL Server comes with a number of custom resolvers. In most cases you will specify a column name as the required input for the resolver. For instance in the case of "Maximum Conflict Resolver", the publisher or the subscriber with the larger column value will be the conflict winner. However if you choose "Subscriber Always Wins Conflict Resolver", you do not have to provide a column name as an input since the subscriber row wins each time there is a conflict. Here is a list of the custom resolvers that come with SQL Server installation.

- Microsoft SQL Server Additive Conflict Resolver
- Microsoft SQL Server Averaging Conflict Resolver
- Microsoft SQL Server DATETIME (Earlier Wins) Conflict Resolver
- Microsoft SQL Server DATATIME (Later Winds) Conflict Resolver
- Microsoft SQL Server Maximum Conflict Resolver
- Microsoft SQL Server Merge Text Conflict Resolver
- Microsoft SQL Server Minimum Conflict Resolver
- Microsoft SQL Server Subscriber Always Wins Conflict Resolver
- Microsoft SQL Server Upload Only Conflict Resolver

COM based Conflict Resolver

If the above mentioned conflict resolvers do not suit your needs you can write a COM based custom resolver using Visual Basic or VC++ and register the DLL at the server where the merge agent runs. For a push subscription the merge agent runs at the distributor and for pull at the subscriber.

Stored Procedure Conflict Resolver

You can write a stored procedure based custom conflict resolver that uses T-SQL to implement your business logic which determines who the winner will be. Stored procedure resolvers are always created on the publisher and only for update conflicts. Stored procedure resolvers return a single row that is identical to the schema of the base table. You can also change the values in any of the columns when you return the final result set. This row will be the winning row and the values will be used to update both the publisher and the subscriber.

The custom stored procedure that you create uses the following required parameters

Parameter	Type	Comments
@tableowner	sysname	Owner for the conflicting table
@tablename	sysname	Name of the conflicting table
@rowguid	uniqueidentifier	Rowguid for the row having the conflict
@subscriber	sysname	Subscriber server that is synchronizing
@subscriber_db	sysname	Name Database on the conflicting subscriber
@log_conflictOUTPUT	INT	Merge logs the conflict based on the value provided.
@conflict_messageOUTPUT	nvarchar(512)	Message to be logged

Let us take a simple example of an ordering system for a retail company ABC. The publisher will be the database server at the corporate office. The subscribers will be the servers at the individual stores. We will just look at one table "Products" from the Northwind database for our discussion purposes. The schema for the products table has been slightly altered and is as follows

Products

Column	Type
ProductID	int
ProductName	nvarchar (40)
SupplierID	int
CategoryID	int
UnitPrice	money
UnitsInStock	smallint
UnitsOnOrder	smallint
ReorderLevel	smallint
Discontinued	bit
OrderQuantity	smallint
rowguid	uniqueidentifier

Let us assume that the retail stores can request products by updating the OrderQuantity column. Company ABC wants to write a custom stored procedure that handles conflicts when multiple stores (subscribers) change the same data. ABC has decided to code the following business logic in the conflict resolver.

- Each time a conflict occurs, add the values of the OrderQuantity column from the publisher and the subscriber. Basically if store x orders 50 and store y 100, the final value in the OrderQuantity column should be 150 (x+y)
- Compute the Units to be ordered based on the units already ordered and Units in Stock
- If the Units that need to be ordered is greater than the ReorderLevel, place an order and update the UnitsonOrder column

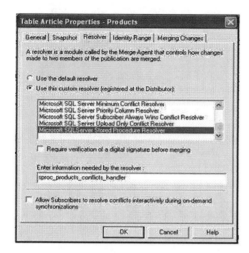

Figure 5. Choosing a Stored procedure Custom Resolver

Once you create your stored procedure in the publication database, you can choose the Custom resolver option from the Products table properties and enter the name of the stored procedure as illustrated in figure 5. Alternatively, you can set the values of **@article_resolver** and **@resolver_info** arguments in the merge sp_addmergearticle stored procedure while creating the publication.

Conclusion

Hopefully this article provides enough information for you to choose among the various conflict resolvers and detection types that would meet your business requirements. For DBAs with little or no programming background in VB or C++ my recommendation is to implement the stored procedure custom resolver. However keep in mind that you will need to change the final SQL statement in the procedure every time you modify the structure of your base table.

Satia Madimchetty
Sr. Consultant, Scalability Experts

Moving Replicated Databases

by Andy Warren

I'm sure most of you have detached a database, maybe to move it to another server, or just to move it to another drive. Did you know that if you've enabled replication for the database you can no longer detach it?

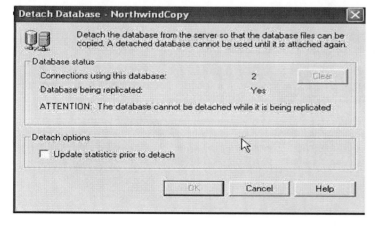

I ran into this a couple years ago. We had added disk space and I needed to move things around, but almost every database I have is replicated. It seemed like there should be an easier way, but sometimes you go with what you know (and is recommended), so I scripted out all the existing publications, removed replication, moved the database, then ran the scripts to add replication back. It takes a good amount of time and effort if you have many publications.

All of the following comments apply only to transactional replication, I would expect similar behavior with merge replication but I have not tested it.

Just in thinking about it, I saw no reason detach shouldn't work. If you detached the database and log file, the log file would contain any committed transaction that had not yet been picked up by the log reader. Provided you reattached the same files back to the same server it seemed like everything would pick up right where it left off.

To start testing I set up a copy of Northwind, enabled transactional replication, and created a publication containing only the category table, and then created a subscription to a new database called NorthwindCopy2. After verifying that replication was working, I went back to make sure I was sure about the detach behavior. I tried three separate methods and all returned the same result – failure. Those methods were:

- Detaching via Enterprise Manager

- Running sp_detachdb from Query Analyzer

- Running DBCC Detachdb which is what really does the work

Clearly it was able to discern that the database was published. I remembered seeing an sp_dboption switch, so I started there. Syntax is straightforward:

```
Sp_dboption 'NorthwindCopy', 'published', false
```

Running it successfully changed the publication status, it also wiped out the publication! Obviously someone is serious about not letting mortals detach a replicated database.

So, time for some deeper study. Assuming the info about replication is probably tied to the database, I query sysdatabases. Nothing obvious, so I jump to BOL. Sure enough, the category column contains a flag for replication and my test environment confirms the settings show below.

category	int	Contains a bitmap of information used for replication:
		1 = Published. 2 = Subscribed. 4 = Merge Published. 8 = Merge Subscribed.

Because I needed to modify a system table, I needed a couple extra steps before I could try the detach again:

```
sp_configure 'allow updates', 1
reconfigure with override
update sysdatabases set category=0 where name='northwindcopy'
```

At this point if you refresh Enterprise Manager the database no longer appears to be published and the publication folder is gone. Detaching the database works without an error as expected.

The first difference I noticed from the early sp_dboption attempt is that the replication jobs were still present. A good cleanup would have removed them. The log reader job had failed indicating it could not run sp_replcmds, which makes sense since the database has been detached!

Before I tried to put things back I wanted to rule out one area of concern I had – what if the database id changed? In my test case the removed database had been 9. I ran a create database statement to create a placeholder database and verified it had been assigned 9, assuring that when I reattached my original database it would get a new id. I reattached using Enterprise Manager, and then ran the opposite script from earlier:

```
update sysdatabases set category=1 where name='northwindcopy'
```

Refreshing Enterprise Manager showed the database as published, the publication was present again, and when I restarted the logreader job it ran without error. I was able to successfully apply transactions to my subscriber database.

Caveats? A few!

- This is only going to work if you reattach to the same server AND you don't change anything else related to replication (distribution database, jobs, etc)

- You're making a change to a system table. Not a reason to shiver in fear, but exercise caution, and be sure to reset allow updates back to false when you're done

- I have not tested this with merge replication

- It's probably not going to be supported if something goes wrong – have a backup and a script of your publications

It's not a technique you'll use often, but maybe one day it will save you some time.

Adventures in Replication

By Chris Rock

A few months ago my company opened a new call center. One of the issues that we knew we were going to face was keeping the data for a client current between two call centers. My boss (Andy Warren) decided to use a combination of queued updates and merge replication. This was running smoothly until last week. For some unknown reason all of the publications became invalidated. This meant that all the subscriptions had to be reinitialized and all the data had to be re-snapshot. This is no problem for some of our smaller tables but the majority of the tables had 1 million+ records. The biggest tables had 9 million+ rows in them. Yikes!!!

Andy and I came up with a plan to get this done and I was almost ready to go. I say almost because I was a little reluctant to take this on as I'm primarily a developer with a second title of Junior DBA (kind of the pseudo-DBA if you will). I'm comfortable with snapshot and transactional replication but merge is a whole new ballgame; one I didn't understand (like croquet).

A couple of other reasons I was reluctant to take this on was if I screw this up, not only do I create more work for my already overworked boss, but I potentially keep 20+ people from working. Luckily I came through and saved the day. Well not really, but you get the idea. I learned a few lessons along the way and I'm a better pseudo-DBA for it.

Here is the plan that we came up with:

1. Rename the tables on the subscriber to keep as a backup.
2. Reinitialize the snapshot (let the publisher re-create the table, etc)
3. To make sure the data was consistent after the snapshot I had to:
   a) Insert rows from the backup tables that didn't exist on the snapshotted (is that a word?) table from the publisher.
   b) Update rows on the table that was snapshotted (seriously, I don't think this is a word) where the data didn't match what was on backup table.

Simple as it looks, I learned the hard way that it wasn't that easy.

Lesson 1
In reference to transactional / queued updates publications; tables that exist in the publication and have already been part of a subscription before a re-initialization, have to be present on the subscriber, otherwise the distribution agent fails. (See error message below). This was perplexing as I thought the publisher would create the table no matter what if the article setting was "Drop existing table and re-create it."

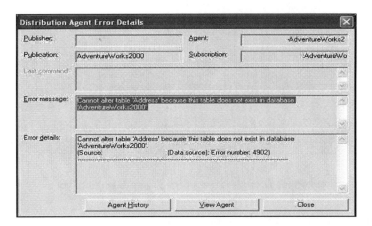

Lesson 2 - Again, in reference to transactional / queued replication; the table has to be almost an exact copy of what's on the publisher (not including indexes) if the table was part of the publication before a re-initialization of the subscription. To solve lesson 1 I created a table with the same name as the table on the publisher. The distribution agent failed with the same message above. I created a shell of the table without the constraints; the distribution agent failed again!!!! What the hell was going on? I was really irritated at this point. What finally worked was scripting the table from the publisher and creating it on the subscriber (constraints and all). I started the distribution agent again and I finally saw the bulk copy starting.

Lesson 3 - To snapshot a lot of rows requires a lot MORE time if the database is 80 miles away. This is kind of obvious, but I was a little surprised how long it really takes. When I ran the snapshot for the 9 million row table overnight I woke up to a surprise. In 9 hours only 6.7 millions rows went over. I had to stop the distribution agent, rename the backup table and recreate the constraints. Fun, Fun, Fun... Out of sync for a few more days. I finally ran the snapshot on a Saturday and for some reason the data went over much faster. This allowed me to run the snapshot for the 14 million row table in the next day. Maybe less network traffic was the difference.

Lesson 4 - The distribution agent does not always give you a status update of the bulk copy. I'm used to seeing the distribution agent give some type of status of the bulk copy with transactional replication (100000 rows copied, etc). The merge replication distribution agent does not give any type of status. This freaked me out for a while. I thought that once again something else went wrong. Finally, I discovered that if I query the table on the subscriber I could see the row count.

Lesson 5 - You can keep data synced between two tables using queued updates with transactional replication. I thought the only way to keep data synced up between two tables was to use merge replication. I found out that using transactional replication with queued updates can accomplish basically the same thing. One major difference is queued updates cannot keep text and image columns synced between the two tables. I found the official explanation on the msdn site. The Subscriber cannot update or insert **text** or **image** values because they cannot be read from the inserted or deleted tables inside the trigger. Similarly, the Subscriber cannot update or insert **text** or **image** values using WRITETEXT or UPDATETEXT because the data is overwritten by the Publisher. Instead, you could partition the **text** and **image** columns into a separate table and modify the two tables within a transaction. Use merge replication to synchronize these values. You cannot be assured there are no conflicts because the update of the **text** or **image** table can occur if the data is not well partitioned.

Lesson 6 - Maybe I should read more articles on sqlservercentral.com about replication.

Conclusion

All in all I'm sure everything would have gone much smoother if I read about what I was doing beforehand, but I had Andy to help me along the way. I was happy with the solution. Whether you agree that it was the best solution is another matter, it worked. I hope that by reading this you understand the struggles that an Until next time...Happy databasing!

Everything Else

The stuff that doesn't really fit into any category, mostly things that might be related to the softer side of being a DBA, your career, getting better at the non-technical parts of your job.

Hopefully these are the articles that give you some ideas, make you think, and help you to differentiate yourself from others. This year it's mostly a collection of job and career related advice from Steve Jones

Employee Retention

By Steve Jones

Not that I'm an expert, but I've been in large and small companies, both as a grunt, doing actual work for the company and as a manager, supervising others. I also read and think about this stuff since I think it matters.

Hopefully this will be a fairly timeless series that you can refer to throughout your career and pass along to your managers and others that are interested. Please be sure that you read the feedback as this is one place where lots of other opinions, not just mine, will be cast and there will be good information as well. You can see what others have posted in the "Your Opinion" tab at the bottom of the article.

Why Retain Employees?

It would seem like a silly question, I mean, why not retain employees who have worked for you? The traditional business employee relationship in history was based on the fact that the employee would work for the company, get paid, remain loyal, and the company would provide employment, training, etc., and everyone would work together for the majority of their lives. Except for slavery or if you couldn't or wouldn't do the job, you typically had a job for life. Even in the craft trades where someone would apprentice, it was expected the master would get years of service.

With the rise of capitalism, especially in the technology area, it seems that there is no loyalty, people switching jobs on a whim. And when demand exceeds supply, it's horrible, as I've seen people accept one job, and then accept another, withdrawing from their first commitment before they start!! With supply outstripping demand, as it has the last few years, the situation becomes reversed with layoffs, forced performance rankings, and no security for the worker.

But both of these markets are bad for everyone. When there is turnover, it has an impact on both the employer and employee. The employee that suspects that they will not remain in their position for a long time and as a result, does not do their best work. Nor do they remain loyal, working in the best interests of the company. We all tend to work in our own best interests. Even most of our "going the extra mile", working longer hours, taking a little more time or doing a little extra work, is mainly a benefit for ourselves. We feel better, expect a bonus, recognition, or maybe enjoy the time spent with our co-workers, but there is something in it for us. If we do not feel this loyalty, then we tend not to work that little bit extra.

Employers also suffer when the employee is not loyal or doesn't work as hard. But there is another issue that is associated with employees that are not retained. There is a knowledge loss, business knowledge, product knowledge, even social knowledge that is gone whenever there is turnover. Many large companies ignore this fact, instead treating all people as "resources", for the most part interchangeable, and easily replaceable. The forced turnover of many large companies, the desire to have teams composed strictly of "high achievers" and superstars, is a good idea at first glance, but one that fails in the long run.

In a corporate environment, the business knowledge is invaluable. It takes time to learn how a particular business works and the quirks of a particular company. A large part of the training time, the lost work often pegged at a few weeks, but in reality, much longer, is acquiring knowledge about the particular business. And the more turnover that you have, the more time is "lost" in terms of growing and enhancing your business, because of new employees having to relearn the same things over and over.

The cost of new employees is often quantified in big companies with a day or two of dedicated training and an allotted week or two to get trained in your particular environment. In IT it's usually learning the domain structures, passwords, procedures for various work, etc. For developers it's time learning the code control, staging processes, styles, and getting familiar with the particular product being worked on. But this ignores another factor. The lost time by current employees in answering questions, training, slowing down their work to accommodate a newcomer, etc. Even simple social time, introductions, coffee breaks to chat, small talk at the beginning of meetings, add up to overall lost productivity.

There are certainly cases where this time is minimized in some jobs, but in a large number, it's not. It is lost time just as a virus in a white collar environment "costs" money to eradicate. It's a soft cost, a time lost cost, but it's still one to consider.

Morale

Morale is seemingly less and less a consideration of the modern corporation. I used to work in a large power company where the majority of employees at the power station were blue collar. And morale was something that was important with a large number of events and functions that were designed to bring people together, managers spent time getting to know people and minimize turnover. People were unique and treated as such, with the recognition that people will always complain and there will be issues, but a higher level of morale means more productivity.

As I moved on to more white collar environments, I noticed less and less effort being put towards morale. It was less often that I saw managers beyond my own working with and getting to know the people that were employees. Less and less concern over how they felt and how their lives outside of work were of some importance. It goes with the job, became a phrase uttered more and more, with the expectation that you should just go the extra mile when it was asked of you. And surprisingly, with the emphasis on individual performance and measurements, there is a constant talk of "teamwork".

In my years of working, there are a few things that I've learned and one of which is that people act in their own best interest. Almost always that is true as I've mentioned above. If you want to get the work focused on what is in the best interests of the company, you have to move some of that self interest from bonuses and commissions to the softer, more ethereal rewards of loyalty, teamwork, and pride. Just as salesman sell the products whose commission serve their paycheck the most, a company wants to get an employee to perform better by changing their rewards from strictly financial to more emotional

I truly believe that this is achieved by building teams of individuals, using their strengths, and showing some loyalties to your employees. Synergies are created that will motivate and reward the employees without financially straining the budget or creating salary inequities that strain relationships. A higher morale means that you can count on your workforce, the same thing that you convey over and over to your customers. That the company can be counted on to be there and perform.

Studies have shown the people work better when they are happier. It may not be required for everyone, but most people work harder, are more loyal, and accomplish more if they have a high morale on the job.

Conclusions

This is a hard subject to write on and I'm not sure how well I've conveyed my thoughts here. I've solicited opinions from friends in a variety of situations and I've struggled, and rewritten, with how to make the point that retaining employees benefits everyone. I'm hoping with your feedback and some more thoughts that this series will be something that will be referenced by both managers and workers.

I do want to make a few things clear. I do not think that everyone should be retained, or that there should never be layoffs. Both of those things will occur in any company, but they should be rare events. I also do not think that people should go to work for one company and stay there. The chances of you finding the perfect company are slim and while you should make every effort to look for a good fit, life intrudes on that and both you and the company will make mistakes. Also, situations change, and what was once a good fit, might no longer be the case.

I've seen many estimates that the cost of replacing an employee is around 150% of their salary, i.e. $45k to replace a $30k person. However I think this is low in the IT area where recruiters and headhunters can charge 20-30% of the first year's salary. Add that to the 50% in lost time as well as the risk that you'll pay a new employee even more because they are more talented and that 2005 $80,000 salary could easily be $160k!!

Retention is not something that everyone believes in. There are many companies that do not expect to keep most of the employees for the long term. They view turnover as a good things, a healthy event that makes the company stronger. They may have a better philosophy, but I do not think so. Anything worth achieving takes time and effort and requires investment. Discarding a resource too soon has been proven to be a poor way of building something that lasts. Which is what a corporation is supposed to be, a lasting enterprise. There are many managers that see retention that way.

Except when it comes to retaining themselves.

Being Retained

by Steve Jones

The Employee View

Most employees want to feel safe at work. I say most because there are exceptions out there in any area, but of all the people I've worked with and talked to, they want to feel safe. Even the ones that are looking to move on to another job, another company, whatever, while they are working at their particular company, they don't want to feel like their job is in jeopardy.

Job security, far above money, is something that many people crave. There are people that are looking for long term security, possibly retirement with this company, and people that are looking to get a year in a position before they move on. Whatever their timeline, security is a big part of their being satisfied at work. Some people, like myself, can't stand the slightest little bit of chaos regarding job security. It drives me insane and as soon as there are rumors or feelings that there might be a layoff, or even a reorganization, I'm updating my resume and sending it out. It sounds crazy, but that's a big part of what I look for in a job. Andy even had one guy that quit and took another job, only to return a few years later when things calmed down.

Yet it often seems that many of the decisions and actions the "corporation" or management undertake, work in the exact opposite way. I'll give a couple examples of this to let you know what I mean. One time I was working in a team of people in a typical corporate environment. We were a younger group, used to fire fighting often and tackling the work that was put in front of us, working to get it done and meet our estimates. We came in worked until 5 or 6, usually a 9-10 hour day, and then headed home most nights. We also had our share or late work every month at night and a massive 3 day workfest once a quarter to meet a particular need of some clients.

We hired a new CTO that managed me and the lead developer, between the two of us, we managed another 15 or so people. He decided that we had to keep track of our time and setup MS Project in a shared environment going against a backend, requiring all of us to enter our time daily against various tasks. I know this is standard in many environments and I had previously dealt with it, but it had been a few years. Same for a number of others and this went over like a f___ in church.

Despite all the explanations and justifications that this would help us, improve efficiency, etc., it made everyone nervous. All of a sudden we weren't focused on building great software, but coding quick enough to get our tasks finished close to the estimate in whatever shape they could be in. The result was that not only did everyone get upset and start looking for other jobs, but the quality of the software was lower. No one built anything in anticipation of change or took the time to query clients over potential enhancements. And I not only had to deal with all of this, but I also had to field questions about whether the percentage of work on time would be used in bonuses, whether it would be used to lay off people, and everything else.

The second example is similar and was in another company. In this one we were keeping track of our time like good little girls and boys, entering our time in a system by Friday every other week in order to get paid and keep our manager off our back. It was a source of constant ribbing to the guy or gal that didn't get theirs entered as our weekly meeting consisted of an announcement of those that hadn't. And a punishment. As an aside, the punishment was to be "soda jerk" for a week, meaning that anytime someone called you and asked for a soda, you had to go to the fridge and bring it back. Surprising how well that discouraged mistakes.

Well in their infinite wisdom, management decided that they wanted to be sure that we were properly staffed and not only would we need to enter time worked on various projects, but that now we would need to forecast the next 6-8 weeks of project time and enter that in another system for review. Supposedly this way management could see if we were overutilitized and justify more people.

Surprisingly no one was every underutilized in their 6 week forecast except the managers. I'm sure they did their best to ensure they predicted their time accurately. However every employee that I worked with was sure that this was a way to weed out slackers, maybe target people for layoffs, and it certainly wasn't going to be them. To ensure that our job security wasn't threatened, we all of a sudden were booked 40+ hours a week on various projects. with a very minimum of time spent on administration activities. Bearing no relation to reality, this was the reaction to a threat to job security. It was the employees way of balancing things out.

So the lesson here is that employees, whether they realize it or not, value job security very highly. They want to be retained for some timeline. Management's job is to work with that timeline, and figure it out, but you do that by gaining trust, not micromanaging others.

Growth

Most employees I know want to grow in their jobs. But growth can mean a number of things. Some people want raises, some more vacation, some more responsibility, some more control over their area, and a host of other things. Employees feel more secure when they think that their manager is looking out for their interests. They understand that not everything can go their way, but winning some battles, maybe not even half, but some goes a long way to keeping us happy.

Face it, most employees don't want to change jobs. Most of us would be happy to stay in the same job for most of our lives if it were secure. However most professional IT people that enjoy their jobs aren't content to just go to work each day. They want to be challenged, they want to grow their skills or career and learn new skills. However, investments in employees are often based on seniority, which only comes when you retain the same job for a long time.

So keeping yourself employed in one job pays additional benefits in the form of additional training, which may even be conferences or other special events. Over time I've often seen that employees that have shown they want to stick around, and do a good job, often get more leeway for local events, like MSDN ones. They also might get to go to a conference in addition to a class each year. That's almost like an extra week of vacation a year if you can swing it. Enjoy yourself, get some SWAG, and push yourself to learn new things.

And it's not just the learning that you get. When you grow your skills and prove yourself over time to be a valuable employee, you'll find yourself getting better and more interesting projects. More business knowledge, the likelihood that you'll stick around for the future, better skills, all increase the chances that you'll be the go-to guy or girl and have the chance to feel challenged instead of bored with the mundane tasks of maintaining an application or checking logs.

Benefits

Not every company offers that grow over time, but many do. By sticking with the same job for a long time you'll get the thing that is probably more valuable as your career progresses: time.

Most companies will increase your vacation or paid time off allowance over time, usually growing it at specific milestones, like 5 years, 10 years, etc. I've seen companies in the US grow vacation time from 2 weeks up to 6 if you remain employed for 10 years. That time may not be something that concerns you in your 20s, but as you mature in life, get married, have kids, etc. you'll really grow to appreciate that time.

If you're lucky, as my wife was, your company will give you a sabbatical periodically. After 6 years at one company she got 30 days off to do whatever. She used it to tackle some small projects she wanted, recharge, get away with the kids and in general get away from work. Even if your company doesn't offer it, after you've been there 5 or more years, you might ask for one. You never know and your tenure with the company goes a long way towards convincing someone that it's worth their while to give you a little extra something.

Trust is something you earn with your employer and it takes time. But as you earn it, you might also earn some softer benefits. Like flexible hours or telecommuting opportunities. Many managers are reluctant to allow remote work or leaving early for some event on a regular basis. However, as you prove that you'll get your work done, that you're not just slacking off and they can trust you to be professional, they'll be more likely to give you some of those benefits.

Conclusions

I'm sure most of this is obvious for the employee, but there may be a few things that are not. It seems obvious that most of us would prefer to remain employed at our job rather than looking for a new one, but sometimes it needs to be spelled out. And I'm sure there will be some good feedback, so use the "Your Opinion" button below to read that.

I mostly wrote this for the managers out there. Or for you to pass along to your manager. Let them know which points you agree with and those you don't. Let them know that you value your job and you'd like to stay there. A little communication goes a long way and may give them something to think about at your next review, or if it happens, a downsizing decision.

Next time I'll tackle a few things from the managerial point of view. How they see employees and what are some of the things that they (should) be thinking about.

Employee Retention From the Managers Perspective

by Steve Jones

The Manager

A corporate lifetime is a series of small periods of time in which an individual works for the company.

I hate to put it out there so simply, but a company has an infinite lifetime and its passage in time is marked by the management of it by different individuals. And by individuals who perform work for a short period of time (relatively). For most of the employees, time is marked by various projects that we complete and further our career. That's kind of how we measure our time at a job.

And it's how managers usually see their time. A series of short events or projects that further their career. Most managers aren't much more terribly loyal to the company than the employee. Some are, but most are just as concerned about their own careers as you are and their actions and decisions are designed to protect themselves.

I can speak about managing in a few situations. Three small companies, from 20-100 people, where I had various levels of management and one large company, over 10,000 people, where I was a first level manager, underneath a director, VP, CIO, CFO, and CEO in that order.

For The Company

As a manager, you have access to information that most employees do not. To some degree you always are informed about the direction the current management so you can be sure you are directing your employees to move in that direction. The directions you are being asked to move people in are not always the most efficient, nor are they always the best for the corporation to survive in the long term. They may just as likely be directions that put the success of the current CEO's career ahead of anything else.

Nevertheless, since managers are concerned about their careers, and most of them are professionals trying to do the best job they can, they act as agents of the company, doing things "for the company", to be sure they are perceived as an effective manager.

How does this translate? I can give you a few examples of what I've seen firsthand or had to deal with firsthand. One of the more controversial and contentious practices in many large corporations, especially technical ones, is performance management. This essentially means that people are "graded" on some curve that ensures all employees are ranked according to performance. The typical method I have seen moves people into 5 categories, that match up as roughly "Excellent", "Exceeding Expectations", "Meeting Expectations", "Below Expectations" and "Performing Poorly". If you end up in the bottom ranking, you can guess what your career at that company will look like.

Managers are called into this situation by being asked to rank people, but not just slotting people into what they think. They are called to slot people according to percentages that are predetermined as in 5% of the department or company will fall into the "Performing Poorly" group. There are similar numbers in other groups and this means that in many cases the manager has to "downgrade" someone to the slot below if they have a group of people that are all similarly skilled or performing. Despite telling your team that they have all been doing good, or great, all year, you might end up moving someone down a level at review time for no reason other than to meet a percentage. Similarly if you had a very average team that was large enough, you might slot someone a little higher, playing favorites, even though they hadn't done anything outstanding over others.

Most managers I know hated this process. They hate breaking bad news to people, they writing people up for putting them on a performance plan. They'd just as soon try to hint and push you to do a better job. That's kind of a human nature thing, but their concern is also that their job is easy, which it isn't when they are receiving complaints about one of their subordinates. However the manager is being graded on his or her ability to accurately, or at least apparently accurately, grade the employees and get the job done. So managers make the best of the situation and do their job. The employee may perceive a lot of spin, and there may be spin, in their review to break the news of their ranking, but the manager has to protect themselves from a poor ranking as well.

Another example of how managers work for the company is their nitpicking on administrative items. The manager isn't trying to make your life difficult, or prevent you from enjoying privileges. Whether it's nagging you to enter your time allocations or not letting you leave early one day, it's the manager concerned over how they look to their boss more than it is their decision to be difficult with you. At least for most managers.

A manager's performance is often measured on administrative metrics. Not just how much software they've gotten completed or bugs they've fixed or uptime, but also how their people have performed: time sheets not being completed, absences, meetings missed, and numerous other paper-pushing administrative things.

There's also a measure to the manager's manager of how his or her peers see them. If someone on your team rubs another manager the wrong way, your boss will get complaints about you managing your team. A "black mark" that tends to keep coming up as review and bonus time approaches. The corporate mentality seems to be dog-eat-dog at the top levels and that is what is subtilely, or maybe not so subtilely, endorsed at the manager level. It's also something pushed at the employee level to try and get employees to compete with each other, but it's less successful there, IMHO.

Retention

OK, so managers try to out do other managers and get on your case so they look good. What does that mean for retention? I haven't forgotten the topic of this article, but you have to get a feeling for what it's like as a manager.

Some managers care deeply about keeping their team of people around. Some could care less whether they lost a person every week and got a new one. But what they mostly care about is getting the items their team is assigned completed. In most cases in technology, there's a fair amount of knowledge that grows over time that isn't easily transferred to a new person.

That means that managers want to keep you around if you are helping them get work done. And when you are received as an employee that gets things accomplished without complaints from others in the company, you are valuable and managers will fight for you.

I hate to say it, but above friendships and likes and dislikes, effectiveness matters to managers. If you've been a manager for any length of time, you know people will leave, or get asked to leave, and you have to put that out of your mind and out of your decision making process.

Managers also like to keep you around for a long time for other reasons. A big one is it's easier. You know the routine, you know how to not make waves, and you're less paperwork. Again, longer term employees tend to make the manager's job easier. There are exceptions and people that slack off as they age in a job usually survive because managers get lazy too. It's a managerial change that usually weeds them out.

The last big reasons that managers like to keep employees around is interviewing is a pain. A large, royal, PIA! These days recruiters get tons of resumes and do little filtering and even less qualification of a candidate. After working to write a job description, something HR departments never seem to keep around, the manager must start sifting resumes. Even if you recruit some employees, you still need to dig through lots of them, make calls or emails, setup appointments, and sit in on interviews. And that's with a large HR department. If you're a small guy, it's worse. And your paperwork piles up!

Finding new employees is no fun. If you are growing and adding to your team, and thus your importance, and thus your career, it's easier to put up with. But if it's to replace people it's downright annoying. And once you find someone, the two week or longer babysitting period has just begun.

Why Don't Managers Try Harder

So why don't managers try harder to get you that raise, that title, that perk?

We do. Most managers I know, even the ones that I think do a crappy job of managing, do advocate things for their employees. They try to get things pushed through. But it's hard.

It's hard.

It needs to be said twice because HR departments, equal opportunity laws, and more hamstring most "exceptions" that a manager tries for. Raises are almost impossible to get outside of a set period each year. The manager may or may not have any say in bonus allocation and likely no say in the bonus amount. Perks, time off, prizes, etc. are often completely ignored by manager's managers.

The rules and regulations that the employee abides by are the same ones the manager has, but the manager has more. As a "representative" of the company, he or she is usually more tightly bound against exceptions than others. You skip a day of work, you're probably yelled at or something. A manager lets you skip a few days, or a few people skip days and gets caught? Probably launched pretty quickly.

A manager's job is enforcement. And that's why I was probably a good manager, a well-like one, but not a successful one :)

The managers that can really help you prosper in the company and want to stick around are those that find a good balance between the company's requirements and the employees'. They slip through exceptions by working the system, turn the other way without getting caught, and motivate you without breaking too many rules. And retain you because you're happy.

Managers can't often compete with money in terms of retaining employees since they have no power in that area. But they can make the rest of your job more fun and enjoyable, which can be worth a lot more.

Retention – Keeping Your Job

by Steve Jones

Note: This first section will be a little long, and will kind of prepare a foundation for later parts that help you to get retained. It's a little bit of a deviation and you may decide not to be retained :), but you should think about that first. Before you make decisions regarding your future, you need to determine what that future looks like. At least right now.

Your Dream Job

Before you decide you want to stay at your current job stop for a few minutes and think about it. Try to imagine your dream job. Think about the things that you like and make you want to come to work. Think about the things that you don't like and make you feel like calling in sick. I'd highly recommend making some notes so you really think about it, whether that be the classic pro/con list, a paragraph describing things to yourself, or something else, it doesn't matter, just write it down somewhere. You want to stop and consider your current situation. You should also think about past jobs, computer related or not, and list the things that you felt there as well. Include your thoughts and feelings here if they are strong, and salary is certainly a consideration as are benefits (insurance, vacation, etc.).

Then set this aside for at least a day, better a week or two and just mull things over. Having had nearly 5 computer jobs over a year and numerous ones in other fields, I've learned, a few times the hard way, not to make quick decisions on something like your career. I've had lots of friends that have moved quickly to get out of a job only to land in a worse one. The grass is not always greener, and things can get worse. Not matter what you think the situation is, assuming it's not life threatening, it can get worse. That bears repeating.

It can get worse.

With that in mind, you want to be sure that you are making a good move for yourself and your family, so think about it. When you pick the list up, see if you want to make revisions, add things, remove them, etc. Once you think you have a good list, try and think about those that are most important and you want in a job. That may mean moving outside IT into some other field, and keep those options open. I'm going to get a little long winded here and diverge into two directions, but I'll try to keep it readable.

The first thing you should think about is where you want to take your career. And by that I mean for the short term, the next job (or staying in this one). That could be working to be a senior DBA, or it could be surviving in this job while you go to school in preparation for something else. For the sake of this article, I'm going to assume you decide that you like your current job/employer and are looking to remain there. If you want to get a better job, even with your current employer, read part 5 :)

The second part of this should be to have some longer range goals. I used to want to be a CIO and so my career moves, even when I knew I'd work in one place for the next couple years, were geared to getting me prepared and experienced in areas like management, budgeting, etc. Those goals have substantially changed now, and so you don't want to have a long range plan that you cannot deviate from, but you do want to have some longer range plans. They may change, and you should expect that, but while you have plans, be sure you keep them in mind. If you want to get into management, you cannot hide in the corner, cutting code in a dark cube and ignoring others. Having that longer range plan does help you do decide how much of your current employment you can live with and how much you cannot.

At this point you should have some idea of your dream job. If you are in a good place, then continue to read. If not, look for another job and then come back and see how to keep it.

Business Value

Most people work for an employer whose business is not IT. Even for many software companies, if you are a production DBA, your job is to provide an environment for the products, however ethereal they may be, to get developed. The business is not IT, it's getting things built that may happen to be used in IT, but you are not there as the primary focus of the business. So for most of us the primary thing we have to learn is that IT is NOT THE BUSINESS. I am still amazed how many people, CIOs included, that forget this point.

Now if you are a developer of shrink wrap software you many think you don't need to read this section. That's somewhat true, but you are still not completely the business. Sure you build products that get sold, and that's part of the business, but there are also salespeople, marketing people, etc. that are also in a similar place. But you are still not the business.

The business is selling.

Every company is involved in selling products, services, something to clients or customers. And that is what you have to help happen. I know I sound like some day-one-training HR flunky, but that's a fundamental point. Those guys and gals are dorky in their message, but their message is true. And one other thing is true.

If you are helping to move the business forward, meaning helping to generate revenue, you will probably be retained.

That's a key fact. Most managers, shareholders, etc. will put up with pretty much anything from someone if that person is generating revenue. Now your costs cannot exceed that revenue and you can exceed the limits, but it's hard. Just like the professional sports teams will put up with an incredible amount of @#$#$#$# (substitute your own language here) from a star player, so will corporations. That doesn't mean that you have to be selling products along with maintaining SQL Server databases, but if you are showing that you understand that your ego and place is in supporting and ensuring that business gets done, you will stand out as someone to keep around.

It's hard to understand that in some roles. But as a DBA in a few companie, I have bent over backwards and worked extra hard on any project or task that had a direct impact on sales getting done. It's one of those things that stands out and salespeople, managers, etc. remember as a valuable quality. Even if you are sometimes not the most joyful person to work with.

Understand corporations today do some shady things and I'm not saying you should bend your morals or ethics. But if you get called at 4am or you see the chance to ensure that sales will be done and you give that extra effort, it will be rewarded. Consequently remember that things that do not impact sales are also the place to perhaps balk a little more and save some of yourself for those times you really need it.

Teamwork

Anyone who's worked with me, or probably knows me professionally, knows that I value teamwork, probably above all else. Including technical skills.

Sounds strange, especially in an industry that has often put emphasis on knowledge and what you know (and can do). But more and more people are coming around to my side. I can teach technical skills; I can't teach personality.

Good development or even production teams are just that. Teams. There is a synergy that produces results greater than the sum or the parts over time. And that means that people have to work together.

Being a disruptive force in a team would mean being a short lived force in my world, maybe a force measured in hours. If you are really great, I mean Jim Grey great, perhaps people will put up with it, but most of us aren't in that class. Heck, I think some times I've out-worked more than out-thought others, and I've always tried to be part of a team. And I've also worked in places where being part of a team made up for a lack of skills. I used to work with a team of people that was large, over 20. We had some great technical workers and some that weren't so great. One person in particular wasn't that great a technical person, but they were very loyal and team oriented. Pitching in, helping others, no matter what the job. That person was valuable and I think just about anyone would hire them again. Despite some technical lacking, the teamwork component was very valuable. Not that I'd look for that person to work out of their area, as in hiring them as a senior C# person, but I'd hire them as a junior anything and work to teach them what I could because that team component is valuable.

Now I've spent more time in a production environment than a development environment, and the needs are different. There are places where you do need some good technical skills. But there are lots more places where I need someone to accomplish work and more importantly, I need to be able to count on them. A brilliant flake is still a flake. A dumb drone is perhaps not capable of doing as much, but I know they'll do their part.

The long and short of my advice is that when managers look for people to let go, teamwork matters. Having a person that everyone else thinks is a #$%#$%, means that person is likely to be on the "go" list.

Uniqueness

Everyone is replaceable. Period.

But only in the medium to long term. In the short term it is hard to replace some people, perhaps most. And corporations are reluctant to let people go unless they really have to for some reason. The way to do this is simple.

Be a team player.

Ensure you add business value and drive the business forward.

Specialize.

That means that you work hard to build a set of skills or work on a unique system and show that you are valuable for some combination of unique skills. In other words, you stand out. I've had teams of 10 or more where everyone stood out in some way and you'd be hard pressed to let anyone go. I've also worked in teams of 10 where I thought everyone could be let go. And that would include me.

Note that this doesn't mean that you hoard information or skip documentation. In my book, and more than a few managers' as well, that's the quickest way to get launched out of a job. If you want to keep your job and you show that the business come first, you'll document and ensure that nothing is strictly in your head. That everything is documented in case you get hit by the proverbial bus. I've done this over and over and never felt that I was less valuable. On the contrary, the more that I showed I can do things and was ready to turn them over to someone else, the more valuable I was. That means I could move to new projects, that I put the business first, and most of all, I knew what I was doing by putting my work out there for anyone to see.

Conclusion

Hopefully you are in a job that you want to keep and this article gives you some ideas. Whether that's true or not, I've added a 5th part to this series and it will cover more of the job securing process. I split that apart from this one because I think retaining a job takes less work and is a slightly different focus.

Retaining a job can be a long term goal. I've met more than a few people, myself included, that were very good at their jobs and had no ambition to move on. I would have been happy as a JD Edwards production DBA for probably 10 or more years and I've met DBAs and developers in similar positions. Companies that get those people are lucky for the stability they provide. Not ambitious to move inside the company, but professional and highly valuable and productive employees.

Working in a company isn't a war. As I've aged, I'm not sure that Sun Tzu is the best model for corporate America. Perhaps Benjamin Franklin was better.

Retention – Finding Your Job

by Steve Jones

Your Dream Job

You should have an idea of what this includes. Not that you have a specific job at a specific place, but you might. More that you know what you like and don't like and can list them somewhere. I'll give you a few things that are important to me and suggest a few more, but you should have your own list.

My Important List

- Flexible Hours - I don't punch a clock and my life is fluid. I work when it's needed, but when things aren't critical, I expect to have a boss that handles some movement of my hours.
- Minimal Commute - I might be able to deal with a longer commute, like downtown Denver, if it were only 2-3 days a week and telecommuting the rest of the time.
- Good Team Chemistry - My goal is to meet everyone that I will work with on a daily basis, but most importantly the entire team of people. And I have to get along and want to be with them. Maybe not everyone, but overall there needs to be a good fit.
- Salary and benefits - I'm flexible here, but I do have some minimums I need to meet for my family. This is far from the most important, but it does factor in there.

Note that I haven't mentioned what the job is. That's because this is my list for a DBA job, which is primarily what I'd pursue at this point in my life. I enjoy the work, I do well at it, and it's basically the same job everywhere. A few items that have been important in the past and you might find to be important for you.

- Size of company - I prefer small companies, but I've worked at companies with > 10,000 people as well. I can deal with both areas.
- Production/Development - I've done both, but I prefer the production environments, working in Operations and keeping things stable and running. They are very different jobs, so be sure you are clear on which one is important to you.
- Database Size - This used to be something I was concerned with, wanting each new job to have bigger and bigger databases to learn about them and add some bragging points to my resume :)
- Technology - I'm not terribly concerned if I'm running SQL 6.5 or SQL 2005, but some people are. If you are growing your career and trying to move it to bigger and better things, then .NET, SQL Server 2005, and other cutting edge technologies might be important. Some companies are content to work with a known quantity and some are looking to move to newer technologies.
- Advancement Opportunities - This could be up in the company, moving into research, or getting to another country. Larger companies tend to have more places you can grow your career, but it can be anywhere. The important thing is that if you are looking to manage DBAs or a team of people that you don't go work for a 20 person company with 2 developers and 1 DBA (you). Think this through.

One last note on important things. You may need to update these as you search for a job over time. A small commute may be important early on, but it becomes less important with each week that I'm out of work.

Looking Around

I've said this to many peers and it always seems to be met with some skepticism. I'm always looking for jobs. I am on the Monster and Dice job lists, but have used others as well. I just like those. I keep an eye out for jobs and when I'm enjoying the Sunday paper, I'll take a glance at the computer jobs because you never know what's in there. Often the government/city jobs will appear there and one might be interesting. I still somewhat kick myself for not applying to run IT for the city of Littleton, CO many years ago.

The point is to be proactive in your career and be knowledgeable. Just like your databases are always gathering new information, you should be aware of the job market. It's relevant if you get laid off, if you are looking to ask for a raise, or you want to justify using other technologies. Not just if you want a new job. Current jobs can clue you in to the state of the DBA world around you.

In line with that, I urge everyone to "touch" their resume every quarter, 4 times a year. I still have a reminder setup in Outlook and I'll take 5 minutes to glance over my resume, see if anything is changed, and check the length. If I add something, then I usually look back at past entries and see if there is anything I can remove. I think these days a 2 page resume is acceptable, especially since most people look at them electronically, but more than 2 pages seems to be a lot. I work to keep mine below two pages.

However, while it's not really a US custom, I do keep a longer CV, or curriculum vitae, that has my complete work history. I typically never remove anything from here, just as I add entries to the resume, they go here as well.

Since I have been called about jobs out of the blue, I want to have a current resume on hand that I can get back to them immediately with. I have also seen friends that were told a job was available and urged to apply and then then spent the next day or so getting a resume together. Having one ready might just land you your dream job, so keep your resume up to date.

Getting Noticed

Assuming you have found a job or two that you are interested in, how do you stand out? Part of standing out is having a good resume that's relevant to the job. I have often created 2-3 different resumes for different jobs, emphasizing different things in each. For example, I have a "manager" resume that highlights positions in which I have managed people. It mentions the things that are specific to managers like budgeting, bonuses, reviews, etc.

Now I have managed people while also having to work as a DBA, so my "DBA" resume highlights the SQL Server work rather than the manager stuff. I'm not lying or misrepresenting what I've done, but since in most of my jobs I've worn a few hats, I emphasize a particular hat for a particular position.

You do want to include some buzzwords, however, because so many people run a search on a resume these days at larger companies that you want to come up in the first pass for the positions you are applying for. So if they use a buzzword in the posting and you have experience in it, put it in your resume where appropriate. Resumes that have paragraphs of buzzwords are likely to be launched by myself and quite a few managers I know.

If you have had relatively few jobs, there isn't much your resume can help with. But make sure it's relevant while being accurate. A cover letter, especially in these days of hundreds of resumes coming for a position, you want to make a personal, relevant cover letter. If you want to be a DBA, but haven't been one, then you should tell why you want this job and that you are realistic. You know you have to learn, you've done some work on your own, and you'll pay your dues.

I should mention that you do want to be somewhat realistic in your search. It's ok to shoot a little beyond your experience for a position, but you have to be somewhat in the range. If you've had less than a year of experience, you aren't ready to be a senior DBA. If you've never managed people, you aren't ready to be a director of managers.

But you can write a real letter, spell and grammar checked, that shows you are interested and have some knowledge about what position and company you are applying for. Fairly short, 2-3 paragraphs, honest, simple letters that are to the point without being full of flowery language and buzzwords do work. Someone will look at this letter and if they can read it in 30 seconds and understand it, you have a chance of moving forward.

Separating Yourself from the Pack

Assuming that you get an interview, how do you ensure you stick in someone's mind and have a shot at the job? These days I see more and more "group" interviews where there are multiple people talking to you. That's usually after a phone interview with an HR person or perhaps a manager, so you usually have at least 2 chances to make a good impression.

So I'll look at both of these interviews and give you a few things I've done as well as things I hear work well from friends that interview people.

One note here: there is no magic formula or trick to guarantee success. This is a subjective area and you should take my advice and modify it to fit yourself and your situation.

Screening on the Phone

Phone interviews are usually spur of the moment and unscheduled. I've had HR people take a few minutes to call me and check the basic facts of my resume and schedule a live interview, and I've had managers call me to see if I was worth the time for a live interview.

If this is scheduled, be sure you are ready and in a place where you can talk. Not in your cube where others will interrupt you, not taking your kids to school, etc. If you have a conflict of some sort, or need to shift things, ask. Small requests like moving the interview 15 minutes later so you can drop kids off at school will not cost you the job.

The same thing goes if you are called out of the blue. If you cannot talk, tell them and reschedule for 30 minutes later, end of the day, tomorrow, etc. Be accommodating, but don't feel like you have no choice and put yourself in a bad place for the interview. However you do it, the first thing is to make sure you have each other's numbers in case of a disconnect. Since many people use cell phones these days, you want to be able to continue if you get disconnected: ask for their number, just to be safe. And if you're on your phone, stop driving or moving. Don't do anything to wreck your reception.

This is a good place to get a basic feel for the job first. I usually ask for a short description of the job to be sure that the position matches what I saw in the ad or was told. You can cut the interview short here of bring up major concerns from your important list (remember that from above?). Commute, salary, etc. are good things to confirm here. If there is a deal breaker, don't waste your time or their time and hope you can work things out.

Just as in a live interview, you want to represent yourself accurately. Listen to the questions and answer them the best you can. "I don't know" is an acceptable answer and please use it rather than trying to fool someone with a BS answer. You really won't know if the person is technical and understands the question or not. Or if they have someone else in the room cueing them!

Be polite and deferential with the person since you can't read body language. A few guidelines that will probably apply in the live interview as well:

- DO NOT CURSE - This was brought up in another article, but it's not appropriate in an interview and you don't know who you offend. Or if you're being baited.
- Do not lie about what you know - Answer honestly and if you don't know, say that. You can always say you'd check BOL, call PSS, etc.
- Have stories ready - what you liked best from each job in the last 2-3 years, what you didn't like, why you left, etc. You'll be asked some of these and you should have practiced some things so you can deliver them.
- Be friendly, excited, and eager - It shows on the phone. Not so much you stumble over your words, but you want to convey you want this job. If you don't, you shouldn't be on the phone.
- DO NOT TALK BADLY ABOUT ANYONE - If you had a problem with someone, admit to the conflict, but do not blame anyone. Don't say other departments screwed your amazing wonderful project up. Don't say someone is an idiot, that they don't know what you're talking about, etc. This isn't being dishonest if you feel this way, it's being tactful. You NEVER know who's listening in or might be working at that company. Your worst enemy from down the hall might have accepted a job there last week and is starting tomorrow.
- Have a plan to shore up your shortcomings - In areas where you are weak, or in case you don't know an answer, be ready to show you have a plan to get better, become more skilled, or prevent mistakes from happening in the future.

Lastly, basic manners. Don't be eating or drinking while you're on the phone. Listen to the interviewer and respond to what they said, not what you want to say.

Live and In Color

OK, you've impressed them and you're invited to a real interview. Same scheduling rules as above, be sure you have time and can talk. Ask how long the interview will be, where it is, etc, and be sure you can accommodate both the company and yourself. If something doesn't work, you can usually delay for a day or two, but don't ask for a week. There's other candidates who won't. Ask how long you should expect and then add a pad to that. Good interviews will probably go long.

Get directions and print them out. Unless you absolutely know where the company is located, be sure you have directions with you. And be on time. Nothing is more annoying than having someone not be there for an interview. You're better off being 10 minutes early and sitting in your car for 7 than being 2 minutes late. Give the receptionist a couple minutes to ask you for paperwork, announce you, finish a phone call, etc.

Dress. This is an interesting one. I usually go to every interview with a collared shirt or polo shirt and jeans, and most of my friends think I'm crazy. I usually ask if it's casual dress in the phone interview or email schedule to be sure, but I'm not a dress up guy. However, you do want to be, in general, perhaps slightly more dressed up than the company. I don't think you have to wear a suit and tie to every interview, but it doesn't hurt. However, even if the team wears obnoxious t-shirts and shorts, wear at least a polo shirt and jeans. It won't hurt.

I shouldn't have to mention this, but since I've seen it, I will. Make sure you're groomed. Showered, shaved, light cologne or perfume, clean clothes, etc. the visual impression will matter. For me, I usually hit the gym at lunch, but I'd skip it if I had an interview later in the day. I'd get myself groomed for the interview in the morning and not take any chances on messing that up.

If you have questions, and you should have some, be sure you know what they are, even if you need to write them down. Use the general list above to be sure you're prepared. You want to be sure you've practiced answers and questions as well. Slow down your speech and eliminate your fidgeting in practice with your wife, husband, friend, etc. The live interview is important to sell yourself and that means a good visual impression. Don't slouch too bad, watch your body language and habits. Don't pick at your clothes, spin your chair, etc. Remember, even the best qualified of us get nervous and all our habits are amplified. Be conscious of your body.

I'm a native English speaker, but I've interviewed and been interviewed by many people who weren't. Some people may have horrible accents or command of the English language. But that didn't necessarily make them a bad candidate. If you don't speak English well, be sure you have paper and pencil in case you cannot make yourself understood. Speak slower than you want because you'll probably be speaking faster than you normally do and be cognizant of what you are saying. You need to emphasize your ability to communicate for most positions, especially if you want to be a DBA.

You want to be comfortable. So be sure you are. If you're chair is not comfortable, tell the interviewer before you start. If you need water because your throat is dry, ask for it. Once things get going, you want them to go smooth. Try to tell yourself to relax and remember that you are trying to connect with your interviewer(s) and develop a rapport as well as wow them with your knowledge. Or your honesty about things you do not know.

I always ask myself these two questions, but I'm somewhat convinced that lots of people unconsciously ask them as well. They are: Would I go have a beer with this person? and Would I drive cross country with this person? They sound similar, but they reveal two different things to me. The first one tells me if I have a rapport with this person socially. I don't mean a beer literally, but would I want to sit and relax and just hang out with this person. That's the important one for a team player to me. The second question reveals if this person is interesting and engaging enough for a longer time period. Not necessarily socially, but could we talk about technology or something else and keep each other interested for a long time. If not, then this person might not be someone that I'd want to work with over time.

When you are asked if you have questions, you should have a few. Hopefully they'll be as a result of what you heard, but you should have thought about the job and developed at least one question. This is the time to be sure that benefits, hours, salary, etc. are as you expect. Any concerns you have should be brought up as well. See if you can resolve something that you think is important here.

I also ask about the future here. What's their timeline for a decision, more interviews, etc. I also ask if there's anyone that I'll be working with a lot that I haven't met and try to arrange time with that person. If I'm not in the running, then no harm no foul, they'll not call me. If I am, however, this is a chance for me to continue my interview, and ensure that I'm getting the dream job that I want.

Your Personal Life

First a fence sitting statement. Your personal life is your own and no one's business in an interview. But being a human being and relating to people helps you sell yourself.

So what can you talk about? First, there are many questions that you are not supposed to be asked. Are you married, pregnant, want/have kids, etc. If you are asked, don't get real offended, but answer politely that it's inappropriate to ask that. Don't get into an argument if the person says they can ask, but decline to answer if you feel it's inappropriate.

In general, you want to keep much of your personal life out of work, at least until you know how much work infringes upon work and vice versa. And you won't know that until you work in the job for a few months. So whether you want to have kids or not, whether you like to hunt, fish, play World of Warcraft, etc. is something you want to minimize. If someone asks you what you do for fun, or outside of work, mention something, but don't dwell on it or describe it in great detail. Give them a sentence or two and move on.

Again, because I've seen it, don't mention anything you do that is time consuming, dangerous, potentially controversial, etc. It can give the wrong impression, right or wrong, so avoid it. I'd include political or religious activities, hobbies, etc. Fundraising, Sunday School, etc. all can be misconstrued or taken the wrong way, so avoid them.

I don't want to offend anyone, but I do want to mention something about the "God Bless You" or similar parting that many people use. It's inappropriate in an interview. And this is the reason.

I'm an atheist. I respect your religion, bow my head when a prayer is said, etc., but I don't want to hear about it at work. If we become good friends, then I can accept it from you or feel comfortable telling you that I'd rather you didn't. But if we're not friends, I don't want to hear it and it makes me uncomfortable, no offended. So it's one more strike against hiring you.

Remember, this is all about selling yourself. So don't move into controversial areas. If you are asked, be honest, but minimize or shorten your answers about anything that could turn off the interviewer.

Blogging

It's a hot phenomenon and it's something that so many people seem to be doing these days. But it's a two edged sword and you need to be aware of that.

A good blog can catch the eye of a potential employer, maybe even without you knowing it. Someone that reads what you write learns something about you, things that you might not be able to get out in an interview. You can showcase your knowledge, your skill with code, or even the software side. Thoughts and notes on how you deal with situations can help to show that you have people skills. I have done well with SQLServerCentral.com and always mention it in interviews. Heck, for me it usually is the interview because my knowledge, philosophy, etc. are all out there for people to read. But before that I mentioned places that I had published in an interview or where I had answered lots of questions on a Q&A site to show something I've put out there publicly.

However a blog can have a downside. Complaining about work, making simple coding mistakes, revealing information that you shouldn't be can affect you in a negative light. People have been fired for writing in their blogs, so if you have your dream job, be careful about what you blog about. I've been careful to let my managers know I'm blogging and asking if I have a question. And if you use events, code, ideas, etc. from work, be sure you have permission.

I have never read a blog by someone I've interviewed, but I haven't hired anyone in the last couple years. However, if I were interviewing someone, I might search to see if they had a blog and how they wrote, what they thought, etc. This doesn't mean you should contrive a blog. Faking something like that isn't easy and probably not possible over any length of time unless that's going to be your job. Someone will catch on that the things you write aren't really your own thoughts or ideas. But be sure to mention it in your interview, or any public works you've written or contributed to. But only if it's relevant to the job. Don't mention your family's picture web site.

Conclusion

This is slightly off the topic of retention, but it does tie in. If you get the dream job, then you'll want to be sure you get retained :)

There are really two very important things to remember. First, be honest. I know it's cliche'ed, but I mean be honest both to the interviewers in your answers as well as to yourself as you evaluate the job. And that evaluation should continue up until you decide to accept a job offer. Keep being honest with yourself as to what you really want and what this position really is. The second part is to do your best while being honest. Make your best impressions, your best answers, your best sales job of yourself. A good product sells itself, but only by itself. When you're faced with lots of competition, you need to be sure you make the best impression.

Interviewing

by Steve Jones

Interviewing as a DBA

How you should interview for a DBA position?

Honestly I don't have all the answers, but I do have a few things I have done in the past as well as recommendations that I have given others. Recently with some friends looking for new jobs, I wrote some recommendations and gave advice, so here are a few things that I think are important to share with you.

This isn't everything you need to know. I'm assuming this is a job interview for a position that you want, or at least think you want and you've done some research there. I do have an article on <u>Finding Your Dream Job</u> out there.

Background

First some background on how I view a job interview. I think this is important because you might be in a very different place in your life and have to approach things differently. Keep in mind my advice works well for me and has gotten me many more job offers than I have accepted over the last ten years, but that doesn't mean it works for you. So let me take a minute to let you know where I stand in life.

My wife works. That's an important point because it means there is much less pressure for me to "take" a job immediately, or take any job. We cannot live off her salary without changing our lives, but it does take pressure off. If you are the sole wage earner then your situation is different and you might need to approach an interview differently. This also means I have less concerns about a company's stability than some of my friends.

Another important point is that I value my time away from work, so I ask questions that relate to the workload and on-call responsibilities for that reason. When I was younger, I was less concerned about this, so I would assume I might work doctor's hours (100 hours a week) and anything less was a bonus. It was one way to learn and get ahead, so I didn't mind it.

I have a lot of experience with SQL Server and most of the time the job is the same for me. I am less concerned about working on a VLDB or dealing with the latest technology, so I tend to worry more about the intangibles than specific "about the job" questions.

The last thing is that I tend to go into jobs at this stage of my life looking for a long term fit. I want a job to last me forever, so I really am open and honest to try and ensure I make a good decision. If you are looking for a shorter term engagement, you may or may not disclose that. A one year target might end your interview immediately, but I have told interviewers that I was looking for a 3-5 year job and I'd evaluate it as I went along.

Preparation

I can't really stress preparing for an interview enough. Lots of people get nervous in an interview, and to some extent that is natural. Preparation can help here in getting you used to people asking you questions, even if it's your spouse or friend, but also give you confidence. Remember that you are interviewing the company as well as they you.

The other thing that preparation can give you is an advantage over other candidates. I learned this in my first interview for an internship in college. I researched every company that I had an interview with, or even wrote a cover letter for. Even to the point of trying to learn something about the interviewer if I knew their name. Before the Internet, this was a library and ask friends search, but now you can Google a name and see what comes up. Just knowing a few things about the company can help to answer questions, or even give you ideas for questions.

You don't want to constantly "drop hints" to show you know something about the company, but if the opportunity comes up, show that you have done some research one or two times. Ask if you will get to work on some technology or project you read about, or show that you understand their business. That is very important to success. After all, for most companies, running the database isn't the business. Understanding what the business actually is helps you to proactively help the business run smoother or even prioritize issues.

The last part of preparation is spend some time listing things that you want to know about the company or the job. Really think about what is important to you and then have some questions you want to ask. A few that I have used in the past:

- How often would I be on call?
- Is there travel required to other sites or customers?
- Can I telecommute for personal reasons (kids sick, snow, etc)?
- How often can we take servers down for maintenance?

Most of these questions are geared to feeling out the job. For example, the last one tells me something about the stress of this environment. I have had people say we can never take the servers down, or that it's once a year. This is a more stressful job, both in ensuring that things run well and trying to make them better. Regular downtime makes a DBA's life easier because you will have some flexibility in scheduling. I used to work at one company where we could go down once a quarter: Sat night from midnight to 5 am. That wasn't as much fun as another job where we pretty much ran 7am-7pm each day and nights off. Maintenance was done on my schedule, not the other way around.

The Interview

The best thing in an interview is to relax. Take the approach that you need to interview the company and be prepared to ask them questions in between their questions. This will help keep things flowing and make it more of a conversation than a quiz.

Answer the questions promptly. It is acceptable to pause briefly to think, but if it will be more than a couple seconds, note that. "Let me think about that" is something to give you a chance to collect your thoughts. I often will walk through my thought process out loud, letting the person know how I am viewing things and the approach I will take.

Answer honestly and if you don't know, then tell them immediately you've never solved that issue, worked with that problem, whatever the reason, but trying to fake your way through a questions, especially a technical one, usually is worse. You can always learn, they can train you, whatever, but that dishonesty cannot be repaired easily.

If you do not know something, it is not necessarily a mark against you. I have had interviewers ask me questions they did not know the answer to and I've done it myself to someone. It's a technique to see if you can get some free consulting or even to ascertain if the candidate is more qualified than you. So be honest and answer the questions. I once interviewed to go to the South Pole and the first question was the meaning of the acronym ACID.

And I missed it. I knew 3 of the 4 and stammered for a few seconds before just admitting I couldn't remember. I could explain the idea behind it, but didn't know the term. Isolation was the one I missed. Later in the interview they asked me a replication question they didn't understand. Once I answered it, they admitted they had been stumped and were glad I answered it.

It's possible you will find yourself in a situation where you are smarted than the interviewer. Especially for a DBA where often a manager or system administrator interviews them not knowing much about SQL Server. Be deferential and do not embarrass anyone. Answer questions tactfully and if the interviewer "mis-asks" a question because they do not know SQL Server that well, be polite about pointing out a misunderstanding or mistake. Or clarify the question and see if they were asking what you interpreted. Showing off or bluntly telling someone they made a mistake is not a good way to handle things in an interview or even in a job. Mind your manners at all times.

Another thing to remember is to let questions go. If the question is asked and answered, or partially answered and the interviewer moves on, then move on as well. Don't go back to the question and try to get it "more right". If you are familiar with Seinfeld, the TV sitcom, there were numerous situations where George or Jerry couldn't let something go and kept going back to it. Even if you are bothered by it, move along in the interview. You can discuss it another time or check on it later.

Often you will get asked about bad experiences: why you were fired/laid off, the classic "tell me about a bad personal interaction", describe a problem, etc. In addition to answering honestly about the situation, do not speak poorly about others, insult them behind their backs, or anything along those lines. It's unprofessional as well as a poor reflection on your character. The interviewer will wonder what you may say about him or her one day. A couple quick stories on this.

I once interviewed someone that told me his old boss had really annoyed him with overworking him. So he wrote a C++ program that connected to a modem (this was back in '94/'95) and dialed his boss' pager every 10 minutes for a whole day. Needless to say I was less than interested in hiring him. Practical jokes or tricks plyed in "getting revenge" are usually a bad idea in the first place and a mistake you learn from, not mention in an interview.

Another time I interviewed a candidate that I thought would be a great hire. Smart, good resume, etc. that had been let go from another company before his last job. In other words, he'd been let go, found another job and came to me awhile later looking for a third. In asking about some bad experiences at the first company, he talked poorly about some colleagues there. Their lack of skills, both technical and social. I would have had some doubts about his character fitting in with our team anyway, but unknown to him, one of his former co-workers from that job was already working for me. And that co-worker was a valued employee!

You never know who you might run into at a new company, so keep your opinions about others' technical skills or character to yourself unless you are willing to say them to the person. When I was looking to leave Peoplesoft, I made no secret of my displeasure with management at some interviews. But I was polite and never denigrated anyone's skills or character. I explained the specific problems I had with policies and why I was leaving. Peoplesoft was not "wrong" in running their company that way, but it was not something I wanted to be a part of, so I expressed that. Both to my Peoplesoft director and VP as well as other companies that I interviewed with.

The last thing in the interview is to be specific in your answers. Don't use general comments to gloss over things. This is both in technical and non-technical questions. If someone asks you if you have done replication, answer with more than "yes." "I have setup snapshot replication", "I have setup simple two server replication," or something like that. Be specific.

Have I written C++ code? Yes, but I answer with the caveat that it has been a long time and I wrote simple utilities to return values. I'm not a programmer to build you an imaging application.

If you are not sure how to answer specifically, ask for a clarification. Even if you are halfway into your answer, do not be afraid to stop and ask about some details or what they are looking for with the question. It will help to show that you are paying attention, thinking, and willing to work with them.

Conclusions

Remember that all of these techniques are guidelines or rules of thumb. They have worked for me, but I have also had to use judgement calls with them. I try to be specific, but within time guidelines. Most questions should be answered within a minute or two. I answer honestly, but do not necessarily give every detail that might make a bad impression. If I think someone I worked with is an idiot, I would not say that, or even blame them for issues. But I would point out what I did right or well and what I didn't.

If I were looking for a one year job, but thought the company might not hire me for that, I would probably not disclose that and hope that I weren't asked the question. Is it unethical to disclose your timeframe? I'm not sure, however I also know that a year is a long time and all kind of plans can change, so no matter what my thoughts were, they might change over time. I also know I have seen people hired and then let go in 4 months because the company decided to reduce head count. In either case, you want to be as honest as you can. You have your own moral compass that will let you know how much to disclose.

We have all made mistakes in life and in our jobs. They are part of what builds our character and skills and helps us grow. Accept responsibility for them and show that you do in an interview. And point out how you have learned and grown from the experience. Remember that you want to fit in well, so treat the interview as your chance to determine that. Relax and enjoy the process.

And keep in mind that the best time to interview for a job is when you don't really need a job.

Spotlight on SQL Server

While SQL Server 2005 development was finishing up, the SQLServerCentral.com staff had quite a bit of contact with various team members at Microsoft. As we quizzed them on the new product, features, capabilities, and what-not, we found that most of them were very interesting people. Aside from being very, very intelligent developers, they were fun to talk to.

So we decided to embark upon a series of interviews to learn more about the people that bring you SQL Server. So here's the list of people we've gotten to interview to date. We hope we can continue and get more done throughout the year and compile a larger section next year.

Euan Garden

SSC : What's your official title and responsibility at Microsoft?

Euan :I am Group Program Manager for SQL Server, my responsibilities include product readiness and planning for the next version.

SSC : Give us a little background on yourself, how did you get into computers?

Euan : I started with computers when I was 15 I asked(and got) a ZX81 computer for Christmas, I think it was called a TS1000 in the US, it had a nasty membrane keyboard 16k of RAM and a Z80 processor but I learnt a ton, especially patience, waiting 20-30 mins for programs to load from cassette!

I started getting into databases when I undertook a year in industry as part of my degree, my first job was making some single user dBase III systems multiuser, which was really quite a challenge.

SSC : Where did you attend college and what degree did you receive?

Euan :I have a degree in Computer Science from The Robert Gordon University in Aberdeen, Scotland. The way the course works is a little different from most US degrees and many UK based ones. It's a dedicated Comp Sci class, so although there are Maths, Stats, Psychology, Legal etc subjects they are all taught from a Comp Sci perspective, plus of course the std Software Engineering classes, this means the course is very focused. It included 15 months in year 3 working as a regular employee in industry and then in the final year we got to choose between real time systems or systems analysis and design as a specialization, I chose the latter.

SSC : Did you see yourself as a programmer/developer when you were growing up?

Euan : Actually no, despite having my own computer at a fairly early age I always wanted to be an Air Force pilot and when I left school I was accepted for an RAF(Royal Air Force) Bursary, I made it as far as Jet Training, which was a blast but didn't make it to operational fast jets so I left and went to University to study Comp Sci. I was lucky enough to hold military and civilian licenses at the same time and have the dubious honor of having survived 2 plane crashes, both of which I was at the controls of. On one occasion it was caused by a flock of birds being ingested into the engine and on the other a log in the middle of a grass strip.

SSC : Were you piloting in both crashes?

Euan : I was the pilot in both, yes.

SSC : Do you still fly today?

Euan : I used to fly but have not for some time.

SSC : What plane would you most like to fly?

Euan : Jet Provost T Mk5, it could do almost 360kts and was fun to do aerobatics and stuff in.

SSC : How do you like living in Redmond?

Euan : I actually live in Bellevue which is right next to Redmond and it happens that because of some boundary weirdness I am REALLY close to Redmond. I love it here, in many ways its like the North East of Scotland where I come from, its very green, rains and snows a lot with a great pace of life, although I have to say that Seattle summers are much hotter and longer than those in Aberdeen, and that's a good thing.

SSC : Who's the most fun to work with at Microsoft?

Euan : Wow, tough question, I think rather than individuals I would say the team aspects of what we do. I can think of many occasions on many different projects where 2/3 folks have gotten together and had fun solving a problem, designing something etc, its amazing how these Ad Hoc teams form and solve issues then move onto the next team, its great to be part of.

SSC : We've all heard stories of some characters at Microsoft. Any interesting ones that stunned you or surprised you when you first went to work in Redmond?

Euan : I've never worked with him but Brian Valentine from the Windows group has provided hours of amusement and motivation for many folks at Microsoft. He has done a series of internal only videos and he does a mean John Belushi impression.

SSC : What's your current favorite tech gadget?

Euan : I'm disappointed with myself right now as my current favorite gadget is 9 months old and that's an Audiovox SMT5600 smartphone. I have spent years trying to find a great PDA, I started with a Psion 3c, followed by the first gen iPaq and finally a Toshiba e740 and none of them has really been the perfect solution, however the Audiovox meets all my needs right now and I have no desire to replace it.

SSC : What does Euan like to do when he's not working on SQL Server?

Euan : I'm a casual gamer, I have an XBOX and I also play PC based games, our dog is always great entertainment as he is either trying to steal stuff and hide it in the garden or trying to cause trouble some other way! I've been pretty lucky in my time in the US to have been able to travel around a fair amount so there is always the hope that I can nip off for a trip somewhere.

SSC : Where in the world do you most want to visit?

Euan : The Giza plateau in Egypt

SSC : Can we get you in a kilt at PASS in Dallas?

Euan : Might be a little hot for that.

Thierry D'Hers

SSC : What's your official title and responsibility at Microsoft?

Thierry :I'm a Lead Program Manager on the Analysis Services team. I have been part of that team for over 6 years.

While my role at the beginning of the Yukon release was around defining the new development tools for Analysis Services, it evolved along the way. I now spend most of my time doing evangelization activities around all of SQL BI. Meeting with customers, helping early TAP customers deploy early builds of Yukon, and

working with our ISV community is keeping me very busy…

SSC : Give us a little background on yourself, how did you get into computers?

Thierry : I studied Engineering and computer science in a French engineering school and once out of school decided to join a French subsidiary of a company called Hyperion Software. Hyperion back then was the leader in building BI applications. I was doing a lot of custom development for them and then moved on to doing Consulting and PreSales type of role. Soon they asked me to move to their headquarters in Connecticut. When Microsoft entered the BI market, I figured this is the future of enabling BI to reach a much larger audience and many more companies. I joined Microsoft just when the SQL team was about to ship SQL Server 2000 Beta 2.

SSC : Did you see yourself as a programmer/developer when you were growing up?

Thierry : Not at all. I wanted to be a mountaineering guide, but as soon as I realized I could make a more decent living with a more serious job in a new emerging business that most people referred to back then as "computer stuff".

SSC : I've done two 14ers in Colorado, peaks above 14,000 feet. What's the tallest mountain you've ever climbed? What's your goal?

Thierry : I climbed Mount Blanc, the tallest European summit in the Alps a few years back. I'm training for Rainier this summer and I have my eyes on Denali (Mc Kinley) :)

SSC : How do you like living in Redmond?

Thierry : Well we actually like it a lot (except for the weather :)). The lifestyle is much more relax and enjoyable than that one of a city. I grew up in Paris and while it is a nice city to visit on vacation, it is a very stressful environment to work in… I love the mountains around us and other outdoor possibilities that are offered by the Puget Sound area…. I just wish the area got a little bit more sun in the year and that it wasn't a 17 hour flight to Paris :)

SSC : Who's the most fun to work with at Microsoft?

Thierry : I would have to say that working with our General Manager Bill Baker is definitely the most enriching experience. He has been in the BI space for very long and as a very rich and wide experience covering many industries and technology. He is definitely someone whom with you always get a very interesting discussion.

SSC : We've all heard stories of some characters at Microsoft. Any interesting ones that stunned you or surprised you when you first went to work in Redmond?

Thierry : In the very first two months of my arrival at Microsoft, I am walking between building 3 and 33 and I am following a tall bald person. As you may imagine it is Steve Ballmer who is walking between building, probably heading to an EBC (since building 34 where he is now, didn't exist at the time) . It probably sounds silly, but it stroked me since I am coming from Europe where executives never mix with the average worker, much less walking without an escort. I definitely got a sense that Microsoft is a different style of company than what I had known before…

SSC : I've heard for a number of years each year that "this is the year for BI", but it still doesn't seem to be a widely adopted technology in many companies. Any theories on why most DBAs don't seem to embrace or push Analysis Services?

Thierry : You can't tell by my experience. We fill every room we can at TechEd events around the world with people clamoring to know more and learn more about SQL Server Analysis Services.

SSC : What is the next cool thing for BI that will be in SQL Server 2008?

Thierry : Well we have our ideas already... but right now the focus is really on shipping SQL Server 2005 and making sure our new and existing customers have the best experience possible.

SSC : Forester recently released, or rather started selling, a report about the SQL Server scalability. In this Redmond Magazine report (http://www.redmondmag.com/reports/article.asp?EditorialsID=156), they mention that SQL Server doesn't even play in the 3TB or 10TB spaces. How true is that? What's the biggest

SQL Server DSS system you know of?

Thierry : All I can say is look at the following case studies we have published on Microsoft.com:

Sage Telecom (5 TB DW on Superdome) -
www.microsoft.com/resources/casestudies/CaseStudy.asp?CaseStudyID=16792
USDA GDW (12 TB DW) -
www.microsoft.com/resources/casestudies/CaseStudy.asp?CaseStudyID=16212
Premier Bankcard (4 TB DW) -
www.microsoft.com/resources/casestudies/CaseStudy.asp?CaseStudyID=16168

SSC : What's your current favorite tech gadget?

Thierry : Currently I would have to say it is my GPS enabled smartphone, but I got my eyes on the new upcoming XBOX 360…

SSC : What does Thierry like to do when he's not working on SQL Server?

Thierry : Take care of my two girls and go hike or ski depending on the season…

SSC : As a father of 3, I understand how it's tough to balance work and family. We've heard stories of the long hours at Microsoft. Is it tough balancing life while working at Microsoft?

Thierry : It is challenging but nor impossible. Microsoft is very demanding but very flexible at the same time, thus making it easy to organize professional life around personal life. I personally work 9-5 on campus, then take care of my girls until they got to bed, then I'm back at work on my laptop which is where I'm answering your questions now :). This arrangement works for me and seems to work for Microsoft. Everybody is happy….

SSC : Where's the best skiing in the world?

Thierry : Even though I am from Europe and would love to name one of the French ski resort here, I found the best snow ever at Whistler-Blackcomb.

Brian Welcker

SSC : What's your official title and responsibility at Microsoft?

Brian : I'm Group Program Manager for the SQL Server Reporting Services team. This means I manage the team that writes the functional specifications for the product. I also do presentations at trade shows, answer newsgroup questions, and order pizza.

SSC : Give us a little background on yourself, college, degree.

Brian : I'm originally from Raleigh, North Carolina and graduated with a BS in Computer Engineering from Carnegie Mellon in 1990. I joined Microsoft in 1996 after working as a developer for a company that made software for hospitals.

SSC : How did your interview at Microsoft go? Any wild questions you can share?

Brian : If I told you, I'd have to kill you afterwards. The only thing I can say is I'll never look at manholes the same way again.

SSC : How did you get into Reporting Services?

Brian : I was part of a trade that sent 2 developers and a tester to the Microsoft Bob team. Actually, I've been part of the Reporting Services team from the very beginning (2001).

SSC : Do you actually help write the code behind reporting services?

Brian : For the good of everyone involved, they keep me away from the code. I did fix a bug in the V1 setup and I do get to write a sample every once in a while.

SSC : Why did Microsoft decide to add the Reporting Services engine to SQL Server?

Brian : It was customer feedback really. What we heard was that customers wanted a reporting solution that integrated with their Microsoft data sources, productivity applications, and developer tools. As we had already added OLAP and data mining to the relational database in SQL Server 2000, it was a logical place for reporting.

SSC : How did Reporting Services get started?

Brian : The funny thing is that when we started Reporting Services, no one on the team had ever built a reporting product before. Of course, we got some inspiration from Access but I think one of the things that has made Reporting Services a success was that we got to start with a clean slate.

SSC : I've seen you speak a few times and it was enjoyable each time. What inspires you for the interesting demos you give?

Brian : People tend to think reporting is a dull subject. I actually think that presentation of data is one of the most exciting and important parts of information technology. You can change the entire meaning of a data set with small changes in fonts, colors, or layout. When I present Reporting Services, I try to get people excited about the topic and expand their ideas about what reporting can do.

SSC : Who's the most fun to work with at Microsoft?

Brian : It's a treat any time you can be in a meeting with Steve Ballmer. If you only see him in front of a big audience you might think he is just loud and crazy. But in a small group setting, he comes across as a very down to earth and funny guy.

SSC : Ever been to Bill Gates' house? Is it as amazing we we've heard?

Brian : Unfortunately, I have never been to Bill Gates' house. I have, however, been to Bill Baker's house and it is very nice.

SSC : What's your current favorite tech gadget?

Brian : My wife bought me a Playstation Portable for my birthday and the graphics are amazing. Maybe someday we'll release an XBOX portable...

SSC : What does Brian like to do when he's not working on SQL Server?

Brian : Not working on SQL Server? Now there's a concept... Actually, my two daughters Riley (who's 4) and Ella (who's 2) keep me pretty busy when I'm not at the office.

SSC : The PASS next year will be in Seattle. Where's the best Pizza in Redmond?

Brian : My favorite in the area is Zeek's. But Acapulco Fresh has the best burritos in Redmond.

SSC : Big question: Panthers or Seahawks?

Brian : Panthers who? If you are referring to the Carolina Panthers, they didn't exist when I lived in North Carolina. I've been a Seahawks season ticket holder since the new field opened in 2002. Look for me in the south end zone, right above the guys in the "hawks nest".

Shyam Pather

SSC : Tell us a little about your position and what you do?

Shyam : I'm the development lead for SQL Server Notification Services and I manage the development team building the upcoming release of Notification Services in SQL Server 2005. At the moment, we're mostly focused on tying up the loose ends and putting the finishing touches on the product. As development lead, my job is to make sure the remaining bugs in the product are found and fixed by the development team. Also, I'm spending an increasing amount of my time working with early adopter customers who are deploying Notification Services applications on the SQL Server 2005 CTPs.

SSC : What product (or portion) are you mostly working on in Notification Services?

Shyam : Over the past 2 years (since the first release of Notification Services) we've been working on an exciting set of feature enhancements that make Notification Services better address the needs of its customers. These include a GUI administration tool built into Management Studio, support for end-user defined subscription matching logic, the ability to embed Notification Services functionality into existing database applications, and an API that provides full programmatic access to all the management and administration capabilities of the Notification Services tools. I've worked on the design of these features and contributed to parts of the implementation.

SSC : Is Notification Services (NS) more of an application development platform or something that's a core part of SQL Server? I know it's integrated tightly in there, but is it used by the server itself or is it more to build something on top of?

Shyam : NS is built on top of SQL Server and the .NET framework. As you said, it's tightly integrated – it's a core part of the BI suite in SQL Server 2005. But, it is not used within the server. It's a development platform on which anyone can build a custom notification application.

SSC : Where did you attend college and what was your major in college? Which college?

Shyam : Computer Engineering at the University of Kansas.

SSC : Happy for Roy Williams or upset? (The coach that left Kansas and won an NCAA basketball tournament at North Carolina)

Shyam : Actually, I have to admit that I'm probably the one graduate of KU who made it out without getting caught up in the basketball craze. So, I guess I'm indifferent.

SSC : What was your first computer?

Shyam : The Commodore 64 with a cassette tape drive. A great little machine for its time!

SSC : Since you've been programming so long, you've been exposed to a lot since the Commodore 64. What's your favorite language to work in?

Shyam : Definitely C#. It's a thoroughly modern language and just makes sense.

SSC : In what ways?

Shyam : Many programming languages have some kind of an "impedance mismatch" with the prevailing development paradigms. A good example is C++ and COM. C++ lacks fundamental language constructs to many express COM concepts. So, to implement COM objects with C++, most developers end up using something like ATL, which can be a mess. You end up wasting a lot of time coding around the limitations of the language. In general, this situation arises because the languages and the development patterns evolve separately.

C#, on the other hand, is built around modern development techniques. The language directly supports many of the things you need to do development in the .NET world. Things like strong typechecking, generics with constraints, and the is and as operators come to mind. It's possible that in 10-15 years, C# will also be out of alignment with the latest development patterns, but that's not the case right now. I've found that coding in C# makes me way more productive. The language seems to be evolving in every release, so it's likely to stay current for much longer than other languages we've seen.

Besides all the innovations in the language itself, the experience of using C# is so positive because of the fantastic tools support and the .NET framework. Visual Studio's support for things like Intellisense, code snippets, refactoring, and so on, make coding much faster and less error prone. The class libraries in the . NET framework offer a wealth of functionality in a form that's easy to reuse.

SSC : Did you see yourself as a programmer when you were growing up?

Shyam : My dad used to be a pharmacy professor and spent a lot of his time in a lab when I was younger. Listening to him talk about his work, I always thought I would end up as some kind of scientist. We got the Commodore 64 when I was 10. The idea was that my dad would eventually learn to program it and we kids would use it for games. One day I tried typing in a BASIC program I found in a book and, not surprisingly, it didn't work. I went through the Commodore manuals to try to figure out what was wrong. That got me started in programming and I've been doing it ever since.

SSC : Do you use any particular development methodology for building software?

Shyam : We don't really use formal design methodologies, but there are some fundamental principles that we follow. The first is to always work from a written design. If you can't write down a description of what you're going to build, you haven't thought it through properly. Another key principle is that we always involve the test team in the process, from the very beginning. Testers often provide valuable insight that often leads to better, cleaner designs. Keeping test in the loop also helps them build better test cases, which ultimately improves the quality of the product. Also, we don't check anything into the mainline source tree unless we have more than 80% of the corresponding priority 1 tests implemented and passing at a rate of 98.5% or higher. We've set up a process we call the "playpen", in which developers can try out bug fixes they've made against the full set of automated tests, before checking in. This helps ensure a consistent level of quality at all times.

SSC : What's your current favorite tech gadget?

Shyam : My Panasonic Lumix digital camera. It's small enough to fit in my pocket, has a fantastic lens, great color rendition, and an image stabilizer that lets me take handheld shots in low-light. I love that I can take this camera anywhere – something I can't do with my bigger cameras.

SSC : Bill Baker introduced you as a kick boxer at TechEd, any truth to that?

Shyam : Some. I used to be a regular at the kickboxing class at the Pro Club (the gym near Microsoft's campus). It's definitely the best workout I've found.

SSC : Anybody you'd like to kickbox against? Could you hang in there with Hillary Swank (Million Dollar Baby)?

Shyam : My kickboxing class was more about the workout than the actual combat. We learned some interesting moves, but never had to actually use them. I'm pretty sure Hillary Swank could take me down.

SSC : What do you like to do when you're not working on stuff for Microsoft?

Shyam : I'm passionate about photography. I've been shooting seriously for about 5 years now and I'm trying to improve all the time. I used to do some fashion photography for designers around the Seattle area, but nowadays, it's mostly just for fun.

I also spend a lot of time writing. Last year I wrote a book about SQL Server 2000 Notification Services. I'm working on an update for the 2005 release at the moment.

SSC : Where's the best food in Redmond for a geek?

Shyam : In Redmond? I don't know. I live in downtown Seattle, so I'm more familiar with restaurants on the West side. In Seattle, my favorite is the Kingfish Café. They serve southern style "soul food". It's fantastic.

SSC : Will we see you at PASS 2005?

Shyam : Absolutely. I'll be there delivering a talk entitled, "Add Alerting Functionality to Database Apps w/ SQL Server Notifications Services". It'll cover the Notification Services basics and show how to work with the platform as a developer. There will be lots of code and live demos.

SSC : What's down the road for Shyam? Will you continue with Notification Services or would you like to move onto some other product/technology?

Shyam : I'd really like to see Notification Services grow and become more widely adopted. There is a lot we could still add to the platform that we didn't have time to do in SQL Server 2005. Based on what we see customers doing with the 2005 release, we'll add new and better things to future releases. As for me personally, I'd love to still have a part in the development of Notification Services, but it's also a goal for me to grow into a bigger role. A big part of the future of Notification Services will be looking at ways to make the technology fit better into the rest of the BI suite. I'd like to be deeply involved with more than one technology so I can help make that happen.

Donald Farmer

SSC : What's your official title and responsibility at Microsoft?

Donald Farmer : Group Program Manager, SQL Server Business Intelligence. My responsibility is to lead the program management team for SQL Server Integration Services. "Program management" is a satisfyingly vague job description: it really comes down to ensuring that all things happen, that need to happen, to make the product a success. That includes plotting out the strategy, identifying and specifying the features, and generally herding cats until the program makes it to release. And then, in addition to working with customers, it starts all over again!

SSC : Give us a little background on yourself, how did you get into computers?

Donald Farmer : My father was a telecom engineer: forever tinkering with electronics at home, and at work he was involved in the development of digital exchanges. As soon as home computers were available, we had one. From then on, computers were an essential part of my living machinery.

SSC : Did you see yourself as a programmer/developer when you were growing up?

Donald Farmer : Not at all. Computers for me were always a means to an end, not an end in themselves. In fact, I am not very interested in computers or the mechanics of computing – right now I could not tell you the processor, speed, RAM, or disk capacity of the machine I am writing this on! I can see it is a Toshiba from where I am sitting, so I know that. However, I am enthralled by what can be done with computing power, whether as a programmer or as a user of software. When I was a kid, I used to be fascinated by the hydraulic jack in the garage – look, I can lift a car with one hand! For me computers and software are like that jack – they enable one to leverage intellectual power beyond what is ordinarily possible. Look, I can detect the patterns in 100 million data points and make sense of them! That's spellbinding. It releases our creativity to work with more information than we have ever been able to in the past. At Microsoft, uniquely, we can release the intellectual power of millions of users. So did I see myself as a programmer? No. But, I was always gripped by the sheer drama of harnessing knowledge and information, so in that sense I am doing pretty much what I always longed to do.

SSC : What was your first computer?

Donald Farmer : The first computer I had for myself was a Sinclair ZX81, but we had a lot of other stuff lying around including a Sinclair MK-14 and a ZX80 that I tried out. The ZX81 was a revelation. For one thing, I discovered that your own code can startle you, and that even simple routines can have emergent consequences that are as delightful as they are unexpected. My example was trivial, but charming. I wrote a little fishing game, the object of which was to guess where a fish was hiding in a pond by entering some coordinates in 3 axes. The computer responded with clues. I spent hours coding and debugging it and even prepared a little graphical fish that flopped on the shore if you guessed right. The first time I tried to play the game I entered the coordinates and the ZX81 responded with "That was too deep and too far out!" Too deep and too far out for sure – it was the seventies after all. I, never mind the fish, was hooked.

SSC : Where did you attend college?

Donald Farmer : "Attend" may be too strong a term – it implies a degree of commitment to which I never quite aspired. I did enroll at the University of Glasgow, and very happily studied Gaelic, History and Philosophy. Other studies I was less keen on. The lack of a degree has never really been an issue, however, as I have never had an uninteresting job since I left. All the time I used computers – whether to build databases of medieval artifacts or for desktop publishing or to develop rainfall models for hydroelectric dams.

SSC : How do you like living in Redmond?

Donald Farmer : I don't – I live in Woodinville! We're hugely lucky to live about 25 minutes from campus, but still have a secluded house with a wild landscape.

SSC : What do you miss most about Scotland?

Donald Farmer : The closeness of history and my own culture. That includes the Isle of Lewis, where I can be totally immersed in my family's life for generations and their groundedness in the landscape. Or in Edinburgh, the most beautiful city on earth, which I miss very much.

SSC : So, beer or scotch?

Donald Farmer : Scotch always. A well-aged Islay malt is hard to beat, but I do love Isle of Jura, because we could see the whitewashed distillery glittering in the sun across the Sound of Jura from our home in Scotland. Springbank is also wonderful, and Mortlach well worth the effort of finding, although both are little known in the USA.

SSC : Who's the most fun to work with at Microsoft?

Donald Farmer : If you have ever been to one of the chalk talks that Bill Baker's team give, you will realize that we all have a blast. There are a ton of great people here and that entire team is fun to work with. Bill's weekly staff meeting is frequently hilarious, but the thinking that goes on there is equal to the hilarity. They are among the smartest people you will ever meet, but they can also reduce a conference audience to tears of laughter.

SSC : We've all heard stories of some characters at Microsoft. Any interesting ones that stunned you or surprised you when you first went to work in Redmond?

Donald Farmer : Euan Garden really stunned me when I first arrived at Microsoft! We used to work together in Scotland in a company where even developers had to wear suits and ties to work. First day in Redmond, there was Euan tootling round the office in casual shorts, t-shirt and sandals. Not a sight I had planned on seeing!

SSC : Which event was the most fun for you at which you attended or spoke?

Donald Farmer : That's difficult – most of them are fun in their own way. My first for Microsoft stands out – at a technical preview of Yukon in 2002. Honestly, I had been struggling in my first year at Microsoft, but I had the chance to do this presentation with Ashvini Sharma. I was a little nervous; it was a large audience, the first big public showing of the new product (still called DTS back then), it was the last presentation of the day, and I was generally unsettled anyway. Once we got on stage, poor Ash must have thought I had a dual personality. Rather than the rather quiet program manager he was used to working with, I was up there telling jokes, making fun of him during his demos, and in general having a good time – and people really enjoyed it. I came back from that presentation knowing that I had turned a corner in my career, and it has been enormous fun ever since. It's a huge privilege to present SQL Server BI to an audience. SQL Server users are amongst the smartest, friendliest, and most appreciative technical crowd out there.

SSC : SSIS is a radical departure from the DTS model. Is this an evolution or a completely new beast?

Donald Farmer : The Ohio board of education may disagree, but this is evolutionary and a completely new beast! It has not one line of code in common with DTS, so for sure it is new, and its capabilities are far in advance of what DTS had to offer. However, we have worked hard to keep many good things about DTS – the ease of use, especially in a DBA-friendly wizard, a good programming model, and excellent integration with other SQL Server tools.

SSC : In developing SSIS, did you do a lot of visits to client installations or work with any users of DTS or was this mostly developed internally?

Donald Farmer : We did a lot of work with clients. One of the great things about SQL Server BI is that people come to us. We have a highly developed, active and vocal community and we rarely have to seek out feedback – we're more often overwhelmed with it. However, we have also done a lot of customer visits, and we gather very specific requirements and pain points from those visits. And of course that continues throughout the development cycle.

SSC : Who's more fun, the relational team or the BI team?

Donald Farmer : Sorry, you'll need to repeat the question. I dozed off at the word "relational." (Yes, I am a BI-bigot, but I'm too old to change.)

SSC : What's your current favorite tech gadget?

Donald Farmer : My noise-canceling headphones. I travel a lot and they really help on the plane – especially the little turbo-props or seaplanes out of Seattle. I tried them at home, but they don't work there – I can still hear my wife asking me to fix the fan in the shower-room!

SSC : What does Donald like to do when he's not working on SQL Server?

Donald Farmer : I cook. And I work in my garden – or our patch of wilderness to be more exact. We have about 1.5 acres and we're keeping it as a wild landscape, but even that requires a lot of work. We have paths and resting places and sculptures all through it. In the evenings, I like nothing more than to sit out there with a large cool glass of good Beaujolais and a favorite book.

SSC : What's your culinary specialty?

Donald Farmer : Fideo – a kind of paella made with short noodles instead of rice. Or pamboli, which is a sort of Mallorcan open sandwich of bread and olive oil. See http://www.pamboli.com to see why!

Christian Kleinerman

SSC : What's your title and position at Microsoft? (What do you really do?)

Christian : I'm a Program Manager in the SQL Engine team and I work in a variety of areas. Throughout SQL Server 2005's development cycle I've owned several features, such as SQL/CLR inproc data access, some TSQL enhancements, and the SQL Server protocols (TDS and SOAP). A couple of years ago I spent some time driving and shipping the initial release of the SQL Best Practices Analyzer. Feature-wise I currently own the 'max' data types (e.g. varchar(max)), query notifications (the server portion of SqlDependency), server-side cursors, MARS, and what we internally call MSQL-transactions, which refers to the user visible transaction programming model. I also run a small team in charge of working through customer scenarios and cross-feature interactions.

SSC : Give us a little background, how did you get into computers?

Christian : I was intrigued by computers from a young age. My dad got me a Commodore 64 – more as a gaming device, but shortly after I was spending more time programming and trying to hack and learn the ins and outs of the machine than actually playing – though the games were great too. I started writing little accounting and inventory management applications for family members and friends. I've been working with computers in one way or another ever since.

SSC : Did you see yourself as a programmer when you were younger?

Christian : I'm not sure. I was convinced from an early age that computers could really improve the way things were done. However I was more interested in algorithm design and optimization than in actual computer programming. Given the close relationship between these two I ended up doing my fair share of programming.

SSC : Can you tell us about where you went to college and what you studied?

Christian : I grew up in Bogota, Colombia where I got an Industrial Engineering degree.

SSC : Why databases? Why SQL Server?

Christian : I've been using SQL Server since the beginning of 6.0 and I was always fascinated by the technology. There was this magic about dealing with large volumes of data, the power of query processing, the simplicity - from the user's perspective - to deal with concurrency and isolation, and "survival to crashes". I slowly became interested, learned about the internals, helped MS-Colombia give talks about SQL Server 7.0 Betas, and at some point made my way over here. This is truly a fascinating problem space and technology area; every single day we face very interesting challenges.

SSC : What's your favorite tech gadget?

Christian : I'm a big music fan – electronic music in particular, so I'm constantly impressed by the gear that keeps coming out for music producers. Guitar midi encoders, guitar synths, vocoders, software synths, samplers, etc. It's a great application of technology.

SSC : How's life in Redmond compare to home?

Christian : I like Redmond. There's no place that has it all and clearly this area completely missed the weather thing. J But it is a nice place with good quality of living, and you can always go to Florida once in a while to warm up.

SSC : Best place to visit in South America

Christian : Two places actually. Cartagena in Colombia: beautiful city, beaches, history and wonderful people. Also Buenos Aires in Argentina is a fascinating place and a paradise for those who like to enjoy a good steak.

SSC : Have you ever been to Bill Gates' house?

Christian : Never. I've heard from a few friends that went there as interns that it is a great experience

SSC : What's your favorite feature in the new SQL Server 2005 relational engine?

Christian : There are many ways to evaluate features, but I would probably rank the Service Broker as number one, mostly because it changes very significantly what you can do with SQL Server and the way you think about building applications. I usually think back about some of the projects that I worked on before I came to MS, and I usually end up thinking of how much simpler or better things could have been if SSB were available. It really opens up the server for a whole new set of capabilities and possibilities. Of course all my features are favorites as well. J

SSC : What does Christian do when he's not working on SQL Server?

Christian : Not working on SQL Sever? I didn't know that was possible. J I think time is split between reading and playing around with music: producing, mixing, and remixing. I love to spend time playing with all the gear and see how it comes out.

SSC : Best guitarist, in your opinion? Anyone you'd like to have the chance to play with?

Christian : I like a lot Paco de Lucia. Though I cannot say I'm a flamenco connoisseur, I've very much enjoyed some of his performances.

SSC : Any big plans for a vacation after November? (when SS2K5 RTMs)

Christian : Nothing in particular… maybe I'll go and help on some of the international launch events and spend some time away. Maybe I'll visit my dad and family down in Argentina… just in time to hit summer down there.

SSC : Who's more fun, the relational engine team or the BI team?

Christian : One of those questions where no matter what you say the answer turns out to be wrong. J I guess SQL Server as a whole is a lot of fun; we're both building systems that complement each other and are part of a complete data platform. In a recent internal conference I was reminded of how good the complete SQL Server offering is. Btw, the relational engine team is more fun. J

SSC : Is SQL Server ready to compete with Oracle? Any plans for distributed clusters like Oracle Parallel Server?

Christian : Yes. There's always the feature by feature comparison where there are differences but the question usually comes up in terms of scalability, reliability, availability and we're there. SQL Server 2000 competes well with Oracle and SQL Server 2005 is even better. On scale out clusters, SQL Server has distributed partitioned views today and unfortunately I can't comment on future plans for this.

SSC : If you weren't a programmer, what would you want to do?

Christian : I haven't really thought much about it… I like organizational sciences, working with people, understanding people. On the other hand, technology and the way it makes things better is definitely a blast. So I guess that the way SQL Server makes organizations and people better and more efficient is a great area to stick with.

SSC : Microsoft abandons SQL Server, who do you go to?

Christian : I would try to go find out who was it that failed to see such a bright future.

Kirk Haselden

SSC : What's your official title and responsibility at Microsoft?

Kirk : I'm the Development Manager for SQL Server Integration Services, which means I'm responsible for ensuring our engineers are happy and busy, while removing obstacles that keep them from doing their job well. I also get to design parts of the product now and then, make sure we hit our dates, ensure that we're putting out a quality product and talk to customers once in a while.

SSC : What's the best part of SQL Server Integration Services vs. DTS?

Kirk : Hmmm, where to start. You know, DTS is a cool product. Given the resources the DTS team had, they did great work. Comparing the two is difficult, but I'd have to say the dataflow task and looping is the main difference. The dataflow task is truly an amazing piece of technology and Mike Blazsczak, Jim Howey, Ted Lee, Matt David and the rest of the folks that contributed to that effort should really feel proud of what they've managed to pull off. Just a while back, the Barnes & Noble team came in and showed us some of the packages they have for their ETL process. Truly amazing. One of their dataflow tasks contained over 100 transforms pushing hundreds of thousands of rows through. The other part I like is the ForEach loop. While it's not such a technological wonder as the dataflow task, it's extremely useful and practical. Almost every package has one for some reason or another.

SSC : What's the most data you've seen pumped through one package?

Kirk : Mmmmm, I don't know for sure. I've physically witnessed ~650 megabytes go through a dataflow. I've heard from our customers about multi-terabyte dataflows. Ashvini Sharma built a package with two script transforms that simulates real data by generating it in the source and consuming it in the destination transform. He has a bitmap on his office door of the package as it's running with something like 1,834,405,400,323 rows. That's certainly a chunk of data.

SSC : I've seen quite a few demos and white papers that show the performance has improved dramatically. Is there any reason for a SQL Server based application to purchase another ETL tool?

Kirk : No. SQL Server Integration Services is a true enterprise platform. In fact, we're constantly going in against pure play ETL vendors and winning big. Our customers are eating SSIS up like candy and they all seem to like the fact that we include a DBMS with our platform.

SSC : Give us a little background on yourself, how did you get into computers?

Kirk : I started working with computers as a sophomore in high school, when I took an introduction to computer programming class. We had a PDP something or other, PDP 8 was it? It was a shared machine for the entire school district. We dialed in on dumb terminals over handset coupling modems. We programmed in basic with the line numbers and such. I barely passed because while everyone else was doing the exercises, I was trying to write a board game. I thought I was going to fail when my teacher lost to the game. As it turned out, that was the only way I salvaged a passing grade. Toward the end of the year we got one of those newfangled home computers with the color monitor. I think they called it an "Orange", "Banana" or "Apple" or something. I was a closet computer geek though. I was a jock at school - football, wrestling, track - but I'd go home and hack around on my parents computer whenever I could.

SSC : Where did you attend college and what was your degree/major/concentration?

Kirk : I started at a small Junior College in Kansas on a football scholarship. After going home with severe head aches every night of the season, I decided that my football career had ended. That's also where I learned the lesson that, no matter how big you are, there's always someone bigger. The college was a feeder school for the Big 8 colleges like Oklahoma, Nebraska, Indiana and such. Can you say six foot eight, 325 lbs and dumb as nails? That's what I was up against and I played center. I decided it was time to start thinking about a life change.

I went home and served a LDS mission to Nagoya, Japan. When I returned, I attended the University of Utah and received a business degree in accounting, which I hated. I wanted to go into computers, but people told me there wasn't any money in it. He he. On the night of my mergers and acquisitions accounting final, I was putting the finishing touches on a hex editor I was writing in assembly. When I graduated, I finally realized that software was for me and I interviewed at a small educational software company in Utah called Wasatch Education Systems. They asked me if I could write C code and I said "sure," but they didn't ask me to write any code, so I got the job. That night I bought a C book and crammed all night. I'd never written a line of C code in my life.

SSC : Did you end up working a lot in C?

Kirk : Yes, and there were some very talented developers there who's code I emulated and learned from immensely. It was a great experience for me because I was constantly asking the developers questions. Why did you use this approach vs. another? Why are you using this particular idiom? They got sick of me I'm sure, but I learned tons.

SSC : What language do you mostly work in these days?

Kirk : I mostly use the English language. Folks on my team like to give me a hard time about the amount of time I spend reading and drafting email. When I do write some code, it's in C++ or C#.

SSC : How do you compare C to VB.NET or C#.NET?

Kirk : Well, the .Net languages are definitely more modern. A lot of what's improved has little to do with the language and everything to do with the tools. For example, the type system in C# simply rocks. Trying to traverse the typelibrary interfaces for COM objects wasn't much fun, but that was the only way to dynamically discover objects in COM. .Net makes it much simpler to discover and build around the type system. C is close to the metal and was obviously created at a time when security wasn't such an issue and there were a lot fewer developers in the world. I've never really thought about comparing C to .Net though. Usually I hear comparisons between C++ and C#, since those are the two languages we use. If C was the telegraph, .Net would be a broadband connection.

SSC : Did you see yourself as a programmer/developer when you were growing up?

Kirk : Early on, I never saw myself as a programmer. I wanted to be an inventor, body builder or a professional football player. My heroes were Westinghouse, Johnny Unitas, Benjamin Franklin, Walter Payton, Lynn Swan, A.G. Bell and Thomas Edison. Microsoft gives out cubes made of granite to those who contribute to the patent effort. It was a proud day of my life when I was able to complete my patent cube pyramid. Obviously, becoming a body builder or professional football player didn't work out, but getting patents in my name was a dream come true.

SSC : What patents have you worked on?

Kirk : Quite a few actually. I can't remember all of them, but here are a few. The very first one was the one I did with Brian Hartman who is now working on SQL Server Reporting Services. It was the "Extensible Breakpoints on an Object Model" patent. Sergei Ivanov and I worked on one for "Package Obfuscation using Compiling", as well as the foreach loop and enumerators ones. I also worked on the "Variable Scope in an Object Model" and "Variable Namespaces in an Object Model" patents.

SSC : What was your first computer?

Kirk : My parents had an old 8080. My first one I bought in college was an IBM 286 with a 20MB hard drive and 640K of RAM.

SSC : How do you like living in Redmond?

Kirk : I actually live south of Redmond in a little suburb called Issaquah. Well, now it's called Sammamish, but both are equally difficult when trying to order something over the phone. We enjoy it because we live right by a lake, wakeboard in the summer, and my kids love their school and friends. Washington is an extremely diverse place by way of the people and geography. People complain about the rain in Seattle, but frankly, it's just my kind of place and I barely notice the rain anymore. I still wear my customary shorts, sandals and Hawaiian shirts all year long – people know it is winter if I'm wearing socks.

SSC : Why doesn't anyone who works at Microsoft live in Redmond?

Kirk : I know a lot of folks that live in Redmond and work at Microsoft, but more to the point, Redmond is really quite small and is surrounded by a number of other small towns like Sammamish, Issaquah, Bellevue, Kirkland, Renton, and Bothel. And then there's Seattle of course. Microsoft also has an office in Sammamish where much of the internal management functions live, such as the IT infrastructure and team websites, etc. Microsoft also has offices in other locations such as "Silly Cone" Valley and Texas.

SSC : Who's the most fun to work with at Microsoft?

Kirk : That's a tough one. I hate to point out any one person because my whole team is a blast. They're extremely professional, yet ready to crack a joke at the tip of a hat. Kamal Hathi who just left our team to head up the Analysis Services team was perhaps the best manager I've ever had and since he's not my manager anymore, I don't even get any brownie points for that comment. Sergei Ivanov and I have worked together for about five years and he's very fun to work with because he's always discussing cool ways to do stuff in a collaborative and exciting way. I've worked with Mark Durley for over seven years and he's endured more jokes about his beloved country of origin than anyone should, but he takes it all in stride and occasionally deals out his own little treasures. The list is too long, but those are a few.

SSC : We've all heard stories of some characters at Microsoft. Any interesting ones that stunned you or surprised you when you first went to work in Redmond?

Kirk : This one is easy. The very first day I came to Microsoft, I was rooming with "Joe." Joe liked to sew and he designed his own ladies wear. He didn't wear it, but he did have some of his friends model the clothes he sewed and then made a screen saver out of it. He also had a habit of turning his phone ringer up to its highest volume setting, while setting his computer sounds to play various songs for approximately 15 seconds for every notification. He also brewed his own beer, which meant 10-15 empty beer bottles were always present in our room. To top it off, Joe liked to listen to satanic ritual music. The day before we were to ship our product, we found a string he had placed in the resources - "Hedonism rules." Yeah, he was interesting.

SSC : What's your current favorite tech gadget?

Kirk : I just bought a communication system for my motorcycle. Now, my wife and I can actually communicate as we're riding. It makes the ride a lot more enjoyable because we can both listen to music at the same time, but then the music will mute when one of us talks. My next purchase will be the TomTom Rider, which is a navigation information portal for motorcycles.

SSC : I had an old Suzuki 500 when I lived in San Diego and used to love riding out to Mt. Palomar and see the telescope as well as out to the Joshua Tree. Where's the best motorcycle ride?

Kirk : Around here the best one I've found is about a mile away from my house. It's extremely twisty and it has the virtue of being devoid of cars most of the time. Smile. A little further away is a ride I've yet to take, but have seen pictures. It's the stretch of road between Kooskia and Missoula on highway 12. Nothing but twisties for miles. Highway 4 in Northern California, just north of Yosemite is a spectacular ride. Then there's the granddaddy of all rides I'd like to make someday over in North Carolina called Tail of the Dragon at Deal's Gap.

SSC : What does Kirk like to do when he's not working on SQL Server?

Kirk : I have a large family, so we like to spend time together, especially outdoors. This includes wakeboarding, snow skiing, and boating on the sound and on Lake Sammamish. I also play the cello with my children who are all much smarter and more talented than I could ever hope to be. I recently purchased a Yamaha FJR 1300 motorcycle after a 13 year cycling hiatus and I'm presently trying to make up those lost years of cycling enjoyment. And I'm a photographer and enjoy nature, landscape and portrait photography. I'm also writing a book about SQL Server Integration Services - it's fun but grueling. You truly get a feel for just how big SQL Server Integration Services is when you try to write a comprehensive reference for it.

SSC : Ever been to Bill Gates' house?

Kirk : Yes, but I signed a non-disclosure agreement before going in, so I can't really talk about what I saw. When I worked in the eHome group, we merged with Rich Hasha and his folks that did all the work to automate the home and otherwise install some pretty bleeding edge technology. It was all very cool stuff that we'd hoped to be able to somehow use in a productized version for the average home user.

It's funny you ask this. Every family member or friend that visits us from out of town wants us to show them Bill's house. We go out on Lake Washington in the boat and drive over to his house about a hundred yards from shore and my visitors invariably ask "Is that it?" It doesn't look all that big or impressive relative to the other houses there. Looks can be deceiving. Somewhere, in the databanks of the Gates residence security team, there are multiple pictures of me in my boat and friends/family with disappointed looks on their faces.

Dan Jones

Dan Jones and Jim Gray

SSC : What's your official title and responsibility at Microsoft?

Dan : Officially I don't like official titles. Seriously, my title is Lead Program Manager for the SQL Server Manageability Platform. Isn't that a mouthful? After we shipped SQL Server 2005 we split up the team who built many of the new GUI tools into two separate teams. One team is devoted to building an extensible manageability platform. This includes Management Studio, SMO, SQL Agent, and a few other technologies. The other team is responsible for manageability of the relational engine. They'll build on top of the manageability platform exposing features and functionality specific to the relational engine. The BI teams will also build on top of the same platform for their manageability features.

SSC : What's the best new thing you worked on in SQL Server 2005?

Dan : During SQL Server 2005 I was the lead PM on the setup team. It was one of the hardest positions I've ever held. Basically everyone needs a piece of you. Setup is one of the last things the dev team thinks about and the first thing customers interact with. We really pushed the envelop of setup technology with SQL Server 2005; I think we have the most complex setup requirements of any Microsoft product.

SSC : Is the 64-bit version of setup different than the 32-bit? Or is it just porting things over

Dan : The core setup is essentially the same (there are a few subtle difference to work around platform specific issues) – just compiled with the correct tool set. There are a few differences with what is installed. For example, the 32-bit setup includes both the 32-bit and 64-bit MSIs (Windows Installer Packages) for some components (MS XML, SQL XML, SQL Native Client, SQL Writer, and the Backwards Compatible components). Remember, on x64 we support installing the 64-bit and 32-bit editions of SQL Server side-by-side. A 32-bit MSI cannot install components to the 64-bit space, but a 64-bit component can install to the 32-bit space. We needed to ensure what's installed supports both 32-bit and 64-bit. Also we had to be sure that everything was ref counted properly so that uninstall wouldn't break components. Therefore, when installing a 32-bit edition on x64 we call on the 64-bit MSI to install the necessary 64-bit and 32-bit files and registry settings. Getting all of this to work properly was incredibly challenging.

SSC : Give us a little background on yourself, how did you get into computers?

Dan : When I was in third grade a friend of mine had an Apple II. He didn't even have a floppy drive; all of the data was persisted to cassette tape. But I was awestruck with what it could do. About a year later I convinced my dad to purchase an Apple II Plus. There weren't many books out on programming Apple DOS so I taught myself how to convert programs for the IBM PC to run on my Apple. I also taught myself DBase III, we've come along way since those days.

SSC : Where did you attend college and what was your degree/major/concentration?

Dan : I received my undergraduate degree from Cal Poly, San Luis Obispo, California. My degree is a BS in Business Administration (concentration in Information Systems) and a minor in Computer Science (concentration in relational databases). While I love writing code, I truly love using technology to solve business problems, hence the business degree rather than a pure CS degree. I also have an MBA from Santa Clara University in Santa Clara, California.

SSC : Did you see yourself as a programmer/developer when you were growing up?

Dan : Absolutely, my two addictions growing up were the computer and television. I loved writing my own programs (in hindsight, none of them did anything overly interesting) and playing computer games.

SSC : So which program that you wrote as a kid comes to mind?

Dan : I wrote a slot machine game – it was incredibly simple. I was never able to get the dials animated correctly – to look like they were spinning - so instead I had to opt for them to flash as they changed. I wrote it in Apple Basic. I don't remember how many lines of code it turned out to be, but I'm sure it was several hundred.

SSC : What was your first computer?

Dan : It was an Apple II Plus with 48KB RAM, no hard drive, and dual 5.25" floppy drives. I had a monochrome CRT and an Epson dot matrix printer. I think it's still somewhere at my mom's house.

SSC : How do you like living in Redmond?

Dan : I live in Sammamish which is about 8 miles from the Microsoft campus. My family and I love it. Moving from California we were a bit concerned how we'd like the weather, but it's been awesome. Yes, it rains a bit, but everything stays so green, lush and beautiful. I was down in CA last summer and just couldn't handle how brown everything was. It was so depressing. Since we moved, roughly two years ago, I think California has received more rain than Washington.

SSC : Who's the most fun to work with at Microsoft?

Dan : That's a really tough question. There are two people, one I work with each and every day, and the other I don't get to work with enough anymore. The first is Bruce Prang. I report to Bruce, by choice. He is very energetic and infectious. He constantly challenges me and our team to do our best each an every day. The second person is James Hamilton. James is now a GM over in the Exchange group but when I joined MS he was on the SQL Server team. James is nothing short of brilliant. Loves life, loves technology, and exudes an incredible sense of commitment, dedication and pure excellence.

SSC : We've all heard stories of some characters at Microsoft. Any interesting ones that stunned you or surprised you when you first went to work in Redmond?

Dan : Having grown up in Los Angeles it takes a lot to stun me, though I'd have to say that Peter Spiro surprised me the most. Before coming to MS I knew the name but had never met him. He's quit a character – speaks his mind with very limited filtering and really doesn't dress up for anyone. I've never seen him in anything other than shorts and a t-shirt. But that's really what MS is all about – hiring talented people to create amazing products; we don't care much about your appearance.

SSC : So what's your daily dress code?

Dan : Jeans (shorts in the spring and summer), tennis shoes, and a t-shirt. Sometimes I'll put on a collared shirt if the mood hits me.

SSC : What's the story with you and Jim Gray?

Dan : Jim and I originally met over the phone back in early 2005. He was trying to install the latest CTP of SQL2K5 and was running into problems. He sent a mail to the setup team and I picked it up to help him. He ran into a problem we had never seen before – after several attempts we worked around the problem and got it installed on his tablet. The picture was taken at a recent Microsoft dinner hosted for him. A good friend of mine is part of a group of technical leaders here at Microsoft. He was allowed to bring one guest to the dinner and when he saw that Jim was the host he knew he had to invite me. It was a very small group of probably 12 people. When I met him at the dinner I reminded him of our phone meeting a year earlier – he gave me a great big hug and thanked me.

SSC : What's your current favorite tech gadget?

Dan : My favorite gadget has held the honor for a couple of years now, my Tivo. It totally changed my life. Eventually I'll switch over to Media Center, but for now I'm sticking with the Tivo.

SSC : What does Dan like to do when he's not working on SQL Server?

Dan : My hobbies include music (I play the drums), not-so-reality TV, and brewing my own beer.

SSC : Neal Peart, John Bonham, or someone else?

Dan : That's a really tough question. I've always had a fondness for Neil Peart. There's a certain elegance to his style that very few drummers can replicate. I love John Bonham for his power and presence (no pun intended). Another of my favorites is Chad Smith from the Red Hot Chili Peppers. Chad can take a really simple beat, add a few spices and turn it into a completely new dish that when you taste it you say "Hmm, now that's familiar but much better than when I make it."

SSC : Ever been to Bill Gates' house?

Dan : Only using local.live.com - http://local.live.com/?v=2&sp=aN.47.628991_-122.240844_Gates_

About The Authors

Alex Grinberg
Alex Grinberg is known and recognized in the Philadelphia metro areas technical community for his teaching, development, and SQL Server DBA efforts since mid 90-s. Alexs persistence and diligence along with his ongoing education made him a valuable asset to every major firm where he has been employed. This includes his current experience at IDP (Insurance Data Processing), Inc. (Wyncote, PA), a major insurance software company.

– pg. 148

Alex Kersha
– pg. 63

Andre Quitta
– Pg. 78

Andy Warren
Andy was a DBA for nearly a decade with Hancock Information Group before leaving to work fulltime for SQLServerCentral.com training a new generation of DBAs.

Moving Replicated Databases – Pg. 211

Anubhav Bansai
– pg. 33

Aries Manlig
– pg. 23

Brian Knight
Brian Knight, MCSE, MCDBA, is on the Board of Directors for the Professional Association for SQL Server (PASS) and runs the local SQL Server users group in Jacksonville. Brian is a contributing columnist for SQL Magazine and also maintains a weekly column for the database website SQLServerCentral.com. He is the author of Admin911: SQL Server (Osborne/McGraw-Hill Publishing) and co-author of Professional SQL Server DTS (Wrox Press) and Professional SQL Server 2005 Integration Services. Brian is a Senior SQL Server Database Consultant with Idea Integration and spends most of his time deep in SSIS and High availability for SQL Server.

Upgrading SQL Server 2000 DTS Packages to SSIS - pg. 122

Charles Hawkins
- pg. 95

Chris Rock

Adventures in Replication - pg.

Christoffer Hedgate
Chris Hedgate works in Sweden as a .NET consultant and SQL Server specialist at Dotway, a company specializing in technical consulting services related to the Microsoft .NET platform. He has more than 8 years experience with SQL Server, including SQL Server 2005 since Beta 1 came out in 2003, and has worked with the .NET platform since it was announced in 2000. Read more from Chris at his blog at http://www.hedgate.net/.

- pg. 30

Darwin Hatheway
- pg.

David Poole
Dave worked first for a French manufacturing company as an analyst/programmer working with mini-computers. He then spent five years as systems manager for an American 'direct mail' printing company, followed by five years with an global advertising agency as a database administrator and business analyst. He specialised in database analysis,

particularly in the area of direct mail and response analysis, using a variety of tools, including SPSS, VB, SQL Server, Access, and Excel. He currently works as a DBA specialising in web content management systems for a technical documentation company near Manchester (UK).

The Pitfalls of Foreign Keys - pg.

Dinesh Asanka

I am living on a beautiful island called Sri Lanka, just beside India. I started my carrier as a simple data entry operator and was in the almost all the sections of Software. I have mote than ten years of experience in the IT field. Currently I am functioning for a company called Advance Data Technologies (Pvt) Ltd as a Senior Database Designer. I am working in SQL Server for just over five years. I have being involved in databases such as Dbase 3+, Clipper, MS Access, SQL Server, Oracle, DB2, mySQL at different scale. I am passionate in Cricket. I am enjoying the sharing my knowledge in SQLServerCentral.com as well.

SQL Server Agent 2005 - pg.

Eli Leiba

Eli Leiba works at Israel Electric Company as a Senior Application DBA in Oracle and MS SQL Server. He also has certifications from Microsoft and BrainBench in Oracle and SQL Server database administration and implementation. Mr. Leiba holds a B.S. in Computer Science since 1991 and has 13 years' experience working in the databases field. Additionally Mr. Leiba teaches SQL Server DBA and Development courses at Microsoft CTEC and also serves as a senior database consultant for several Israeli start-up companies. (e-mail: iecdba@hotmail.com)

Handling Simple XML Using T-SQL - pg. 183

Frederik Vandeputte

Frederik Vandeputte is a SQL Server Consultant and trainer for Cronos (www.cronos.be) in Belgium. He has been working with SQL Server since version 6.5 and holds certifications as MCSA, MCSE, MCDBA, MCT and recently MCTS and MCITP Database Administrator on SQL Server 2005. His blog can be found on www.vandeputte.org.

SQL Server 2005 Logon Triggers - pg.

Grant Fritchey

I'm a database administrator for a leading insurance company. I have 18 years experience in development, database design and administration. I'm a Black belt in Ken-Ryu kenpo karate. I brew my own beer. I'm a major history geek. My nickname at work, including an official name plate, is "The Scary DBA" and I wear it proudly.

Outer Join Mystery – pg.

Haidong Ji

I was a developer, working with VB, SQL Server, Access and lots of other Microsoft stuff. I am currently a SQL Server DBA in my company in the Chicago area. In addition to SQL Server, I also do Oracle work on Linux and Solaris. I am MCSD and MCDBA certified. In my spare time, I like to do Linux, C and other open source project. I can be reached at Haidong.Ji AT gmail dot com.

 - pg. 208

Hugh Lynch

Windows/Web developer since 1990, focused on developer tools and financial services. CTO of Restricted Stock Systems, Inc. Father of two boys 8 and 7. Interests: inline speed skating, tennis, ultimate, chess, evolutionary biology.
Simplify the Creation of XML from SQL Server Data – pg.

James Greaves
Handling Zero Byte Files in DTS - pg. 81

Jereme Guenther
HomePage: http://users.thelifeline.net/guenther/
Location: Lebanon, Oregon, USA
Occupation: Database Developer
Interests: Computer Programming and SI FI books and movies

Printing in .NET - pg. 209

Jonathan Stokes
Jon has over eight years of multi-functional experience encompassing programming and development with a variety of tools (SQL, VB, Business Objects, etc.)

DTS Standards - pg. 60

Joe Sack
Joseph Sack, MCDBA, is a SQL Server consultant based in the Twin Cities.   He is the author of SQL Server 2000 Fast Answers for DBAs and Developers (Apress) and the co-author of Beginning SQL Server 2000 DBA: Novice to Professional (Apress). He can be contacted via his website, http://www.SackConsulting.com.

Stored Procedure Naming Conventions - pg.

Kathi Kellenberger
Kathi Kellenberger is a database administrator for Bryan Cave LLP in St. Louis, MO. She is a frequent columnist for SQLServerCentral.com and SQL Server Standard Magazine and a co-author of "Professional SQL Server 2005 Integration Services" (Wrox Press). Kathi is a volunteer on the PASS Program Committee and co-chair of the St. Louis SQL Server User Group.

 - pg. 198

Ken Powers
Reduce Database Round Trips Using XML - pg. 185

Kristian Wedberg
SSIS - Code Reuse and Complex Control Flows - pg. 9

Leo Peyasakhovich
Leo Peysakhovich is consultant and president of ACCT INC. As a developer, DBA, and an architect he has been working with SQL Server since 1993. He has published multiple technical articles throughout his career. He provided training for more than hundred of people in SQL Server and Business Application Development. He immigrated to the United States from Minsk, Belarus in 1989. He holds a degree in Electrical and Automated System Engineering (equivalent to an M.S. in System Control Engineering). Leo lives in a suburb of Philadelphia with his wife Liana and 2 sons Felix and Nathan. He can be reached at leop@acctinc.com

An Audit Trail Generator - pg. 160

M. Choirul Amri
SQL Server 2005 for the SQL 2K Developer - pg. 27

Michael Coles
SQL Server 2005 Symmetric Encryption - pg. 156

Nanda Kishore
 - pg. 47

Peter He
 - pg. 89

Peter Ward
Peter Ward is the Chief Technical Architect for WARDY IT Solutions, a consulting and training company specialising in SQL Server Solutions which he founded in 2004. Peter is an active member in the Australian SQL Server community and regularly publishes SQL Server related articles to his weblog (www.wardyit.com/blog) along with the monthly SQL server newsletter that he produces. Since founding WARDY IT Solutions Peter has continued to focus on his passion for automating administrative tasks for SQL Server.

Male, Female, and The Other One (NULL) - pg.

Raj Vasant

I work as a Software Engineer for VR Software Systems, located at Vadodara in Gujarat [India]. I received my Master's degree in computers in 2005 from the M.S. University of Baroda, Gujarat [India]. I have been working on SQL Server and .NET since 2004. My role includes designing the applications following the UML methodology, database design and development. Playing Table Tennis, makes my mind and body ready for exciting new tasks!!!

Using OPENXML - pg.
Using OPENXML Part II - pg.

Rama Nageshwara

Overview of DTS Packages - pg. 163

Ranga Narasimhan

Database Design and Reference Tables - pg. 93

Rob Scholl

Finding the Next Business Day Recursively – pg

Robert Davis

Practical Uses of Patindex - pg. 7

Roy Carlson

No Outlook for Alerts - pg. 167

Satia Madimchetty

Sr.Consultant at Scalabilty Experts. Previously worked with SQL Server PSS, Microsoft and as SQL Server DBA with i2 Technologies.

Handling Conflcts in Merge Replication - pg. 69

Sean McCown

Finding Objects Owned by Non-DBO Users - pg. 16

Serhiy Snisarenko

Customer Database Update – A Practical Solution - pg. 77

Sloan Holliday

The Zero to N Parameter Problem - pg. 43

Steve Jones

With over a decade of working with SQL Server as well as many other aspects of the IT industry, Steve Jones brings a variety of viewpoints to many problems that DBAs face. As a founder of SQLServerCentral.com, Steve has worked to build a community that is practical, professional, and invaluable to SQL Server DBAs

Incident Reponse – The Framework - pg. 82
Incident Reponse – Responding to an Incident - pg. 85

Steve Moore

Steve is an MBA, MCSA, MCDBA living and working in Paris, France. He has worked mostly in the health care industry doing system support and development. He is currently administering the databases and developing in .NET 2.0 for a large multilanguage support web site.

Importing XML Files into SQL Server - pg. 66

Subramanyam Krishnamurthy

The Dodgy GO Statement - pg. 191

Suresh Maganti

MS SQL Server DBA at TCS, Syntel, Capgemini Ernst & Young, Scalability Experts.

Sushila Iyer

I moved to the U.S (from India) many summers ago...lived for a brief spell (2 yrs) in Holland and backpacked my way through the European youth hostels - easily the best 2 years of my entire life and the start of my aspirations to learn other languages - while I was attempting to learn Dutch I discovered that the only times I would come out of my shell was during the once-a-month meetings at the local pub where I would be magically transformed from taciturn to (almost) garrulous and my fellow-students woud gape at me with jaw-dropped amazement equalled only by my own as I heard myself speak Dutch like a native. Alas - these Cinderalla moments vanished with the break of dawn and the dissipation of the spirits. Since the real world compels me to interact with people AND frowns upon leading life in a constant state of inebriation I thought my reclusive nature could be kept happy hiding behind the facade of a programmer churning out code in a little cubicle far from the madding crowd! However, I have been forced out of my hole by misguided (ex) bosses who were convinced that there is more to me than meets my eye and tasked me with seeing a project through from nascency to deployment - this included the design, development and maintenance of a sql server database and it was love from the very first select. Stumbled upon ssc.com during one of my sql troubleshooting days and find that I've found the perfect spot in the shade - I can stay speechless and still communicate!!! "Home at last"!!!

Terri Troisi

Thomas LaRock

Tiago Andrade e Silva

Tim Chapman

Tim Mitchell

Todd Lodermeier

Vince Iacoboni

Zach Mattson